Learn
SOMETHING
NEW
Every Day

365 Facts to Fulfill Your Life

KEE MALESKY

WILEY

John Wiley & Sons, Inc.

Design by Forty-five Degree Design LLC

Cover image: Garden gnome reading a book © Mac99/iStockphoto; book pages turning into birds © Lobke Peers/iStockphoto
Cover Design: Wendy Mount

Illustration credits appear on p. 266.

Published by John Wiley & Sons, Inc., Hoboken, New Jersey
Published simultaneously in Canada

For general information about our other products and services, please contact our Customer Care Department within the United States at (800) 762-2974, outside the United States at (317) 572-3993 or fax (317) 572-4002.

Wiley also publishes its books in a variety of electronic formats and by print-on-demand. Some content that appears in standard print versions of this book may not be available in other formats. For more information about Wiley products, visit us at www.wiley.com.

Library of Congress Cataloging-in-Publication Data:
Malesky, Kee, date.
    Learn something new every day : 365 facts to fulfill your life / by Kee Malesky.
        p. cm.
    Includes index.
    ISBN 978-1-118-11275-5 (cloth); ISBN 978-1-118-22434-2 (ebk);
    ISBN 978-1-118-23812-7 (ebk); ISBN 978-1-118-26241-2 (ebk)
    1. Handbooks, vade-mecums, etc. 2. Curiosities and wonders. I. Title.
    AG106.M355 2012
    031.02—dc23

                                                        2012025740

Printed in the United States of America

10 9 8 7 6 5 4 3 2

To Robert Malesky,
my dear heart,
my favorite person,
my best friend

Strive for tone

Contents

Introduction

"LEARN SOMETHING NEW EVERY DAY" is the motto and motivation of many librarians. We spend our professional lives surrounded by and constantly exposed to new ideas, concepts, facts, and details—an amazing, swirling vortex of information.

Librarians are hardly alone in this attitude; great thinkers across the eons have made it clear that they value education and the results it can produce, that being a lifelong learner is not only good for you, it's beneficial to our global society. Life is infinitely interesting; being open to absorbing new information and knowledge wherever you find them means you'll never be bored or jaded, your brain will be stimulated and will stay healthy, and you'll be a more useful, content, and productive citizen. Dr. Seuss, in *I Can Read with My Eyes Shut*, sums it up nicely: "Young cat, if you keep your eyes open enough, oh the stuff you would learn! The most wonderful stuff!"

Adult or lifelong education doesn't only mean signing up for formal classes; it can also involve attending a lecture at a museum, practicing a new skill, joining a discussion group, or just browsing the shelves of your local library or bookstore—finding new ways to bring learning into your life every day.

In 1996, the International Commission on Education for the Twenty-First Century produced a report for the United Nations called *Learning: The Treasure Within*. In his introduction, Jacques Delors, the French economist and former president of the European Commission who headed the project, expounded on the goals of education: "to attain the ideals of peace, freedom and social justice . . . a deeper and more harmonious form of human development . . . to lift their minds and spirits to the plane of the universal . . . to develop all our talents to the full and to realize our creative potential, including responsibility for our own lives."

As I learned with my first volume, *All Facts Considered*, information can be hard to pin down and verify, and it's difficult to tell a complete story in just a couple hundred words. I have tried again in this book to compile the salient and most interesting details in each little fact and then point you to sources that will expand your understanding, provide extensive background information, or at least show you a cool video. All of the sources for these facts are available on my website, www.keemalesky.com, where the Internet links are active and updates will be provided (and it saves a good bit of paper if we don't print them all here). Any material quoted in a fact is identified in the notes section at the end of the book.

Out of respect for sources who wrote before our spelling system became standardized, I have reproduced all quotes with the original spelling, however unusual.

As a member of the National Public Radio team of librarians, I handle a wide range of questions every day. I've based some of the facts in this book on queries from reporters and editors, but I also found inspiration from many other sources and gladly took facts wherever I found them waiting to be researched and summarized.

This book is a collection of facts to take you through a full year (with a bonus fact for leap year). Some facts are directly connected to the date on which they appear—the person's birth or death date, the day the incident occurred, or when the item is celebrated. Sometimes

I had a conflict—two facts for the same date—so I had to make a choice (who gets November 5, the New Jersey Turnpike or Guy Fawkes?). Many facts have no relation to their dates. Some have a connection that may not be immediately apparent, and so you may have to discover it yourself (for example, the fact about the Room to Read project appears on International Literacy Day). I hope each fact interests, intrigues, or challenges you, and that you'll be inspired to look deeper into it.

Read—on any platform and in any format: on paper, on an electronic device, on clay tablets or papyrus scrolls. Read about things that already fascinate you and things that you know nothing about. Reread your favorite books or those you hated in high school. Compare, muse, evaluate, consider, analyze, ponder; keep your mind occupied. Read because it's fun, it's exciting, it's a joy to find out something you didn't know before. Keep your eyes open to the wonderful stuff. Never let a day go by without giving yourself an opportunity to say, "Who knew?" If we're not on this planet to learn something new every day, why are we here?

JANUARY

JANUARY 1 | "Free Land!" Was the Cry

The Homestead Act of 1862 opened up the West to settlers, offering 160 acres of land to any adult who had not fought against the government. Homesteaders were required to construct a house, cultivate the land for five years, and then pay a small registration fee to obtain clear ownership. The very first homesteader was likely Daniel Freeman, a Union soldier stationed at Fort Leavenworth, Kansas, who persuaded a local land registrar to open his office at midnight on January 1, 1863, when the law took effect. Freeman laid claim to a piece of land in Nebraska, and after the war, he built a log cabin and lived on the property until his death in 1908. The National Park Service has now preserved his home as a national monument. Although the Homestead Act did help settle the West, it was a poorly written law, with numerous loopholes that allowed land speculators and others to take advantage. About five hundred million acres were disbursed, but only eighty million actually went to homesteaders.

JANUARY 2 | The Book of Bargains

One of the eventual effects of the Homestead Act of 1862 was the creation of a new market in the West for mail-order goods. In 1886, Richard Warren Sears, a railroad agent in Minneapolis, bought a shipment of watches from a local jeweler. He was able to sell them at a profit, so he purchased more and opened the R.W. Sears Watch Company. He soon moved his business to Chicago and hired a young watchmaker named Alvah Roebuck. Sears sent out his first mailer in 1888, to advertise his watches. Sensing the possibilities of the emerging market, Sears and Roebuck expanded the mailer to a catalog (the 1894 edition was called the *Book of Bargains: A Money Saver for Everyone*). Their timing was right. Most of the settlers out West were buying their goods at general stores, which were adding a considerable markup to their prices. Buying and selling in volume allowed Sears to undercut the general stores, and his business took off. In 1896, the U.S. Post Office started the Rural Free Delivery service, and that—along with Sears's acumen for promotion and marketing—ensured the catalog's success. It was the beginning of mass-market merchandising, and Sears Roebuck & Company would be a major part of it. The Sears catalog quickly became a benchmark of the new mass culture, offering everything from eyeglasses to baby carriages and even kit houses and automobiles (known as the Sears Motor Buggy).

JANUARY 3 | The Silver Bible

The Codex Argenteus, or the Silver Bible of Prague, is an evangeliarium (a book containing portions of the four gospels) in the Gothic language, probably created for the Ostrogoth king Theodoric the Great in the sixth century. It was written on high-quality purple-colored vellum with most of the text in silver ink, which accounts for the name. Lost for a thousand years, the bible turned up in the possession of the Holy Roman Emperor Rudolf II and then was seized by the Swedes when Prague was captured in 1648 during the Thirty Years' War. The manuscript went to Queen Christina's library in

Stockholm, and today the Codex Argenteus—Sweden's most valuable and precious book and one of the few extant examples of the Gothic language—resides at the University of Uppsala. In 1995, two pages from the Silver Bible were stolen; they were found by the police, undamaged, in a locker at a Stockholm train station a month later.

JANUARY 4 | Burma or Myanmar?

There has been much confusion over the name of the country in southeast Asia that's known as either Burma or Myanmar. Essentially, the words mean the same thing, and the former is a variation of the latter ancient form of the name. The country is made up of many different ethnic groups, of which the largest is the Burmese people. *Mranma* is the formal written version of their name, although it is pronounced colloquially as bam-MA. When the British occupied the country in the nineteenth century, they anglicized it to Burma. That name was retained through independence from Britain in 1948 and the first decades of the military dictatorship. In 1989, the regime renamed the country the Union of Myanmar, claiming that it represented all of the minorities in the country, not only the Burmese, which isn't completely accurate. Perhaps anthropologist Gustaaf Houtman explains it best: "There's a formal term which is *Myanmar* and the informal, everyday term which is *Burma*. *Myanmar* is the literary form, which is ceremonial and official and reeks of government." The United Nations accepted the name change, but some countries, particularly the United States and the United Kingdom, have not, in order to show support for the democratic opposition to the junta.

JANUARY 5 | The Beautiful Blue Danube

No river in the world flows through more countries than the Danube. It originates in the Black Forest of Germany and then travels through or forms a border of Austria, Slovakia, Hungary, Croatia, Serbia, Bulgaria, Moldova, Ukraine, and Romania (and nine more countries are in its drainage basin). The name probably comes from *danu*,

Trajan's bridge

a proto-Indo-European word for "river" and also an ancient Celtic river goddess. The Danube basin was the home of an important Neolithic culture at least seven thousand years ago. For much of the Roman era, the river served as the empire's northern boundary. Trajan built the first bridge to cross the lower Danube around 105 CE, near the present-day town of Kladovo in Serbia; some of its foundation pillars remain underwater today. The Danube is the second-longest river in Europe (the Volga is the first), about 1,774 miles. The Danube Delta, where the river drains into the Black Sea, is one of the most biodiverse regions on earth, with 5,429 species of flora and fauna, including 331 bird species.

JANUARY 6 | The First American Books

A True Relation of Such Occurrences and Accidents of Noate as Hath Happened in Virginia since the First Planting of That Collony by Captain John Smith, using the pseudonym Th. Watson, was the first book written by a settler in the New World, in 1608. It was "a plain, unadorned account of hardships" that had to be printed in London, because the first printing press didn't arrive in America until thirty years later. The first book published in the colonies was the *Bay Psalm Book*, printed in Cambridge, Massachusetts, in 1640; of course, it had been written elsewhere and much earlier. The first children's book, *Milk for Babes, Drawn out of the Breasts of Both Testaments, Chiefly for the Spiritual Nourishment of Boston Babes in Either England; but May Be of Like Use for Any Children*, by Puritan clergyman John Cotton, was published in the early 1640s.

JANUARY 7 | London Calling

In this age of Skype, smartphones, and video conferencing, it's no big deal for someone in New York City to speak with someone in London, but in the 1920s, it was the bee's knees. On January 7, 1927, commercial telephone service between the United States and Europe commenced, using a combination of land lines and radio transmission. Transatlantic telegraph service had been available since 1858, but this was the start of regular voice-to-voice communication. "Hello, London?" were the first words spoken by the American operator. "London ready," came the reply, and then the first call began between Walter Sherman Gifford, the president of the American Telephone & Telegraph Company in New York, and Sir Evelyn Murray, the secretary of the British Postoffice, in London. Immediately, there was a deluge of cross-Atlantic calling, by politicians, journalists, financial firms, and others. There were no privacy concerns yet, and owners of wireless radios were able to eavesdrop on the conversations. It wasn't cheap, either; the cost of a three-minute call was $75.

JANUARY 8 | A Confrontation of Brains and Fists

Knight takes Bishop, followed by a left hook. That would be Chess Boxing, an actual sport, which combines "the #1 thinking sport and the #1 fighting sport," according to the World Chess Boxing Organisation. Competitors engage in alternating rounds of chess and boxing: four minutes of chess followed by three minutes of fighting, and then a one-minute rest; that continues for eleven rounds unless there's a knockout or a checkmate. Inspired by *Froid Équateur*, a 1992 graphic novel that featured a version of chess boxing, a Dutch artist named Iepe Rubingh created the sport, figured out its rules, staged its first events, and is president of the WCBO. Its motto: "Fighting is done in the ring and wars are waged on the board."

JANUARY 9 | The Booziest Nations

The World Health Organization released its *Global Status Report on Alcohol and Health* in February 2011, providing data on the use of alcohol and its effects in more than a hundred countries. The study found that worldwide consumption is about 6.5 quarts of alcohol per adult (fifteen years or older) per year. Though alcohol use is wide-spread, almost half of the world's population has never consumed any alcohol (35 percent of men and 55 percent of women). Alcohol abuse has serious health consequences; it's a causal factor in more than sixty types of diseases and injuries. About 2.5 million deaths each year are alcohol-related—nearly 4 percent of all deaths: 6.2 percent of deaths among men and 1.1 percent of women, and 9 percent of deaths among 15- to 29-year-olds. This is greater than the number of deaths caused by HIV/AIDS, violence, or tuberculosis. The highest alcohol consumption levels are found in the developed world; at 19 quarts per person, the Republic of Moldova is at the top of the list. The United States also exceeds the world average, with 10 quarts per person.

JANUARY 10 | The Tube

The world's first subway, the Metropolitan Railway that ran between Paddington Station and Farringdon Street in London, opened in 1863. The first lines had been constructed using the "cut and cover" method: a shallow trench was dug, tracks were laid, and then it was roofed over with bricks. Later, they started to use boring machines, which allowed deeper tunnels and caused less disruption and destruction on the surface. The term *tube* was first used for those lines to distinguish them from the earlier ones, but it's now a common name for the whole system. Early trains were steam powered, and vents were needed to allow them to exhaust the smoke and fumes. One such vent still exists, in Leinster Gardens; it's disguised by the façade of two truncated houses, which look exactly like their neighbors except for the blackened windows. Since 2007, the London Underground has carried more than one billion passengers per year.

JANUARY 11 | "Little Stinkers"

In 1963, cigarettes were ubiquitous—people smoked in airplanes, offices, restaurants, elevators, or wherever they chose. Numerous studies from scientific and medical groups had already shown the dangers of tobacco, particularly regarding lung cancer, but 45 percent of Americans were regular smokers. On January 11, 1964, that began to change. On that day, Surgeon General Luther Terry brought two hundred journalists to the State Department auditorium in Washington, D.C., and closed the doors. He chose a Satur-day so the stock markets would not be adversely

A smoker

affected by what he was about to say. For the next two hours, he pre-sented a 387-page report titled *Smoking and Health*, which concluded that "cigarette smoking is a health hazard of sufficient importance in the United States to warrant appropriate remedial action." The report became front-page news around the country, with most of the media predicting that smoking might drop for a time but would bounce back quickly. That view was expressed in person-on-the-street interviews. "I can stop drinking but not smoking," said one. "I love these little stinkers," responded another. Legislators began to take some steps, beginning with a 1965 law that required a health warning on packs of cigarettes. Four years later, television and radio advertising for ciga-rettes was banned. By 2010, the number of Americans who regularly smoked was down to 19.3 percent.

JANUARY 12 | Smelly Cinema

With the advent of television in the 1950s, the film industry was deeply worried about losing its audience. The studios tried a number of experiments to lure viewers back to the theaters, including Cin-erama, 3-D, and, perhaps oddest of all, Smell-O-Vision. This inven-tion was bankrolled by Mike Todd Jr., the son of the famous film producer, and it could deliver up to thirty different smells, triggered by the film's soundtrack and fed to the seats through specially installed tubing. Yet before the first film made with this process, *Scent of Mys-tery*, was released, another smell system was rushed through produc-tion. AromaRama fed the smells through the theater's air conditioning system; it was used to add scents to a documentary on China that had already been shot. *New York Times* critic Bosley Crowther called it a stunt and said its artistic benefit was nil. That didn't help *Scent of Mystery* when it was released a few weeks later, in January 1960. In the battle of the "smellies," both systems were financial failures, with *Time* magazine proclaiming that "most customers will probably agree that the smell they liked best was the one they got during intermission: fresh air." In recent years, a few films have experimented with scratch-and-sniff cards distributed to the audience, who can release aromas according to on-screen cues.

JANUARY 13 | Nomads in the Modern World

We often associate nomads—people with no fixed home who move according to work and the seasons—with bedouins in the Middle East or the Huns in ancient Asia. Yet there are also peripatetic groups living in Europe and the Americas. They are called by a number of names—Roma, Kale, Sinti, Gypsies, Travelers, Tinkers—and have developed their own dialects, art, and culture. The Romani people were originally thought to come from Egypt (thus the name *Gypsy*), but they actually originated in Northern India and found their way to Europe by the year 1000. They followed the harvests of various crops through the seasons and in winter would camp at the edge of urban areas, doing odd jobs. Other nomadic Europeans may not be of Romani origin but were forced into a wandering lifestyle due to famine or unemployment. Ireland's Tinkers evolved from itinerant metalworkers, who repaired pots and pans around the country. Some simply prefer life on the road, rather than being rooted to one spot. All of these nomadic groups are frequently accused of alcoholism, prostitution, petty thievery, and other crimes, a reputation they have found difficult to escape. Intolerance of nomadic groups is endemic to almost all countries where they live, and many governments have tried to force their assimilation. A variety of support groups have been able to promote antidiscrimination legislation, but more and more European nomads are giving up their mobile lifestyle, while trying to preserve their ethnic heritage and identity.

JANUARY 14 | Pathfinder of the Sea

Landlubbers may not know the name Matthew Fontaine Maury (1806–1873), but to anyone who sails the high seas, he was an indispensable man. Maury joined the U.S. Navy in 1825, sailed around the world, and conducted the first systematic studies of oceanography and meteorology. He decided to write a textbook about navigation, which he published in 1836. A few years later, he was put in charge of the navy's Depot of Charts and Instruments, where he pored through old sailors' logbooks to organize information on winds and currents. He published the first charts of the North Atlantic in 1847 and in 1855 released his master-work, *The Physical Geography of the Sea*, which went through eight editions and became the seaman's bible. Its opening lines are poetic and powerful: "There is a river in the ocean. In the severest droughts it never fails, and in the mightiest floods it never overflows. Its banks and its bottom are of cold water, while its current is of warm. The Gulf of Mexico is its fountain, and its mouth is in the Arctic Sea. It is the Gulf Stream." Maury's charts and books revolutionized ocean travel and earned him the title "Pathfinder of the Sea."

Matthew Maury

JANUARY 15 | The Great Molasses Flood

In Boston's North End on January 15, 1919, a gigantic tank full of molasses exploded, spilling more than two million gallons of sticky, viscous fluid onto the streets in a brown wave that was probably fifteen feet high at first and moved at thirty-five miles per hour. "I heard something like machine-gun bullets," said survivor Albert Mostone, remembering the event seventy-five years later. "And then when I looked I saw it was the ripping of a tank and a big piece of the tank blew up in the air and went over and landed . . . in the North End Park. And a house that was on Clarksville Terrace and Commercial Street was blown right into the molasses that was going down the street." Workers who had been near the tank were sucked into the thick, sweet muck and swept away.

The wave crashed into buildings, filling basements and causing people to drown. Shards from the tank buckled a support for the elevated railway tracks, and an oncoming train was barely able to stop in time. Twenty-one people were killed, and 150 were injured. Cleanup of the city took months, and cleanup of the legal claims lasted for years. The court eventually ruled that the tank's owner, the United States Industrial Alcohol Company, was responsible for the disaster, although its exact cause was never determined; the company claimed an anarchist had planted a bomb in the tank. Old-time Bostonians say that this area of the city smelled of molasses, especially on hot days, for decades afterward.

JANUARY 16 | "You Are the Ball"

Ever since people first domesticated members of the family *Equidae*, they have devised games to play on horseback. Polo—probably the oldest team sport—dates back before recorded history. The first written reference to the game is from around 600 BCE, when the Turkomans beat the Persians in a public match. Persia, today's Iran, is where the sport probably originated; it developed as a method of training cavalry. It was a huge game, with as many as one hundred riders to a side, and resembled a real battle. From Persia, polo spread to the rest of Asia, including India, where in the nineteenth century British tea planters discovered the game and introduced it to their home country. Here's how the Museum of Polo describes a match: "Imagine a ball hit so hard that it comes at you at a speed of 110 miles per hour, so fast, you can hardly see it. Your job is to stay at a gallop, get your horse in line with the ball, and either pass it ahead to a teammate, or carry the ball down the field for an attempt at goal." The name *polo* comes from the Tibetan word *pulu*, which means "ball." The Persian poet Omar Khayyam wrote a quatrain about it in *The Rubaiyat* (here, in a literal translation):

> In the cosmic game of polo you are the ball
> The mallet's left and right becomes your call
> He who causes your movements, your rise and fall
> He is the one, the only one, who knows it all.

JANUARY 17 | Glass Armonica

If you run a wet finger around the rim of a glass, it will produce a sound, sometimes a very lovely one. If you fill a set of glasses with different levels of water, the glasses emit various notes. In the seventeenth century, musicians performed with water glasses, arranging them on a table, filling them carefully, and picking out melodies. Keeping the glasses in tune was a challenge, because the water evaporated and changed the pitch of the note. Benjamin Franklin attended a glass concert in Europe while serving as a representative of the American colonies and decided he could improve the instrument. In 1761, his new invention was ready; he called it a *glass armonica* (a play on the Italian word for "harmony"). Instead of upright goblets with different levels of water, he had a horizontal spindle on which were mounted glass bowls of different sizes, without any liquid. The size and thickness of the glass determined the note it would play. A foot-powered treadle rotated the spindle, and a moistened finger applied to the different bowls produced the music.

Franklin's instrument created an ethereal, sweet sound that attracted not only audiences, but the ears of composers such as Mozart, Beethoven, and Donizetti, who wrote pieces for it. Franklin later said, "Of all my inventions, the glass armonica has given me the greatest personal satisfaction."

A glass armonica

JANUARY 18 | "And So to Every Streete"

The word *pageant* is used today to mean a beauty contest, a spectacular presentation, or an elaborate parade. In the Middle Ages, it referred to the structure mounted on a wheeled cart that was used to transport and present such activities: "A stage or platform on which scenes were acted or tableaux represented . . . a movable structure consisting of stage and stage machinery, used in the open-air performance of a mystery play," as the *Oxford English Dictionary* explains it. In the late

1500s, an archdeacon in Chester, England, described a pageant wagon, "a high scafolde with two rowmes, a higher and a lower, upon four wheeles . . . when the first pagiante was played it was wheeled to the highe crosse before the mayor, and so to every streete."

JANUARY 19 | An Ecological Paradise

The world's largest freshwater wetland system is the Pantanal (from the Portuguese and Spanish word for "swampy land" or "marsh"), covering approximately seventy-five thousand square miles in the center of South America, mostly in Brazil but also extending into parts of Paraguay and Bolivia; the region is larger than England. The Pantanal is an immense alluvial plain that is underwater during the rainy season from October to March. This flooding creates enriched soil that supports large numbers of plant and animal species. The area has been described as "an unparalleled wildlife sanctuary of spectacular beauty, an ecological paradise," and it contains an astounding diversity of fauna—the greatest concentration in the Americas—including jaguars, crocodiles, giant anteaters, capybara (the world's largest rodent), huge insects, and hundreds of bird species. The Pantanal has begun to attract tourists; it's easier to observe wildlife in the open floodplain than in the dense jungle of the nearby Amazon, and the city of Cuiabá will host some of Brazil's World Cup soccer matches in 2014.

JANUARY 20 | Our Founding Capitalist

Robert Morris is a little-known but eminently significant figure in U.S. history. Although he had opposed the move by the Continental Congress to break from England, he did sign the Declaration of Independence. An entrepreneur from Philadelphia, Morris—a self-made millionaire and the nation's "founding capitalist"—became the financier of the American Revolution. "It was at the dawn of the whole idea of global enterprise. He was very much a free market, laissez-faire capitalist—he talked about trade being as free as the air," according to his biographer, Charles Rappleye. Morris bankrolled the military, providing supplies for the troops (especially at the crucial battle of Yorktown) and making secret deals for arms with European nations. He functioned, essentially, as the country's treasury and banker. At the end of the war, Congress appointed him the nation's first superintendent of finance, and he proposed the creation of the first national bank. He was later involved in land speculation on a huge scale (five million acres in western New York, the rural South, and elsewhere), went bankrupt, and spent several years in debtor's prison.

Robert Morris

JANUARY 21 | A Fountain of Music

If you think a blaring car alarm in the middle of the night is annoying, then you may appreciate the feeling of the villagers in Tivoli, Italy, about 250 years ago. They lived near the sumptuous Villa d'Este, filled with formal gardens and an amazing array of fountains. The opulent estate had been built by Cardinal Ippolito d'Este II, the son of Lucrezia Borgia, and the governor of Tivoli, beginning in 1550. One of the showpieces of the garden's five hundred fountains was a magnificent water organ (*Fontana dell'Organo*) that used the pressure of the water to force air through pipes and play a tune on a barrel mechanism that resembled a music box. It was based on technology from ancient Greece and Rome that had been lost by the eighteenth century when the estate and its fountains had fallen into disrepair. At that time, the water organ began to play only one note—continuously. Exasperated villagers marched to the organ and destroyed the mechanism, silencing the irritating sound. In 2002, a contemporary organ maker built a replacement water organ that now performs every two hours.

JANUARY 22 | Candy Bricks

PEZ, those little compressed bricks of candy, were first produced as breath mints in 1927 in Vienna, Austria. The name comes from the

German word for peppermint—*pfefferminz*—which was shortened to PEZ. Promoted as an antismoking product, the candy originally came in dispensers that looked like cigarette lighters. By the 1950s, PEZ Candy, Inc. began marketing to children, introducing fruit flavors (chocolate didn't come along until 2008) and making the dispensers more toylike; Santa Claus, a robot, and a space gun were early models. Soon the company licensed such cartoon characters as Popeye, Mickey Mouse, and Bugs Bunny. To date, the most popular licensed PEZ characters are from the Star Wars movies. In 1987, feet were added to the dispensers to make them more stable. The first conference of PEZ collectors (also called PEZheads) was in 1991 in Mentor, Ohio. A roll of candies has only thirty-five calories, with nine grams of sugar, no fat, no sodium, and no protein. A Royal PEZ Set was issued for the wedding of the UK's Prince William and Kate Middleton in 2011. More than three billion PEZ candies are consumed each year in the United States.

JANUARY 23 | Luncheon on the Grass

Sometimes, you just have to break the rules. That's what renowned painter Édouard Manet did in 1863 when he revealed his latest work, *Déjeuner sur l'herbe* (Luncheon on the grass), and caused a rousing controversy that involved style, tradition, and sex. The painting shows two well-dressed men, having just finished a picnic, lounging on the grass with a totally naked woman. Another, semiclothed woman is bathing in a stream a few feet away. What was the controversy? Nudes had certainly appeared before, even with men, but they were usually classical nudes. This was an obviously modern woman. And she is not acting demurely but stares without shame directly at the viewer. Even the size of the canvas was criticized—it was 7 by 8½ feet, proportions that were traditionally reserved for grand historical or mythological themes. Manet's painting had none of that, but by breaking those taboos, he opened up the art world to a more modern sensibility, inspired younger artists—particularly Claude Monet and Paul Cézanne—and brought himself a great deal of fame.

JANUARY 24 | Angelic Voices

For a male, it was the supreme sacrifice for art or for money. From the mid-1500s until the nineteenth century in Italy, an unknown number of boys were castrated before puberty in order to prevent their voices from changing, giving them a possible career in either church music or opera. Without testicular secretions, the male vocal chords will not lengthen, resulting in a voice that maintains the high range of a youth with the increased lung capacity of an adult, a child's pure, angelic voice with the power of a grown man. Because women were not allowed to sing in church at that time, choirs were the first to use castrati, and one was officially admitted to the Sistine Chapel Choir in 1562. Opera composers became enamored of the possibilities of the castrato voice, and many wrote for it, including Mozart and Handel. Thousands of poor Italians had their boys castrated in the hope of gaining substantial financial rewards. In the eighteenth century, Naples alone may have castrated four thousand boys a year. The few who actually became world-class singers were idolized; Carlo Broschi, known as Farinelli, was probably the most famous. Yet people did mock them, and most castrati pretended that their condition was the result of an accident, rather than a deliberate act. The last performing castrato (and the only one to have made a recording) was Alessandro Moreschi, known as "the angel of Rome"; he died in 1922.

Carlo Broschi

JANUARY 25 | Refreshing the Tree of Liberty

The Revolutionary War was winding down in 1783; the national government was massively in debt and was having enormous difficulty paying the soldiers who had fought the war. Superintendent of finance Robert Morris had been able to scrape together one month's salary for each man, but the rest of the back pay was issued in scrip, redeemable at some future unspecified date. Yet the men needed cash quickly, to pay their own debts on the homes, the farms, and the shops that they had been unable to maintain during the war. Many sold their scrip to speculators, and their money ran out fast; local courts began seizing property from those unable to pay their debts. In 1786, the Massachusetts government called out the militia to protect the Springfield courts from debtors who had banded together in protest; a tense standoff followed. In January 1787, the unrest broke into open rebellion, when more than a thousand debtors under Captain Daniel Shays marched on the arsenal at Springfield, hoping to acquire arms so they could force the government to act on their grievances. But the militia arrived first, firing cannons as the protestors approached, killing four and wounding many more. Shays and his men dispersed, and although there were still a few minor skirmishes in the following weeks, the rebellion was effectively over. National leaders were greatly disturbed by Shays's Rebellion, and it gave substantial impetus to those seeking a strong federal government during the crafting of the Constitution at the Philadelphia Convention that summer. It was of this incident that Thomas Jefferson—then the U.S. ambassador to France—wrote, "The tree of liberty must be refreshed from time to time with the blood of patriots and tyrants."

JANUARY 26 | The Orange Orange

From *naranga* (Sanskrit) to *narang* (Persian) to *naranj* (Arabic) to *narancia* or *naranza* (Italian) to *orenge* (medieval French) and *naranja* (Spanish)—the fruit and the color known as *orange* have had a long journey. The word *orange* didn't exist in English until the sixteenth century; before that, they used *geolurēad* (yellow-red) for the color. Until English spelling was standardized, you might have seen references to *orenche*, *orrendge*, or even *horonge*. Oranges are among the earliest fruits to be cultivated; people have been growing and eating them for at least four thousand years. Probably originating in India and China, bitter and sweet oranges (*Citrus aurantium* and *C. sinensis*) made their way to the West by the Middle Ages. Christopher Columbus brought orange seeds and other citrus to Haiti in 1493. Brazil, the

United States (particularly Florida, California, and Texas), and China are the top orange producers, according to the Food and Agriculture Organization of the United Nations. Most of the U.S. crop is used for juice.

JANUARY 27 | Las Vegas of the East

It was the first European colony in China and also the last. Macau, a tiny peninsula connected to two small islands on China's southeastern coast, was a Portuguese colony established in the sixteenth century as a trading port where gaming was popular among the workers. It thrived until the mid-1800s, when it was overshadowed by Hong Kong, which the Chinese had ceded to Great Britain. To make up for lost revenue, Macau's Portuguese government legalized gambling in 1847. It became the city's bread and butter and continues to be its biggest source of revenue to the present day. When discussions were underway to return sovereignty of Macau to China in 1999, many expected the communist government to reject gambling. Instead, the government promised to keep things as they were for fifty years, and casino ownership was opened to some of the world's major operators. Macau now outstrips Las Vegas as the world's gambling capital, bringing in more than $33 billion in 2011. Macau doesn't draw only an international crowd; some of the biggest players are the Chinese people themselves, who see this kind of gambling as an investment akin to the stock market.

JANUARY 28 | The End of the Crawler

When the U.S. Space Shuttle program ended in 2011, it was also the end for NASA's Crawler-Transporter. Two of these massive tanklike machines individually moved the shuttles in an upright position from the Vehicle Assembly Building to the launch pad. The largest self-powered land vehicles in the world, the Crawlers are aptly named—they travel at .8 miles per hour and get only 32 feet to a gallon of diesel when hauling a shuttle. Each one is about 130 by 115 feet and weighs six million pounds (with the shuttle and the mobile launch platform, it's triple that weight). "At first glance, the crawler's imposing size eclipses its high-tech capabilities. It's strong enough to lift space shuttles and moon rockets, precise enough to place them within a fraction of an inch of their destination, and delicate enough to keep its surface level so its towering cargo stays perfectly vertical throughout the roughly six-hour ride," according to NASA. They were in use for forty-five years—the Crawler moved its first mobile launcher in January 1966.

JANUARY 29 | The Mormon Battalion

Only one unit in U.S. military history has been associated with a specific religious group: the Mormon Battalion. Raised in 1846 to support the Mexican War effort, the battalion served the government's need to secure the Southwest region and the Mormons' desire to migrate to the West. Brigham Young, the leader of the Church of Jesus Christ of Latter-Day Saints, also believed that forming an army unit would prove the Mormons' loyalty to the nation, something that had been in question during conflicts in Missouri a decade earlier. After lengthy negotiations with a church elder, President James K. Polk wrote in his diary: "Col. [Stephen W.] Kearny was . . . authorized to receive into service as volunteers a few hundred of the Mormons who are now on their way to California, with a view to conciliate them, attach them to our country, and prevent them from taking part against us." The battalion was raised in Council Bluffs, Iowa, under the overall command of an officer appointed by the government, with individual unit officers chosen by the Mormons. In July 1846, some five hundred men—accompanied by more than eighty women and children—began an arduous trek of nearly two thousand miles from Iowa to California. After a stop at Fort Leavenworth, Kansas, for outfitting, they headed southwest. The women and children split off at Santa Fe to winter in Colorado. As the rest continued, they experienced their only fighting of the march—with some wild bulls in Arizona. The battalion arrived in San Diego on January 29, 1847, having opened a new wagon road from Santa Fe. They were mustered out of the U.S. Army about six months later.

JANUARY 30 | A Great Year for Dinosaurs

It's not unusual to find dinosaur fossils in the state of Utah, but 2010 was a boom time: eight new species were named, all discovered on federal lands in the state. The eight species—*Abydosaurus mcintoshi, Seitaad ruessi, Diabloceratops eatoni, Utahceratops gettyi, Kosmoceratops richardsoni, Hippodraco scutodens, Iguanacolossus fortis,* and *Geminiraptor suarezarum*— include horned dinosaurs, long-necked herbivores, beaked iguanadonts, and a raptorlike creature with a large cranium, the oldest of its type found in North America, which was named for Celina and Marina Suarez, the doctoral students (and twin sisters) who found the fossils. It was a great year for dinosaurs, but Dan Chure, the paleontologist at Dinosaur National Monument, points out, "It doesn't seem that there's any end in sight in terms of finding new dinosaurs, or better understanding the biology of the ones we've found."

Skull of Kosmoceratops

JANUARY 31 | Pioneer Recordists

They were a father-and-son team like no other. John (1867–1948) and Alan (1915–2002) Lomax were responsible for collecting, recording, popularizing, and preserving thousands of American folk and roots songs that would otherwise have been lost. John Lomax grew up in Texas, surrounded by cowboy songs that fascinated him. He started writing them down and published *Cowboy Songs and Other Frontier Ballads* in 1910. Two decades later, he forged a relationship with the Archive of American Folk Song at the Library of Congress. The library provided John with portable recording equipment, and he hit the road to record whatever he could find. On his first trip in 1933, he took his eighteen-year-old son, Alan, with him. Together, they recorded ballads, work songs, and blues and made a stop at the Angola prison farm in Louisiana, where they recorded a convict named Huddie Ledbetter, better known as the iconic blues player Lead Belly. John became curator of the archive, and he and Alan continued to record and write about the music they uncovered. After John died in 1948, Alan expanded on his father's work, recording American musicians Son House, Muddy Waters, Woody Guthrie, and others and traveling overseas to such places as Haiti, Sicily, and Scotland. Neither John nor Alan was immune to controversy and criticism for some of their pronouncements about folk music and indigenous cultures, but they remain a crucial force in the history and preservation of "people's" music. In 2012, the Global Jukebox project began free online streaming of thousands of field recordings made by Alan Lomax.

FEBRUARY

FEBRUARY 1 | **Navel Life**

Scientists from North Carolina State University and the North Carolina Museum of Natural Sciences are running something called the Belly Button Diversity project: they collect samples of the many microorganisms that live in our navels, grow them in the lab, and identify and sequence them. The navel provides a good source for studying bacteria and fungi—it's an area of the body that is isolated from other parts, doesn't excrete anything, and probably isn't washed very often. As the project's website points out, "Each person's microbial jungle is so rich, colorful, and dynamic that in all likelihood your body hosts species that no scientist has ever studied. Your navel may well be one of the last biological frontiers." The researchers also hope this project will help people understand that most of the microbes living on our bodies are not harmful. As one explained, "Having an appreciation for the abundance of life just inside our bellybuttons can help us to see just how connected we are to the living world around us."

FEBRUARY 2 | ## Shakespeare in China

It took nearly three hundred years for the words of William Shakespeare to reach China. Although missionaries had made reference to him during the nineteenth century, it wasn't until 1903 that a rough translation of Charles and Mary Lamb's children's book *Tales of Shakespeare* was published. The next year, Lin Shu produced a more complete version of the Lambs' book, in which he called the works "stories of gods and spirits." *Romeo and Juliet* and *Hamlet* were the first plays to be fully translated, in 1922; stage performances soon followed. Zhu Shengao then emerged as the main translator of the Bard's work in China, bringing thirty-one plays to the country between 1935 and 1944, despite dealing with war, poverty, and illness. He outlined the principles he used in translating: "I do my best for conserving the flavor and features of the style of the original. In case I failed to reach this goal, I would try to communicate the ideas . . . clearly and faithfully in an elegant and comprehensible Chinese. I

considered it indecent to translate word for word without expressing the ingenuity and vigor of the original." Shakespeare's name was originally pronounced *Shashibiya*, but he is now respectfully called *Sha Weng* (Old Man Sha). His complete works were published in eleven volumes in 1978, the collaboration of many Chinese Shakespeareans.

William Shakespeare

FEBRUARY 3 | ## Dueling Pianos

During the golden age of American animation (1928–1960), cartoons were immensely popular, and competition among studios was fierce. In 1946, two cartoons of remarkable similarity were produced by two rival studios. Warner Bros. released the Bugs Bunny cartoon *Rhapsody Rabbit*, with Bugs as a concert pianist in white tie and tails, trying to perform Franz Liszt's Hungarian Rhapsody No. 2 while a mouse living in the piano interferes. That same year, MGM produced the Tom and Jerry cartoon *Cat Concerto*, featuring Tom the cat, also in formal attire, performing the same Liszt piece, with Jerry the mouse as the interloper. Each studio accused the other of plagiarizing, and both studios submitted their cartoons for Oscars. The Academy screened *Cat Concerto* first and gave it the nomination, dismissing *Rhapsody Rabbit* completely. *Cat Concerto* won the Oscar for Best Animated Short Film. Nothing definite has ever been determined about the plagiarism charge. It is possible the similarities were coincidental; there had been earlier cartoons that featured the Rhapsody. At the very least, the cartoons brought a bit of classical music into movie theaters and, with the advent of television, into the homes of a broad range of Americans.

FEBRUARY 4 | The Science of Bacon

"The smell of sizzling bacon in a pan is enough to tempt even the staunchest of vegetarians," says Elin Roberts of the Centre for Life in Newcastle, England. The wonderful aroma and taste of meat, toast, coffee (and so on) are produced by the Maillard (mah-YAR) reaction, a chemical interaction between certain sugars and amino acids, usually in the presence of heat. This oxidative browning is a complex process, similar to caramelization, and releases hundreds of flavor compounds that are unique to each type of food. The Maillard reaction can also occur within the human body; it's part of a process called glycation that's a factor in diabetes and some eye diseases. Some sunless tanning products work on the same principle—amino acids on the surface of the skin react with a chemical in the lotion or the spray. The process was named for French chemist Louis Camille Maillard, who first described it in 1912.

FEBRUARY 5 | Evidence Consumed

The era of Prohibition brought with it speakeasies, organized crime, and some unusual days in the courthouse. Take, for instance, a trial in Los Angeles in 1928. The jurors were considering the case of a hotel clerk named George Bevan (or maybe it was Joseph Bevan) who was charged with violating the Wright Act, the California version of the federal Volstead Act, which banned alcohol. The prosecution's chief evidence was a pint bottle of bootleg liquor. During their three hours of deliberation, the jurors decided they needed to be certain the evidence was truly alcohol and asked the bailiff to bring them the bottle. In their quest for assurance, nine of the twelve jurors consumed almost the entire bottle, thereby destroying the evidence against Bevan, who was subsequently acquitted. The judge hauled the nine before the bench, where they admitted to drinking the evidence but said it was only for the honorable purpose of determining the truth of the matter. The judge called it a breach of conduct and dismissed them from further service.

FEBRUARY 6 | Furry Birds That Don't Fly

When humans first arrived in New Zealand, about seven hundred years ago, among the bird species they found there were the kiwis (genus *Apteryx*, "without wings"), members of the ratite group of flightless birds (think of ostriches or emus). In existence for about sixty-five million years, these nocturnal ground dwellers have hairlike feathers (similar to those recently discovered on some types of dinosaurs) and no visible wings or tail. Unlike most birds, kiwis have poor eyesight but an unusually good sense of smell. Their nostrils are located at the end of their beaks, which helps them find worms and insects in the soil. They have the largest egg-to-body ratio of any bird, and the males tend the eggs, which take two or three months to hatch. Considered a *taonga* or "treasure" by the Maoris, kiwis are in decline and at risk due to loss of habitation and the introduction of predatory mammals, but there are government and private efforts for preservation and recovery. Kiwis have appeared on postage stamps, currency, military badges, logos, and trademarks and have become the national symbol for New Zealand and its people.

A kiwi

FEBRUARY 7 | A Curtain of Flickering Light

"He knew, by the streamers that shot so bright / That spirits were riding the northern light," wrote Sir Walter Scott in 1805, describing the *aurora borealis* (on the other side of the equator it's called *aurora australis*). The phenomenon occurs when the solar wind—highly charged particles shooting out from the sun—reaches the magnetosphere, the magnetic field that surrounds the earth. There the particles energize the electrons and the protons, causing them to glow as they travel down the magnetic field lines into the upper atmosphere around the poles. Best seen in higher north or south latitudes, these geomagnetic storms and their light shows can be small and sedate or quite active, producing ribbons or curtains of light that shimmer and flicker with eerie, brilliant colors, particularly bright green. Although beautiful to observe, intense space storms can seriously affect earth communications, air traffic, power grids, and GPS systems. In 2007, NASA launched THEMIS (Time History of Events and Macroscale Interactions during Substorms), a group of five satellites designed to study space weather and auroras.

FEBRUARY 8 | The Patron Saint of Science Fiction

He wrote about air travel before airplanes were invented, undersea travel before the submarine, and space travel before there were any rockets. Jules Verne (1828–1905) was born in Nantes, France, to an attorney father who wanted his son to make a career of the law. Jules did study law in Paris but fell in love with literature and began to write plays and short stories. He worked as a stockbroker for several years while continuing to write, experimenting with the idea of combining scientific fact with adventure fiction. Then in 1862 he met publisher Pierre-Jules Hetzel, who serialized a collection Verne called *Extraordinary Journeys*; the first novel, *Five Weeks in a Balloon*, became a best-seller. It was the beginning of a forty-year relationship that saw the publication of more than sixty works. In the first decade of their partnership, Verne published some of his best-known and longest-lasting works, including *Journey to the Center of the Earth*; *From the Earth to the Moon*; *Twenty Thousand Leagues under the Sea*; and *Around the World in Eighty Days*. He became a famous and wealthy man, and after his death in 1905, many of his works were adapted for films and later for television. Jules Verne remains the second most translated author in the world, after Agatha Christie.

FEBRUARY 9 | Beatleland

Beatlemania swept Great Britain in the spring of 1963, but it took a few months before the U.S. media caught on. Some newspapers on both sides of the Atlantic referred to the music as noise, mass hysteria, or uninterrupted hell. *Time* magazine said, "their songs consist mainly of 'Yeh!' screamed to the accompaniment of three guitars and a thunderous drum." American television networks discovered the Beatles when they performed at the Bournemouth Winter Garden in November. NBC had a short piece on the *Huntley-Brinkley Report* on November 18. CBS's London bureau chief Alexander Kendrick prepared a segment to air a few days later. It opened with a bit of snark: "Yeah, yeah, yeah, those are the Beatles, those are, and this is Beatleland, formerly known as Britain, where an epidemic called Beatlemania has seized the teenage population, especially female." Kendrick clearly didn't like the music or appreciate the developing phenomenon. His report ran on the *CBS Morning News* on November 22, but its scheduled repeat that night on Walter Cronkite's *Evening News* was postponed because of the assassination of President John F. Kennedy. The story finally aired on December 10, and the Beatles made their first live appearance in the United States on the *Ed Sullivan Show* on February 9, 1964.

FEBRUARY 10 | Found in Translation

We use the names of countries every day, usually without knowing or even wondering what those words mean or how they have evolved. Translating them may reveal something about history and worldview. Here are a few interesting examples:

Argentina: Latin for "of silver"
Australia: Latin for "southern land"
Bahamas: *baja mar* in Spanish, "shallow sea"
Bhutan: Sanskrit for "at the end of Tibet"
Burkina Faso: from two local languages, meaning "land of the incorruptible"
Cameroon: from the Portuguese *Rio de Camaroes*, "river of shrimp"
Canada: Iroquois word for "village" or "settlement"
Hong Kong: Cantonese words for "fragrant harbor"
Ireland: from the Celtic word *Éire*, "fertile place"
Liechtenstein: German words for "bright stone"
Singapore: from the Sanskrit term for "lion city"
Sudan: Arabic for "land of the blacks"
Venezuela: a variation of the Italian for "little Venice"

FEBRUARY 11 | Corporate Naming

Company names are often taken for granted, but many of them have interesting back stories, too:

- Raytheon (*rai*, "beam of light" and *theon*, "from the gods"), today a maker of defense, intelligence, and information systems, took its name from one of its first products, a rectifier tube marketed in 1925 that made radios less expensive to produce and therefore accessible to millions.
- Mitsubishi means "three (*mitsu*) diamonds (*hishi*)," which is the car company's logo as well. *Hishi* actually means "water chestnut," but it's also used to indicate something that has a diamond shape, and when it's combined with another word, it's pronounced *bishi*.
- Lego created its name by combining the Danish words *leg* and *godt*, "play well," which the company says is also its ideal.
- Sanyo means "three oceans" in Japanese and refers to the Pacific, Atlantic, and Indian oceans, expressing the company's intention to be a global enterprise.

- Bally is now a gigantic casino gaming company, but it started out as Lion Manufacturing, which originally produced punchboards, sort of an early version of a lottery ticket. The company found great success selling pinball games, and the Ballyhoo was its first and most popular machine. The shorter form of the name became the company's trademark, and in 1968 it was officially changed.
- Samsung, which means "three stars" in Korean, started out in 1938 exporting dried fish and vegetables before it expanded into electronics and other products. The founder hoped the company would be "powerful and everlasting like stars in the sky."

FEBRUARY 12 | Mr. Bones

Barnum Brown (1873–1963) was the greatest dinosaur hunter who ever lived. Fascinated by fossils as a youth, Brown joined the staff of the American Museum of Natural History (AMNH) in New York while still a college student. In a career that spanned six decades, he traveled the world, collecting fossils from India to Patagonia. He uncovered numerous species, none more significant than his discovery of *Tyrannosaurus Rex* ("tyrant king of lizards"). In 1902, Brown dug up some unusual bones in Hell Creek, Montana, and realized that it was an amazing find. He eventually unearthed an almost complete *T. Rex* skeleton, including the four-foot-long skull, which weighed more than a thousand pounds; it became the prime dinosaur display at the AMNH for decades. He took copious, detailed field notes, and although he rarely published his results, he earned the respect of pale-ontologists around the world. Brown collected so many fossils that dozens of crates still remain unopened in the museum's storerooms. At the time of his ninetieth birthday, Brown's successor at the museum told him, "There are, in our Tyrannosaur Hall, thirty-six North American dinosaurs on display. . . . You collected twenty-seven, an unsurpassed achievement." The original *Tyrannosaurus Rex* he discovered in 1902 is now exhibited at the Carnegie Museum in Pittsburgh.

FEBRUARY 13 | Minié's Ball

It wasn't a ball but had more of a cone shape. And it wasn't pro-nounced MIN-ee, as the Americans thought, but min-YAY, like the name of its French designer, Captain Claude-Étienne Minié. The minie ball represented a revolution in ammunition when it was devel-oped in the late 1840s. Smoothbore muskets had been the standard firearm; they were quick to load, but because they had no rifling grooves in the barrel, they were not very accurate at more than eighty or a hundred yards. Beyond two hundred yards, as one British officer put it, "You might just as well fire at the moon and have the same hope of hitting your object." Rifles did exist by that time and were far more accurate, but they required bullets that fit tightly into the barrel so that they would emerge spinning from the grooves. Jamming the bullets into the muzzle was a very slow process, making the guns unworkable in most combat situations. The minie ball changed all that. It was narrower than the barrel, so it slipped in easily. It had a concave bottom that nestled against the gunpowder charge so that when the rifle was fired, the minie expanded and fit into the grooves, propelling it far more accurately than a smoothbore musket could. The British were the first to use the minie in combat, during the Crimean War. Its success there led to the minie ball becoming the preferred projectile of the American Civil War, where it caused more than 90 percent of all wounds.

A minie ball

FEBRUARY 14 | Water from the Cosmos

The Earth is a wet planet; oceans cover more than 70 percent of the surface. When the Earth was first formed, it was too hot to retain sur-face water, so how were the oceans filled? Scientists have speculated that the water came from icy comets that struck the planet early in its history. There was a problem with that theory, however, because they were unable to find a comet with the same chemical signature as Earth water. The D/H ratio—the level of deuterium to hydrogen—is consistent in all of the Earth's natural water, but comets seemed to have a different ratio, leading scientists to consider that perhaps only 10 percent of our water could have come from comets. Then, in October 2011, a team of researchers used the Herschel Space Observatory to study comet 103P/Hartley 2, and it showed a D/H ratio very similar to Earth's water. The Hartley 2 comet originated in the Kuiper belt beyond Neptune, an area with many comets and other fragments from the formation of the solar system. Questions remain, but the discovery suggests that far more than 10 percent of the Earth's water came from comets. One of the report's authors, Paul Hartogh, points out that "in principle, all of Earth's water may come from comets. However, it is still possible that a large—or the largest—fraction came from asteroids."

FEBRUARY 15 | A God of Darkness

In Siberia and Lapland, there are versions of an interesting myth about the origin of evil. Ulgan, the creator, saw a bit of mud floating on the primordial ocean, imbued it with life, and created a helper for himself called Erlik (meaning "first life"). When Erlik was sent to gather more mud, he hid some in his mouth so he could create his own universe. The mud swelled as he chewed it, however, so Erlik spit it out, creating all of the swamps and the dank spots around the Earth. Meanwhile, Ulgan created proto-humans from mud and left a dog to guard them while they dried out. Erlik wanted the humans as his servants but couldn't persuade the dog to give them up, so he covered them with his saliva. When Ulgan saw what had been done, he turned the humans inside out; we have been that way ever since—dry on the outside, and moist on the inside. Ulgan then condemned Elrik to the underworld, where he became the god of darkness and death.

FEBRUARY 16 | Comparing Apples and Oranges

Let's say you really love Winesap apples. You decide to grow a tree in your backyard, so you plant a Winesap seed. Once the tree comes to maturity, you discover that the apples it produces aren't Winesaps.

Frankly, they don't even taste good. What's up with that? Most apples are self-unfruitful, that is, they can't produce fruit from their own pollen and must be fertilized with a different variety of apple in order to get a good fruit set. Two different, compatible varieties need to be planted close to each other to achieve proper pollination. Apples aren't the only fruit that does this—many pear, sweet cherry, and plum trees are propagated the same way. There are some self-fruitful apple types, such as Golden Delicious, but even they will bear more apples if they are cross-pollinated. Citrus fruits are somewhat different; some varieties will come true from seed. But they are usually grown by grafting seedlings onto a different rootstock that contains the qualities a grower is looking for, resistance to cold or disease, for example. The rootstocks can be from a different citrus species altogether, and that's why if you plant a seed from an orange, you might get a lime tree.

FEBRUARY 17 | "A Jumble of Lines and Patches"

Walter Kuhn (1877–1949) was an American modernist painter remembered mostly for his studies of performers, chorus girls, and circus acts, but it was his role in helping mount a ground-breaking exhibition that has given him a permanent place in the history of American art. Held in the 69th Regiment Armory in Manhattan, the show was formally titled the "International Exhibition of Modern Art." What came to be known as the Armory Show alternately thrilled, angered, inspired, and horrified America in 1913. A passionate champion of modern art, Kuhn wanted to bring contemporary European work to the United States and shake up the rather staid and conservative art establishment here. He traveled around Europe, meeting with artists and gallery owners, and selected a broad spectrum of the latest work for the exhibition. The thirteen hundred pieces from such now revered artists as Cézanne, Van Gogh, Matisse, Picasso, and Duchamp (as well as Americans Edward Hopper, Joseph Stella, and others) were viewed by two hundred thousand people. The Armory Show didn't merely create a sensation, it turned American art upside down. Artist and writer Bolton Brown complained to the *New York Times* that the Armory paintings "consist of a jumble of lines and patches, and that they are very ugly. . . . Brains and taste, labor and skill, love and patience, are back of all art. Omit these and you get—these other things."

FEBRUARY 18 | In-flight Guernsey

On February 18, 1930, a cow—first name uncertain, surname Ollie—became the first bovine to fly in an airplane, as part of the International Aircraft Exposition in St. Louis, Missouri. Ollie, a resident of the nearby town of Bismarck, and a member of the Guernsey family, was fed and milked during the flight. The milk was packaged in paper containers with tiny parachutes attached and dropped to the spectators below. Some reports claim that aerial pioneer Charles Lindbergh was presented with one of the containers. Journalists on board reported that "the demonstration was undertaken to illustrate the stability of modern aircraft, the feasibility of transporting livestock by air, and for scientific study of the cow's behavior." Ollie behaved very well. Her feat is celebrated annually by a fan club in Wisconsin (the Dairy State), and there's even an operetta based on her adventure called *Madame Butterfat* and attributed to Giacomo Moocini.

FEBRUARY 19 | Little Armored Ones

The armadillo (*Dasypodidae*) is the official small mammal of Texas, even though it is not native to the state or even to North America. The sharp-clawed, armor-plated insect eater is a creature of South America, and it migrated north in the Great American Faunal Interchange, millions of years ago. The most distinctive feature of armadillos is their leathery plating. The plates are made of bone covered with horn (keratin), and the various species have different numbers of plates. The Texas armadillo is a nine-banded variety, while the three-banded armadillo is the only one that can curl itself into a ball to

avoid predators. Although hard, the plates are
not impervious, and the animal's underside is
not armored, making it more vulnerable than
its appearance indicates. *Armadillo* means "little armored one" in Spanish; the Aztecs called
them *azotochtli*, or "turtle-rabbit." The mascot
of the School of Information at the University
of Texas at Austin is the "reading armadillo."

The Reading Armadillo

FEBRUARY 20 | An Unsuccessful Assassination

Four American presidents have been killed by assassins. There
have been other, unsuccessful, attempts, including one on President
Harry Truman on November 1, 1950. Two Puerto Rican national-
ists, Oscar Collazo and Griselio Torresola, approached Blair
House, across the street from the White House, where President
and Mrs. Truman were staying while the executive mansion underwent renovations. Truman was scheduled to go out later that day
to dedicate a statue, but the gunmen didn't wait; they opened fire
on the guards on the sidewalk. One White House policeman was
hit but kept shooting back. Another officer, Leslie Coffelt, went
down with shots in the chest and the stomach. Bullets were flying
everywhere in front of the house on Pennsylvania Avenue. A
Secret Service agent took cover behind a tree and fired, hitting
Collazo as he reloaded. Another White House policeman was shot
in the hip, the shoulder, and the neck and fell to the ground. Yet
Coffelt managed to get off one shot, hitting Torresola in the head
and killing him instantly. It was all over in less than forty seconds.
Truman was safe and said later, "a President has to expect those
things." Coffelt died that day, but the other guards recovered from
their wounds, as did Collazo, who was sentenced to death for the
assassination attempt. Truman commuted his sentence to life
imprisonment, and in 1979 President Jimmy Carter granted him
clemency, and he was released. He died in Puerto Rico on
February 20, 1994.

FEBRUARY 21 | A Decade of Change

The 2010 census revealed that the immigrant population of the United States underwent some significant changes in the first decade of this century. Although its rate of growth has slowed since the peak era of the 1990s, the foreign-born population increased by 8.8 million, to 40 million people. Large cities retained much of their immigrant population, but smaller metropolitan areas and suburbs experienced tremendous growth. The Scranton–Wilkes Barre area of Pennsylvania saw a 140 percent increase in its immigrant community; Indianapolis, Indiana, had a 117 percent increase; and Jackson, Mississippi, 110 percent. Miami remained the city with the largest concentration of immigrants, 38.8 percent. Washington, D.C., saw its proportion of immigrants change from 17 to 22 percent. The highest number of immigrants listed Mexico as their birthplace, but Africans were the fastest-growing group. Europe's share of the U.S. immigrant population dropped from 16 to 12 percent. America remains a melting pot, but the ingredients of the national stew are changing.

FEBRUARY 22 | The Coldest Place on Earth

In 1908, the most frigid spot on the planet was in Leiden, Netherlands, in a physics laboratory run by Heike Kamerlingh Onnes (1853–1926). Kamerlingh Onnes was fascinated by the effects of extreme cold on different materials, and as head of the experimental physics department at the University of Leiden, he focused on cryogenic research. After years of experimenting, he liquefied helium for the first time, producing a temperature of minus 268.8 degrees Celsius, the closest humans had yet come to absolute zero. While working with mercury in 1911, he ascertained that as it approached absolute zero, electrical resistance disappeared. He had discovered the principal of superconductivity: without resistance, electricity will flow with no loss of energy. That discovery opened up a whole new field of scientific exploration that has led to Maglev trains, magnetic resonance imaging, and particle accelerators. Future applications include improved power transmission and storage, satellite gyroscopes, and even Internet communications. Kamerlingh Onnes won the Nobel Prize in Physics in 1913 for his work.

FEBRUARY 23 | The End of the Earth

What is the southernmost city in the world? That depends on whether you ask an Argentine or a Chilean. Both Ushuaia and Puerto Williams are located at the tip of South America, on the archipelago of Tierra del Fuego, which is divided between the two countries— Ushuaia on the Argentine side, Puerto Williams in Chile. They're only about forty miles apart, separated by the Beagle Channel. Technically, Puerto Williams is a little farther south, but is it really a city? Founded in 1953, Puerto Williams has been primarily a base for the Chilean navy and has only around two thousand inhabitants, mostly naval personnel, although tourism has boosted the civilian population in the last decade. On the other hand, there is no doubt that Ushuaia is a major city. It is the capital of the province, with a population of more than sixty thousand and all of the amenities of urban life. The commonly accepted view—at least, outside Chile—seems to give Ushuaia the title of most southerly city.

FEBRUARY 24 | The Other End of the Earth

The northernmost permanent settlement on Earth can hardly be called a city. Alert, Canada—officially, Canadian Forces Station Alert—is at the very northern tip of Ellesmere Island, only five hundred miles from the geographic North Pole. The outpost is named for the HMS *Alert*, the ship captained by Sir George Nares, which was the first to visit the uninhabited area while on an expedition to the North Pole in 1875. In 1950, Canada and the United States jointly founded a weather station there, which was eventually taken over by the Canadian military. Alert is permanently inhabited, but fewer than one hundred people are assigned to live there, and the environment is hostile, with snow cover ten months of the year and temperatures that dip down to 31 degrees below zero Celsius. The base staff provides signals intelligence and search-and-rescue services and works with environmentalists and arctic researchers.

FEBRUARY 25 | Protein Source of the Future

Entomophagy, the eating of insects, is a rather off-putting concept to most Westerners, but the rest of the world isn't so squeamish. A 2008 United Nations conference pointed out that fourteen hundred species of insects, arachnids, and worms are consumed in about ninety countries in Africa, Latin America, and Asia. As the global population continues to climb, meat production—which already uses 70 percent of all agricultural land—won't be able to keep up with the demand. Insects take up less space, they're high in protein and low in fat, and they are certainly abundant. They could be raised for food more efficiently than animals are: one hundred pounds of grain feed can produce ten pounds of beef but forty-five pounds of cricket meat.

Hygienically farmed insects would have far less environmental impact than raising mammals (livestock production releases more greenhouse gases than transportation does), and the bugs also require far less water. Most insects have a taste that's been described as "nutty." Of course, we already do eat insects, as much as a pound a year per person that accidentally finds its way into our food. Pass the grilled cockroach steak, please.

A cockroach

FEBRUARY 26 | "The Vehicles of Life"

The Svalbard Global Seed Vault, which opened in 2008, was created to ensure "that the genetic diversity of the world's food crops is preserved for future generations," according to its website. The vault is a safety deposit box for duplicates of seeds that are held in gene banks around the world and has the capacity to store more than two billion individual seeds. Dubbed "the Doomsday Vault" by the media, the site was constructed inside a mountain on Norway's Svalbard archipelago, about 650 miles from the North Pole, where the seeds can be protected from instability of any kind—tectonic, climatic, political, or economic. The seeds are stored at minus 18 degrees Celsius in sealed packages; the combination of low temperature and lack of oxygen prevents metabolic activity and delays the aging process. At the inauguration of the vault, the head of the United Nations' Food and Agriculture Organization thanked the Norwegian government for its support of the project and remarked that "the wealth that is being safeguarded in Svalbard will be the global insurance to address future challenges. . . . Seeds are the vehicles of life."

FEBRUARY 27 | Nine Lives Had Elfego Baca

"I never wanted to kill anybody, but if a man had it in his mind to kill me, I made it my business to get him first." So said New Mexico lawman Elfego Baca (1865–1945) to a Federal Writers' Project interviewer in 1936. Born in Socorro, New Mexico Territory, at a time when the Southwest was rapidly expanding, Baca became a hero to the often victimized Latino community. His fame started when he arrived in the town of Lower San Francisco Plaza (near Reserve, New Mexico). A drunken Texas cowboy was shooting up the town, and Baca, deputized by the sheriff, disarmed him. The cowboy's friends protested, a gunfight ensued, and one of the men was killed. A large, angry group soon went after Baca and found him holed up in a small shack. For thirty-six hours, Baca held off the group (said to be as many as eighty men), who fired some four thousand bullets into the shack. A warrant was issued for Baca's arrest; he surrendered and walked out, unscathed. At trial, he was acquitted and went on to a long career as a U.S. marshal, a politician (campaigning as 'a friend of the poor'), and a lawyer who was known for defending the Mexican American community. In 1995, then representative Bill Richardson (D-NM) read a tribute into the *Congressional Record* that said in part, "Baca's bravery instilled hope to the native New Mexican people who upheld the laws of the land and refused to succumb to racial injustices."

FEBRUARY 28 | That's One Bad Golf Hole

You stand in the tee box, and you line up your drive. The pin is three miles away and 2,550 feet down. That's because you're on top of Socorro Peak in New Mexico, participating in the one-hole Elfego Baca Shootout. A side event of the Socorro Open since 1960, the shootout presents a number of challenges for the ardent golfer—rattlesnakes, scorpions, and the occasional mountain lion among them. Rather than the traditional cup, the target is a fifty-foot chalk circle on the campus of New Mexico Tech. Given the rough terrain, players are permitted to use a tee to set each shot and have three spotters to find the balls in the rocks and the scrub; a medical team also goes along, in case of emergencies. Players are allowed ten balls; a lost ball that can't be located within twenty minutes costs one penalty stroke. Scores can be in the seventies (which would be great if you were playing eighteen holes instead of one), but the record is an amazing nine strokes.

FEBRUARY 29 | A Day for Leapers

Romulus, the legendary founder of Rome, was said to have created the lunar-based calendar used there for hundreds of years. Yet it had only ten months, or 304 days, so it quickly became out of sync with the seasons. Even though two additional months had been added by the time Julius Caesar was running things, the calendar desperately needed reform. Caesar changed it to something he had heard about while in Egypt: a solar calendar whose year contained 365 days, with every fourth year adding an extra day. The old Roman calendar was by then so far off from reality that Caesar stretched the current year (46 BCE) to 445 days, and not surprisingly it became known as "the year of confusion." He also ordered that the months should alternate between thirty and thirty-one days, with the exception of February, which would be shorter but would have the extra day every fourth year, the leap day. Why February? Because the Roman year then began in March, so leap day would be the last day of the last month of the year. The Romans soon changed the calendar again, to start the year with January, which was closer to the winter solstice. The sixteenth-century Gregorian reform made a further modification: century years not divisible by four would not contain a leap day. Many people born on February 29 call themselves "leapers" and proudly celebrate their birthdays once every four years.

MARCH

MARCH 1 | Monstrous Wigs

Colonial Americans naturally imported many traditions from Great Britain, but some customs are best left in the mother country. Take the practice of judges wearing powdered wigs. When Justice William Cushing (1732–1810) of Massachusetts came to New York for the first session of the U.S. Supreme Court in 1790, he decided to wear his traditional powdered wig, as did most judges in the colonies. Supposedly, local boys harassed him on his walk to the court, and a bystander shouted out, "My eyes, what a wig!" Thomas Jefferson agreed, declaring, in a conversation with Alexander Hamilton (who favored wigs and togas for judges), "If we must have peculiar garbs for the judges, I think the gown is the most appropriate. But, for heaven's sake, discard the monstrous wig, which makes the English judges look like rats peeping through bunches of oakum [loose rope fibers used for caulking ships]." No Supreme Court justice has worn a powdered wig since.

MARCH 2 | Kind of Blue

On March 2, 1959, a group of musicians walked into Columbia Records' 30th Street Studio in New York to begin recording an album with trumpeter Miles Davis. He wanted to try something new. Most jazz up to that point was based on chord progressions with improvised melodies laid on top of them. Davis was experimenting with modal jazz, which was based on scales instead of chords, and was more concerned with melody than structure. He gathered together some of the cream of the jazz crop—pianists Bill Evans and Wynton Kelly, bassist Paul Chambers, drummer Jimmy Cobb, and saxophonists Cannonball Adderley and John Coltrane. Davis gave the players only a few outlines for the tunes and said he wanted to record with no rehearsal and just one take for each piece. The result, though they did not fully grasp it at the time, was not only a seminal recording, but a work that would change the direction of modern jazz. *Kind of Blue* has become one of the best-selling jazz albums of all time, and it appeals to both the jazz aficionado and those completely unfamiliar with the form. As music journalist Ashley Kahn points out, "*Kind of Blue* lives and prospers outside the confines of the jazz community. No longer the exclusive possession of a musical subculture, the album is simply great music, one of a very, very few musical recordings our culture allows into the category marked 'masterpiece.'"

MARCH 3 | Vanishing Alphabets

There are about six thousand to seven thousand languages spoken around the globe, and some linguists estimate that half of them will have become extinct by the end of the twenty-first century. Those languages are written with fewer than two hundred alphabets, and some of those are also disappearing. Roman, Arabic, and Cyrillic are the most common alphabets; many others are used only for a single language. Tim Brookes, a writer and a professor at Champlain College in Vermont, has taken up the cause of

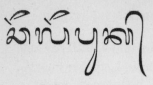

Balinese letters

preserving some of those alphabets by calling attention to their plight. His Endangered Alphabets Project is a traveling exhibition of maple planks onto which he has carved a two-sentence phrase using one of the endangered systems—Baybayin, Cherokee, Inuktitut, Samaritan, Balinese, and a few others. The phrase he's chosen to use is Article One of the Universal Declaration of Human Rights, drafted in 1948 at the foundation of the United Nations: "All human beings are born free and equal in dignity and rights. They are endowed with reason and conscience and should act towards one another in a spirit of brotherhood."

MARCH 4 | A Tough Election

He announced his campaign for president on March 4, 1948. The young candidate, despite his wooden appearance, effectively used the new medium of television to get his message across, tapping into a groundswell of popular support. I'm not talking about Harry Truman or Thomas Dewey. The candidate was a puppet named Howdy Doody, and he was running for president of all the kids in America. *The Howdy Doody Show*, hosted by Bob Smith, went on the air in 1947 on NBC's six-city network. Eddie Kean, the show's writer, decided that having Howdy run for president might be a way to demonstrate the marketing power of television. It worked, with tens of thousands of children writing in for campaign buttons. Howdy ran on a platform of two Christmases and only one school day per year, double sodas, and more movies. Just as the campaign started, the original puppet was replaced with the Howdy that is remembered today: a shock of red hair, a permanent smile, and forty-eight freckles—one for each state. The new Howdy won his election, and the *New York Times* reported that although he received fewer votes than Truman or Dewey, he did much better than Progressive Party candidate Henry Wallace. *The Howdy Doody Show* ran until 1960.

MARCH 5 | A Nation without a State

The Kurds are an ancient people whose ethnic origins are unclear. They are not Arabic, Turkish, or Persian; they speak an Indo-European language related to the Iranian group. If Kurdistan were a state, it would stretch from eastern Turkey across northern Syria and Iraq into Iran. Over the centuries, the area was occupied by Alexander the Great, the Mongols, and the Ottoman Turks. Saladin the Magnificent—the twelfth-century sultan who fought Richard the Lionhearted in the Third Crusade—was a Kurd. The Kurdish people were promised independence after World War I, but ultimately the region was divided and given to Turkey, Iraq, Syria, and Iran. Under Saddam Hussein, the Iraqi Kurds suffered brutal suppression and attempts to annihilate the entire population. Since the fall of Saddam, they have set up civil structures and a democratically elected Kurdistan Regional Government with its capital in Erbil (one of the world's oldest continually inhabited cities). In his inaugural speech, President Masoud Barzani said, "This is a golden opportunity to benefit from the mistakes and the futile attempts of former regimes and bring about a brighter future in this country on the basis of fraternity and equality."

MARCH 6 | Consumer Outreach

Outdoor advertising is nothing new; it goes back thousands of years. In ancient Egypt, papyrus notices offered rewards for the return of runaway slaves. Babylonian merchants hung signs over their shops, as did the Romans, who also painted advertisements on exterior walls. Pictorial signboards were common in the Middle Ages, and after Gutenberg invented movable type in 1450, handbills and posters were seen wherever people congregated. Soon, merchants wrangled exclusive rights to advertise in desirable locations and then began to build their own structures to post their signs. With the advent of lithography in 1796, posters became the dominant form of advertising in Europe and the United States. Painted signage, especially on barns and roadside fences, expanded in the post–Civil War era, and soon advertising became ubiquitous. Public outrage reached the boiling point in 1860 when someone painted a rock at Niagara Falls with an ad trumpeting a patent medicine, St. Jacob's Oil, prompting the first legislation to control outdoor advertising. By 1870, there were three hundred bill-posting companies in operation. In the early twentieth century, standardization of billboard size created a boom in national advertising, and such companies as Kellogg and Coca-Cola began to mass-produce their ads. Objections to outdoor advertising have always been common—for aesthetic and safety reasons—but the ads continue to appear on everything from bus shelters to the sides of buildings; American companies spent more than $6 billion on outdoor ads in 2010.

MARCH 7 | With One Eye Blinking

Art can often arise out of pain; sometimes extraordinary suffering leads to extraordinary creativity. Such was the case with Jean-Dominique Bauby. The editor of the French fashion magazine *Elle*, Bauby survived a massive stroke in 1995 that left him with a condition called "locked-in syndrome," or LIS. His mind was fully active, but his body was completely paralyzed, except for his left eyelid. Bauby was determined to continue to write. At night, he would compose paragraphs in his head and memorize them. The next day he would have his transcriber recite the alphabet and then Bauby would blink when the correct letter was reached. Slowly, painstakingly, he managed to complete a memoir, *The Diving Bell and the Butterfly*. In the prologue, he said, "[M]y mind takes flight like a butterfly. There is so much to do. You can wander off in space or in time, set out for Tierra del Fuego or for King Midas's court." Bauby died two days after the book was published; it received excellent reviews and was turned into a film in 2007 that was nominated for four Academy Awards.

MARCH 8 | "Where I Can Be of Use"

Alexander Thomas Augusta (1825–1890) was the first African American medical doctor commissioned in the U.S. Army. He was born free in Norfolk, Virginia, and, with the help of a local minister, defied the state law that prohibited black people from learning to read. Apprenticed to a barber, he moved to Baltimore and then Philadelphia to pursue his dream of becoming a physician. But no American medical school would admit him, so he enrolled in the University of Toronto, graduated in 1856, and worked in private practice and as head of a hospital there. In 1863, during the Civil War, Augusta wrote to President Abraham Lincoln, asking for a commission:

> Having seen that it is intended to garrison . . . forts with coloured troops, I beg leave to apply to you for an appointment as surgeon to some of the coloured regiments, or as physician to some of the depots of "freedmen." I was compelled to leave my native country and come to [Canada] on account of prejudice against colour, for the purpose of obtaining knowledge of my profession; and having accomplished that object . . . I am now prepared to practice it, and would like to be in a position where I can be of use to my race.

Commended for his faithful and meritorious service, Dr. Augusta left the military in 1866 and soon became a member of the faculty of the new Howard University Medical School in Washington, D.C. Despite his significant accomplishments, he suffered many instances of discrimination during his career and was even denied membership in the American Medical Association. Dr. Augusta is buried in Arlington National Cemetery—the first African American military officer to receive that honor.

Alexander T. Augusta

MARCH 9 | Cranioscopy

Are you selfish or magnanimous? Let me feel your head and find out. That was the basis of phrenology, a pseudoscience that claimed personality and character could be discerned by studying the bumps on one's head. As silly as it may sound to us today, the practice did enjoy

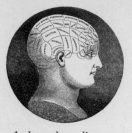

A phrenology diagram

enormous popularity in the nineteenth century. Developed by German physician Franz Josef Gall around 1800, phrenology (or cranioscopy, as he originally named it) was built on the correct idea of localization of cerebral functions—that certain parts of the brain are associated with particular behaviors. Gall thought that character traits could be "read" by feeling the contours of the skull, which he believed matched the contours of the brain beneath. For instance, benevolence was thought to reside in a particular area of the forehead, so if a person had a prominent bump at that location, he was deemed to have a well-developed sense of kindness. Head analysis became a popular and lucrative occupation for a time; it even led to a bizarre device called the Psychograph, a helmet filled with wired contact points that measured the head bumps and rated one's character on a scale from "deficient" to "superior." Though thoroughly debunked by science, phrenology maintained its popularity into the twentieth century in the United States, well after most Europeans had dismissed it as nonsense.

MARCH 10 | Droning Overtones

Throat singing, also called overtone or harmonic singing, is an ancient form of chanting used by different cultures around the world, although its most famous practitioners are in Tuva (a small Russian republic on the southern edge of Siberia) and neighboring Mongolia, where it probably originated. These people are primarily Buddhists with a strong streak of animism: they believe that all natural things—rocks, trees, rivers—have souls. Throat singing creates sounds that imitate nature, so the singer can converse with the natural world. The distinctive notes (described by a reporter as "eerie, buzzing harmonics and guttural rumbling timbres") are produced by shaping and manipulating the vocal cords, the windpipe, and the mouth so that a fundamental drone has added overtones, producing two or more distinct pitches at once, something like the sound of a bagpipe. In Tuvan throat singing, there are different styles, including the high-pitched *sygyt*, the low-pitched *kargyraa*, and the trilling effect of *borbangnadyr*, among others. Traditionally performed outdoors, throat singing became popular in the West in the 1980s, and now Tuvan and other throat-singing groups perform in concert halls around the world.

MARCH 11 | Tsunami Flotsam

When the massive Tohoku earthquake caused a tsunami to strike Japan on March 11, 2011, the seawater surged as much as six miles inland. As it receded, debris of all sizes and shapes—houses, cars, small household articles, and tiny bits of plastic—was sucked out to sea. "If you put a major city through a trash grinder and sprinkle it on the water, that's what you're dealing with," said Curt Ebbesmeyer, a Seattle oceanographer. The debris field is being propelled eastward by the North Pacific Drift. Computer models predicted it would reach the United States and Canada in three years, depending on the weight and buoyancy of the individual bits, but a lost and battered Japanese squid-fishing boat was sighted off the coast of British Columbia in March 2012. After the plume reaches the West Coast of North America, the flotsam will be caught in the North Pacific Garbage Patch, and some of it will slowly head west, back toward Asia. Ocean debris is already a serious problem for marine ecosystems and shipping, and the addition of so much material from the tsunami will seriously exacerbate the situation in the Pacific.

MARCH 12 | The Integratron

On the fringe of the Mojave Desert in California there is a giant rock, perhaps the largest free-standing boulder in the world. Native Americans considered it a sacred place, and it has also attracted a fair number of loners and eccentrics. One of them was George Van Tassel, an aeronautical engineer, who was so intrigued by the rock that in 1947 he leased the property from the Bureau of Land Management, abandoned his career, and moved his family to the area, where they built a small airport and a café. A few years later, he claimed he had been visited by aliens from Venus, who revealed to him secrets of time travel and rejuvenation. He started hosting interplanetary spacecraft conventions, and the area soon became a mecca for UFO enthusiasts. In 1957, Van Tassel began to build a domed wooden structure, fifty-five feet in diameter, which he called the Integratron. It was, he said, designed to rejuvenate the cells of the human body, just as a battery is recharged. He founded the Ministry of Universal Wisdom to merge religion and science and spent the next eighteen years soliciting donations and working on the project. Van Tassel died in 1978, and the Integratron was eventually sold, refurbished, and opened to the public. Musicians, spiritual seekers, and others come to take a "sound bath," in the "acoustically perfect tabernacle and energy machine sited on a powerful geomagnetic vortex in the magical Mojave Desert," as the Integratron's website describes it.

MARCH 13 | First Lady at Work

Abigail Powers Fillmore (1798–1853) was the first wife of a U.S. president who had a career and earned a paycheck on her own. For thirteen years, she worked as a public school teacher in Sempronius and two other towns in upstate New York. In 1826, she married Millard Fillmore, who had been one of her students, and continued teaching until the birth of their first child. She was an important adviser to her husband in his political career and may have influ-

enced him to request funding from Congress to create the first White House library; she was certainly an advocate for libraries and public education for women. Abigail Fillmore was not referred to as the "First Lady," however, because that term wasn't popularized until 1877, when it appeared in a newspaper article to describe Lucy Ware Webb Hayes, the wife of President

Abigail Powers Fillmore Rutherford B. Hayes.

MARCH 14 | Island of the Spirit

Manitoulin Island in the Canadian part of Lake Huron is the world's largest island in a freshwater lake, covering more than a thousand square miles. Manitoulin Island itself contains more than one hundred lakes, some of which have their own islands, and some of these islands have their own ponds. The largest of the island's lakes, Manitou (about forty square miles) is the largest lake in a lake. Another lake on Manitoulin, Mindemoya, contains Treasure Island—the largest island in a lake on an island in a lake. Manitoulin comes from the Ojibwe word for "island of the spirit."

MARCH 15 | Which Carolina?

Unlike the situation with President Barack Obama, there doesn't seem to have been a "birther movement" demanding to see Andrew Jackson's long-form birth certificate, but we don't know exactly where the seventh president was born. North and South Carolina have been arguing for more than a century—and placing statues and naming schools and parks—over the right to claim "Old Hickory." Here's what we know: Jackson was born on March 15, 1767, as his mother was returning from burying his father who had died in an accident. They were somewhere in an area called the Waxhaws in the Piedmont region that straddles the two Carolinas, but a precise border between the colonies had not yet been determined. When Jackson was a young man, he moved to what would become the state of Tennessee and worked there as a solicitor; he later represented the new state in both the U.S. House and the Senate. The hero of the Battle of New Orleans in the War of 1812, Jackson was a founder of the Democratic Party. As president, he "boldly cast himself as the people's tribune, their sole defender against special interests and their minions in Congress." He paid off the national debt, but he was also a slaveowner and a strong supporter of the states in their efforts to remove Native Americans to western territories. Jackson built his plantation home, the Hermitage, near Nashville, and considered himself a Tennessean; he died there in 1845.

MARCH 16 | An Ecological Disaster

Once there were four billion American Chestnut trees (*Castanea dentata*) covering a 200-million-acre range from Maine to Florida and from the Carolinas to Ohio, and it was the dominant hardwood species in the eastern United States. Lumber from these tall, fast-growing, easily worked trees was widely used for homes, furniture, utility poles, railroad ties, and musical instruments. The nuts were an important food source for livestock, woodland creatures, and humans. Devastated by a blight that was accidentally introduced in the late nineteenth century, the trees had almost completely disappeared by 1950. Dr. James Hill Craddock of the University of Tennessee considers it "the greatest ecological disaster in North America since the Ice Age." But efforts by the American Chestnut Foundation and

others to breed blight-resistant strains are having some success, and thousands of saplings are being planted throughout the tree's natural range, in the hope of someday restoring the chestnut to its original prominence. What about those chestnuts you roast on an open fire or purchase from street corner vendors? They're from European and Asian trees that were not affected by the *Cryphonectria*

American chestnut   *parasitica* fungus.

MARCH 17 | Not So Rare Earths

Rare earth elements (REEs) are somewhat misnamed. Neither earths nor rare, they are metallic elements (atomic numbers 58 through 71), and in fact the earth's crust is littered with them. REEs such as cerium, europium, and lanthanum are becoming increasingly important to the global economy, because they are essential in the manufacture of a wide range of modern applications: magnets, batteries, phosphors, and other products used in wind power technology, electric vehicles, superconductors, and defense systems. Finding them in sufficient concentrations is what makes mining them so difficult and costly.

China currently produces 97 percent of the world's rare earths, and restricts exports through quotas and tariffs. The United States was once self-sufficient in REEs, with significant deposits of them in more than a dozen states, but there is only one active rare earth mine in the country. Some scientists and politicians are increasingly worried about the potential hazards of REE shortages.

MARCH 18 | "Almost Like a War"

On March 18, 1925, at 1:01 in the afternoon, the deadliest tornado in American history touched down near Ellington, Missouri. It ripped a mile-wide swath extending 219 miles through Illinois and finally dissipated three and a half hours later near Petersburg, Indiana. When it was over, the Tri-State Tornado had killed 695 people, most of them in Illinois. A schoolgirl in the town of Gorham described the scene to a reporter from the *St. Louis Post-Dispatch*: "Then the wind struck the school. The walls seemed to fall in, all around us. Then the floor at one end of the building gave way. . . . I can't bear to think about it. Children all around me were cut and bleeding. They cried and screamed. It was something awful. I had to close my eyes." The storm was unusual in many ways. It didn't seem to produce a funnel cloud, there were no breaks or periods of lesser intensity, its path was almost dead straight in a northeasterly direction with very little wavering, and it raced across the countryside at sixty miles per hour. In addition to the deaths, 2,027 people were injured and 15,000 homes were destroyed. A Murphysboro resident summed up the devastation: "It was almost like a war."

MARCH 19 | The Threshold of Civilization

Some scholars say it was the world's first city. Çatalhöyük is certainly the best-preserved Neolithic city yet discovered. Nine thousand years ago, when most humans were still living as nomadic hunter-gatherers, this settlement was "at the threshold of civilization." Several thousand people lived there, herding domesticated livestock, hunting wild animals, and growing crops of lentils, peas, and other vegetables. The remnants of at least two hundred mud huts have been uncovered, which revealed painted murals with geometric and floral designs, as well as plaster reliefs and sculpted heads of bulls, sheep, goats, aurochs, and even a few humans. One room contained what has been described as the world's first landscape—a painting of two mountain peaks above a group of houses. British archaeologist James Mellaart first excavated Çatalhöyük (near the modern Turkish city of Konya), beginning in 1958, and because he found no footpaths or streets separating the tightly packed structures, he concluded that the residents used the flat rooftops to move around and entered the houses through holes in the ceilings. Ian Hodder, the leader of the current team excavating and studying Çatalhöyük, addressed the question of whether it was a true city, "In terms of population size and density, it certainly seems to be an urban centre. But in most towns you get functional differentiation between zones—residential, industrial, places of worship, cemeteries and administrative centres. In Çatalhöyük all you have is lots and lots of houses and rubbish dumps."

MARCH 20 | Psst, Your Automatic Continuing Clothing Closure Is Open

Since humans first wrapped themselves in animal skins eons ago, we have needed some method to keep our clothing from falling off or flapping in the wind. At first, belts and ropes made of plant or animal material were used. Then came cloth ties, then buttons. In 1851, Elias Howe, the inventor of the sewing machine, came up with an idea for a fastener that he patented as "An Automatic, Continuing Clothing Closure." It was a set of clasps that were fastened by hand and then pulled shut using a string. Howe didn't pursue the idea, and it died. Forty years later, Whitcomb Judson came up with a "Clasp Locker or Unlocker for Shoes" that was deemed too cumbersome. He tried again in 1893, changing from clasps to

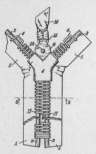

Patent diagram for a zipper

hooks and eyes, but they had a tendency to pop open. Gideon Sundback devised a similar closure he called the "Plako fastener," but it often opened when it was bent. Sundback didn't give up, though, and in 1913 and 1917 obtained patents for a new device: interlocking oval scoops that were opened or closed by moving a slider up or down. It worked well but still took a while to catch on. At first, the new fasteners were used on galoshes and tobacco pouches, and that was about it. The U.S. military in World War I decided they were efficient closures for flight suits, which helped them achieve more widespread use. The B.F. Goodrich Company, which used fasteners in its line of boots and galoshes, named it the "zipper." It still wasn't until the 1930s that zippers became the norm, replacing button fasteners in many applications.

MARCH 21 | Floriography

Plants have been endowed with symbolic and religious meaning throughout human history. During the Victorian era, flowers not only were a way of brightening a garden or a home, but also became a mode of communication. At a time when many things between men and women were left unspoken, flowers could bridge the gap and let someone know what you were really thinking. Of course, one had to speak the language of floriography, that is, know what a particular flower represented. Here are a few examples:

Almond blossoms—hope
Balsam—ardent love
Pink camellia—longing
Yellow carnation—disappointment or rejection
Dill—lust
Forsythia—anticipation
White lily—innocence
Lotus—estranged love
Mimosa—secret love
Orange blossom—marriage

Phlox—souls united
Red rose—I love you
Yellow rose—jealousy
Venus flytrap—caught at last

Flowers could be combined into rather complex messages, which were often sent via a tussie-mussie (also called a nosegay), a small bouquet wrapped in lace and tied with a satin ribbon. *The Language of Flowers*, by Kate Greenaway, was published in 1884 and became the bible for Victorian floral communicators.

MARCH 22 | Goniochromism

Have you ever picked up an abalone shell and marveled at how it changed colors as you turned it in your hand? That's the optical phenomenon known as iridescence or goniochromism. It's found in a variety of places in nature—soap bubbles, fish, beetles, and butterflies, for example. Here's how it works: light travels in waves, and different colors have different wavelengths. An iridescent surface contains multiple semitransparent layers. As light passes through the first layer, some of it is reflected and some continues through to the next layer, where again some is reflected and some passes through. Those reflected light waves interfere with one another, amplifying or diminishing a particular color, depending on the angle at which they are seen. Iridescent colors can also be created artificially and are used in lipstick and custom automobile paints, as well as in a variety of contemporary arts, including glass sculpture.

MARCH 23 | "This Side Up with Care"

Henry Brown was a slave in a Richmond tobacco factory in 1848. When his wife and children were sold to a master in North Carolina, Henry decided it was time to escape. With the help of two acquaintances, he built a box three feet long, two feet wide, and two

and a half feet deep and wrote "this side up
with care" on it. He crawled inside and then
his friends nailed it closed. They shipped him
to the Pennsylvania Anti-Slavery Society in
Philadelphia on March 23, 1849. Air holes
had been drilled in the box and he had a supply of water, but the twenty-seven-hour jour-

Henry Brown's box

ney by rail, ship, and wagon was arduous and agonizing, especially
when he was turned upside down. "I was again placed with my head
down," he wrote after the escape, "and in this dreadful position had
to remain nearly an hour and a half, which, from the sufferings I had
thus to endure, seemed like an age to me, but I was forgetting the
battle of liberty, and I was resolved to conquer or die." The box was
received at the Society, and Brown was a free man. He changed his
name to Henry Box Brown, published a narrative of his life, and
went on to tell his tale to enthralled audiences, carving a career for
himself as an abolitionist speaker with a distinct flair for
showmanship.

MARCH 24 | Operation Acoustic Kitty

We've all heard about the cool gadgets spies have used over the
decades, from cameras hidden in cigarette packs to weaponized
umbrellas. But there were some not-so-cool projects as well, perhaps none more bizarre than the experiment the Central Intelligence Agency labeled "Acoustic Kitty." At the height of the Cold
War in the mid-1960s, American spies thought it would be a good
idea to surgically implant a microphone and transmitting gear
inside a cat. The animal could then be trained to eavesdrop surreptitiously on the Kremlin or at Russian embassies. After invest-
ing millions of dollars, the CIA was ready for the first live trial.
The cat was released and was immediately run over by a taxicab.
The spies cut their losses and ended the program, noting in a
memo that despite successful training, using cats to spy "would not
be practical." Indeed.

MARCH 25 | Tasting Flavors

Your tongue is covered with little bumps called *papillae*, which contain up to ten thousand taste buds. There are also some taste buds in other parts of your mouth. The buds are attuned to the four main flavors we perceive—sweet, sour, salty, and bitter. There's a fifth that's gained some currency recently: umami, a difficult-to-describe savory taste (and there may be others). Each taste bud is made up of about a hundred receptor cells. When food enters the mouth, saliva breaks up the chemicals, allowing the molecules to bind to a receptor cell, which transmits the information to the brain. The receptor cells have a short life span, lasting only about a week or two before they are replaced. That doesn't happen as quickly as one gets older, which is why your sense of taste can diminish over the years, and why kids who hate broccoli can grow into adults who love it. Experiencing the true flavor of something depends as much on the sense of smell as it does on your taste buds. The olfactory membrane in the back of the nasal cavity is made up of 100 million receptor cells that react to the smell of food and transmit information to the brain, along with the messages coming from your taste buds. Anyone who has had a bad cold knows that the inability to smell diminishes the taste of foods.

MARCH 26 | For Men Only

The Olympic Games of ancient Greece were religious and artistic, as well as sporting, events. The first champion was recorded in 776 BCE; the games continued until they were suppressed by Emperor Theodosius in 393 CE. There were five events in the ancient Pentathlon: foot race, discus throw, javelin throw, long jump, and wrestling. Women and foreigners were banned from competing, although young unmarried women had their own games—a foot race in honor of Hera, the wife of Zeus. There's a legend that a woman named Pherenike violated the ban on female participants when she accompanied her son to the games, disguised as his trainer. When her son triumphed, she leaped into the stadium and her robe somehow opened, revealing her true nature.

She could have been condemned to death, but her family's status as important athletic champions meant her life was spared. Her name was changed to Kallipateira, which means "Mrs. Good Father."

MARCH 27 | Olympic Oddities

After a gap of about fifteen hundred years, the Olympic Games were reintroduced in 1896. These were summer games; the winter Olympics didn't begin until 1924. Sporting events—official and demonstration, standard and strange—have been added and dropped over time. The tug-of-war, actually one of the ancient Olympic events, was brought back in 1900 and lasted until 1920, with two teams of eight men competing to drag the other over a distance of six feet in five minutes. Rope climbing and one-hand weightlifting were also popular for a while. But the games with the most unusual events has to be the 1900 Paris Olympics. They had underwater swimming (not much of a spectator sport); an obstacle race where competitors had to swim over and under rows of boats in the river Seine; croquet (the first Olympic sport to allow women to participate); and perhaps most surprising of all, shooting of live pigeons (nearly three hundred birds were killed). None of those events returned after the 1900 Olympic Games.

MARCH 28 | The Broadest Aspect

Egyptian figure paintings—why do they look so weird, so flat and unnatural? The ancient artists followed the convention of the broadest aspect. The Metropolitan Museum of Art in New York has this explanation:

> When depicting the human body on a two-dimensional surface, artists used different points of view to show each part of the body in its most complete form. For instance, the shoulders are seen from the front. The torso and hips turn in three-quarter view so that the legs and arms can be seen in profile. The head is also

An Egyptian figure

shown in profile—to display simultaneously the back and the front, with protruding nose and lips—but the eye is drawn as if seen from the front, looking directly at the viewer.

Egyptian artists followed strict, complex rules that determined how they should depict human figures, especially the pharaohs, who were, after all, imbued with divine power by the gods. The placement of the figures, their relative sizes, even the pigments used (green represented fertility; red meant power, victory; blue indicated the heavens and water, creation) were regulated according to stylized, symbolic meanings. Despite some modifications of fashion, the rules governing the artistic representation of nature and man were unchanged for thousands of years.

MARCH 29 | Truly Wild

The last truly wild horse in the world is the *takhi*, from Mongolia. Other horses that are considered wild—such as the ponies on Assateague Island, brumbies of Australia, and mustangs in the American West—are actually feral horses, descended from domesticated animals that escaped or otherwise were returned to the wild. Horses have been an essential part of Mongolian culture, at least since the days of Genghis Khan in the twelfth century. Takhis (*Equus caballus przewalskii*; called Przewalski's horse in the West) have thicker necks and shorter legs than most equine breeds, and they now live mostly in captivity. Takhis were last observed in the wild in the 1960s in the Gobi region and would probably have died out altogether if not for zoo breeding programs.

MARCH 30 | The Heart of a Champion

Secretariat (1970–1989) was undoubtedly one of the greatest race-horses of all time. The 1973 Triple Crown winner set records that remain unbroken in the Kentucky Derby and the Preakness, and shattered the record in the Belmont Stakes, winning the mile-and-a-half endurance test by an astounding thirty-one lengths. After his death, a necropsy showed that Secretariat had an extraordinarily large heart. Dr. Thomas Swerczek, who performed the postmortem examination, recalls being stunned: "This was a heart completely out of anybody's league. . . . The heart was what made him able to do what he did. . . . We couldn't believe it. The heart was perfect. There were no problems with it. It was just this huge engine." The heart of an average horse weighs approximately 8.5 pounds. Secretariat's was estimated to weigh 22 pounds. A large heart means more blood can be pumped to the muscles while the animal runs. Pedigree research discovered a link between large hearts and a mutation of the equine female X chromosome (called the X-factor), which was traced back to the great eighteenth-century English racehorse Eclipse. In 2007, Secretariat became the first nonhuman inducted into the Kentucky Athletic Hall of Fame.

MARCH 31 | Pre-Code Hollywood

Almost from the beginning, the film industry in Hollywood had a tawdry reputation, for the risqué scenes in silent films, as well as for the real-life antics of some movie stars. Fearing government censorship, the studios instituted the "Code to Govern the Making of Talking, Synchronized, and Silent Motion Pictures" (known as the Hays Code) in 1930 to regulate themselves. It was a severely restrictive set of rules: "No picture shall be produced which will lower the moral standards of those who see it. Hence the sympathy of the audience should never be thrown to the side of crime, wrongdoing, evil or sin." Yet the code had no real enforcement mechanism until it was amended in 1934 to require a certificate of approval before a film could be distributed. During those intervening few years, some of Hollywood's most daring films were made, dealing with topics that would soon be banned—homosexuality, drug use, violent crime, miscegenation, and of course, sex. The era was not as completely open as some film historians suggest; there were local obscenity regulations and public opinion to contend with. Nonetheless, pre-code pictures give some insight into the mores and conflicts of a pivotal era of American history. The Hays Code was replaced by the film ratings system in 1968.

APRIL

APRIL 1 | Fool's Day

I kid you not: no one knows for certain how the tradition of April Fool's Day began. Some say it was related to the calendar reform that moved the start of the year from March to January, others think it's related to the Roman festival of Hilaria (Day of Rejoicing), and still others claim it has to do with the vernal equinox. None of those theories has any definitive proof behind it. It is known that people have been playing jokes on one another on the first day of April since at least the early eighteenth century, but that is primarily in the Western world. Other places have prank days that fall at different times of the year. The news media has latched onto April Fool's Day as a time to trick people into believing false stories. In 1957, the British Broadcasting Corporation reported that the spaghetti harvest was coming early; they showed images of Swiss peasants gathering pasta from trees. George Plimpton wrote about a baseball player for the New York Mets named Hayden Siddhartha Finch who could throw a pitch at 168 miles per hour. A Danish newspaper reported on legislation requiring all dogs to be painted white for improved visibility in the dark. NPR has a tradition of April Fool's stories. My favorites are the report that claimed Rupert Murdoch was buying the NPR network and the one where a decline in demand for maple syrup was causing the untapped trees to explode like geysers.

APRIL 2 | "Most Priceless Asset"

The Norden Bombsight was one of the most closely guarded secrets of World War II. It was the most technologically advanced method yet devised for accurately dropping bombs on a target; one was used to drop the first atomic bomb on Hiroshima in 1945. Theoretically, it could hit a hundred-foot circle from an altitude of four miles. The bombsight employed a crude analog computer into which the bombardier would enter data on speed, wind, altitude, and angle of drift. The device would then take over, pilot the plane toward the target, and release the bombs at precisely the right moment. At least, that was the theory. In actuality, it depended a great deal on the bombardier's accuracy in judging all of the variables he fed to the instrument. Security of the device was so important that it was stored in a concrete vault under guard when not in use. In case of ditching, the bombardiers were instructed to throw the sight overboard. Each man swore an oath to protect it: "Mindful of the fact that I am to become guardian of one of my country's most priceless military assets, the American bombsight . . . I do here, in the presence of Almighty God, swear by the Bombardier's Code of Honor to keep inviolate the secrecy of any and all confidential information revealed to me, and further to uphold the honor and integrity of the Army Air Forces, if need be, with my life itself."

APRIL 3 | Knickerbockers

What do a New York basketball team and British women's underwear have in common? One is the Knicks, the other is knickers, and they both derive from the same word: Knickerbockers. In 1809, Washington Irving published his famous satire, *A History of New York, from the*

A man wearing knickerbockers

Beginning of the World to the End of the Dutch Dynasty, under the pseudonym Diedrich Knickerbocker. Soon, New Yorkers began referring to themselves as Knickerbockers. A British edition of Irving's book contained illustrations by George Cruikshank (who also illustrated some of the books of Charles Dickens), showing the old Dutch-descended New Yorkers wearing baggy knee pants, which began to be called knickerbockers. The *Oxford English Dictionary* defines the term as "loose-fitting breeches, gathered at the knee, and worn by boys, sportsmen, and others who require a freer use of their limbs." A similar style of women's underwear became known as knickers, though that term never really caught on in the United States. Over the years, the name was adopted for a variety of things, including New York's first baseball team, a newspaper, a brand of beer, a chamber orchestra, and, of course, the current basketball team.

APRIL 4 | Movie Music

Music has been associated with motion pictures almost from their beginning. Early in the era of silent films, theater owners realized that musical accompaniment added a great deal to the story on the screen, while also covering up the noise of the projector. At first, they used mechanical devices to produce the music but soon opted for live performers—often a solo pianist or an organist who would improvise along with the flickering images. As the industry evolved, many theaters replaced soloists with small ensembles or specially designed organs. Camille Saint-Saëns was the first important composer commissioned to create an original film score, for *L'Assassinat du duc de Guise* in 1908. He later turned the piece into a concert work, his Opus 128 for strings, piano, and harmonium. Commissioned scores were costly, so other ideas also evolved. Composers provided books of music cues classified by style and mood, and producers distributed lead sheets of appropriate music, tied to the action on the screen and arranged for everything from solo piano to small orchestra. It wasn't

APRIL 67

until well into the sound era that composed film scores became the norm.

APRIL 5 | Salt of the Earth

The history of salt is the history of civilization. Perhaps no other single substance has contributed more to the success of humanity over the eons. Settlements grew up around salt licks; salt was mined in caves that are still active; it was evaporated from pools that are still in use; and the salt trade powered commerce for thousands of years (salt was traded, pound for pound, with gold). Salt is essential to the health of the human body; it was vital for food preservation before refrigeration; it was part of religious rituals; it was used medicinally; it melts ice; and it makes everything taste better (but too much salt can cause health problems). Roman soldiers received part of their pay in salt, the *salarium argentum*, which evolved into the English word *salary*. The English language is replete with phrases related to it: "salt of the earth"; "take it with a grain of salt"; "worth his salt"; "rub salt in the wound." Salt has been taxed, sometimes heavily, by most governments, and major wars and revolutions have been fought over it. As American chef and food writer James Beard reportedly said, "Where would we be without salt?"

APRIL 6 | The Great Hedge of India

India long enjoyed a vibrant salt trade, with production centered near Gujarat and Orissa, and the vital substance was readily available to the people. When the British began to control commerce in India in the early nineteenth century, that situation changed. Looking to dominate the salt trade, they imposed a tax that was so high that smuggling became prevalent. In order to control the smuggling, the British in 1843 began building an Inland Customs Line, connecting already existing customs houses with stone walls and a hedge, stretching from Punjab in the Northwest to Orissa in the Southeast. The Great Hedge, as it was known, eventually extended 2,500 miles and was filled with thorny bushes as high as twenty feet tall; at its peak, fourteen thousand men patrolled the line. Impoverished Indians were forced to spend two months' wages to procure enough salt for a small family. Financial minister Sir John Strachey opposed the line (but not the tax), which he saw as "a monstrous system, to which it would be almost impossible to find a parallel in any tolerably civilised country." The Inland Customs Line was abolished in 1879, and the hedge disappeared, but the tax did not end. In 1930, Mahatma Gandhi led a 240-mile march to the sea at Dandi to protest the salt tax. He was arrested on April 6 for illegally collecting salt, and the issue was brought to public attention; the tax was finally repealed in 1946.

APRIL 7 | Friction Lights

The first self-igniting matches were invented by French chemist Jean Chancel in 1805. He coated the head of a stick with a mixture of sugar and potassium chloride. To light it, you had to carry around a little vial filled with concentrated sulfuric acid, then dip the match into it. The head would flare up and light the stick. It was as dangerous as it sounds. Then in 1826, a British pharmacist named John Walker accidentally discovered the friction match. He was experimenting with combustible substances, and the end of the stick he used to stir them accumulated a coating of the chemicals. When he rubbed the stick on his hearth, it burst into flame. He then developed what he called "friction lights," using antimony sulfide, potassium chloride, gum, and starch. He sold them in a tin, along with a piece of sandpaper; the first sale was on April 7, 1827. Walker didn't obtain a patent for them, so another man began to market them under the name "Lucifers." They were popular with smokers but produced an unpleasant odor. Charles Sauria next developed a match that used phosphorus to eliminate the bad smell, but it was a serious health hazard. During the next few decades, a number of people refined the friction match, using various chemical mixtures and delivery systems. In 1910, the Diamond Match Company patented the first nonpoisonous safety match.

APRIL 8 | There Are No Suits in Baseball

Look at the coach courtside during a professional basketball game; he's probably wearing a suit. Football coaches normally appear in street clothes, well-marked with the team's logo. Now check the dugout during a baseball game; you will see the manager wearing the full team uniform, the only major sport where that occurs. Some have said it's because the manager has to go onto the field to make pitching changes and kick dirt on the umpires, but there's nothing in the rulebook that specifies his attire. The only peripherally related rule is 1.11(a)(1), which states, "All players on a team shall wear uniforms identical in color, trim and style." But the manager isn't a player, right? In the early days of the game, the "manager" was the person who arranged team travel and paid the bills; the man who decided the lineup and made strategic decisions during the game was the team captain, and he was a player. That changed in the twentieth century, when the captain position became honorary and the nonplaying manager called the shots. Most managers opted to wear the uniform, with a few exceptions, and it's now a well-established baseball tradition.

APRIL 9 | The Mysteries of Rapa Nui

Easter Island is one of the most remote inhabited places on earth. More than two thousand miles west of South America, it was named by a Portuguese explorer who first saw it on Easter Sunday in 1722; the natives call it Rapa Nui. The island is known for the imposing, immense statues carved from compressed volcanic ash, maybe a thousand of them altogether (including unfinished, buried, and broken ones), that are scattered all over the island. Known as *moai*, they range in size from six to thirty feet and weigh as much as eighty tons. Thought to be images of ancestral chiefs, their specific purpose, how they were moved, and exactly why many were destroyed are all unanswered questions. Archaeologists believe Rapa Nui was first settled by Polynesians, perhaps as early as

300 CE, when the small island (less than a hundred square miles) still had trees. As the population grew, the island was slowly deforested. Resources became scarce and the tribes set upon one another, and many of the moai were destroyed. Easter Island is now owned by Chile, and it's been designated a national park to preserve the many archaeological sites. "The *moai* are not silent. They speak. They're an example our ancestors created in stone, of something that is within us, which we call spirit. The world must know this spirit is alive," says Petero Edmunds, the former mayor of the capital, Hanga Roa.

A moai

APRIL 10 | The Father of the Dream Car

Henry Ford made the automobile popular and affordable; Harley J. Earl (1893–1969) made it the ultimate object of desire. Earl's father was a coachbuilder who switched to producing custom automobile bodies, and Harley worked with him after college. General Motors' Cadillac division commissioned him in 1927 to design the LaSalle, which was successful enough for the company to hire Earl as head of what would be called the Styling Section. Before this time, car bodies were designed for functionality, not for appearance; they were boxy and not aerodynamic or pleasing to the eye. Earl changed that with a number of innovative design ideas. During the course of his career, he removed running boards, encouraged streamlining, and instituted the use of chrome, two-tone paint jobs, wraparound windshields, and, perhaps most remembered (fondly or not), tail fins, which he first put on a Cadillac in 1948 after being inspired by jet plane design. The original Corvette was Earl's idea—he believed the United States needed its own sports car. He thought car companies should bring out new models every year so that buyers would always be hungering for the latest bit of Detroit flash. The *Encyclopedia of Pop Culture* says that Harley Earl's "cars were designed to inspire desire, build egos, and make ownership feel satisfying and exciting."

APRIL 11 | A Hole in the Head

Trepanation, or drilling a hole into the skull, is one of the oldest surgical procedures known. The word comes from the Greek *trypanon*, meaning "to bore or drill." The practice dates back seven thousand to twelve thousand years and was found among many ancient cultures, including the Egyptians, the Romans, the Chinese, the Celts, the Indians, the Greeks, and the Meso-Americans. It is unclear exactly why these cultures drilled holes in the skull, but scientists conjecture that it might have been medically related, to deal with headaches, fractures, or other injuries, or it might have had a religious basis, to release evil spirits that inhabited the brain. The procedure was often successful, because healing and regrowth can be seen on ancient skulls; it was performed on men, women, and children; and some skulls show multiple procedures. At first, practitioners used flint or another sharp stone to scrape away the skull. Then more advanced tools were developed to drill small holes in a circular pattern and pry out the piece of bone. Trepanation or craniotomy is still used today to treat traumatic brain injuries. There are also people who practice elective trepanation in the hope of achieving higher consciousness; the International Trepanation Advocacy Group claims that "making an opening in the skull favorably alters movement of blood through the brain and improves brain functions."

APRIL 12 | A Sound Ship

In the 1997 movie *Titanic*, after the ship hits the iceberg, the captain says, "Find the carpenter. Get him to sound the ship." That nautical term is probably unfamiliar to most of us. Depth sounding—knowing how much water is below the keel of the ship—has been an important part of sailing from its earliest days. A lead weight attached to a line was lowered over the side of the vessel until it touched the sea or river bottom. Sounding was also used onboard ships to find out how much water might be collecting below decks. In the era of wooden sailing ships, a sounding well was a pipe that ran from the upper decks down to the bilge, and as with a depth sounding, a weight was lowered on a line down the pipe to check the water level. The ship's carpenter was in charge of that operation. By the time of the *Titanic* disaster, sounding the ship meant visually checking for damage and leaks. John Hutchinson was a carpenter on the *Titanic,* and according to survivor Marie Young, "[H]e was the first of the *Titanic's* martyrs, who, in sounding the ship just after the iceberg was struck, sank and was lost in the inward rushing sea that engulfed him."

APRIL 13 | Hey, You Guys

The English word *guy* originally came from the French word meaning "guide" or "leader." As a man's name, it became famous with Guy Fawkes (1570–1606), the head of the unsuccessful attempt to blow up the British Parliament in 1605. Effigies of Mr. Fawkes were burned on the anniversary of the plot, and *guys* came to be a way of referring to the effigies, then to anyone who dressed strangely or behaved weirdly. By the mid-1800s in the United States, the word *guy* had become a generic term for "man" or "fellow." Today, *guys* is used to address any group of people, not only men; perhaps that's due to the fact that there aren't many good words to address a multiple-gender grouping. "Ladies and gentlemen" and "folks" are on opposite ends of the formality scale, and neither seems appropriate for all settings. Variations of the second-person plural pronoun—yinz, youze, yiz, y'all—are regional colloquialisms that are frequently heard. It seems that *guy* is losing its gender specificity and now is used to address a wholly female grouping, though the women may not be pleased. Right, guys?

APRIL 14 | To Investigate and Safeguard

The U.S. Secret Service (USSS), originally a division of the Department of the Treasury, was created in the nineteenth century to investigate the counterfeiting of currency at a time when as much as one-half of all money in circulation was fake. Its original mission did not include protection of the president; the security of the executive branch was not then seen as a necessary priority. President Abraham Lincoln signed the legislation establishing the Secret Service on April 14, 1865, the day that he—guarded only by a Washington police officer—was assassinated at Ford's Theater. Eventually, the USSS acquired its more prominent role of protecting the president, the vice president, former presidents, major political candidates (and their families), and distinguished foreign visitors, and its agents continue to oversee criminal investigations of financial crimes, identity theft, and computer fraud. Since 2003, it has been part of the Department of Homeland Security.

APRIL 15 | Tax Day

April 15 wasn't always a dreaded day in the United States. In fact, for much of our history, American citizens did not pay any income tax. The first real tax on personal income was the Revenue Act of 1861 to finance the Civil War, and it lasted for ten years. Then in 1894, Congress passed a flat income tax, but it was ruled unconstitutional because it was not apportioned among the individual states. The Sixteenth Amendment, ratified in 1913, removed the apportionment requirement and allowed the government to tax American citizens directly. The original deadline to file tax returns was March 1, but that was changed to March 15 in 1918. After thirty-seven years, the date was changed to April 15. The Internal Revenue Service says the date change was to "spread out the peak workload," but it also allowed the government to hold onto our money longer and avoid issuing refunds early in the year. Albert Einstein once told his accountant, "The hardest thing in the world to understand is the income tax."

APRIL 16 | Tut's Trumpets

When British archaeologist Howard Carter located the tomb of King Tutankhamen in 1922, he poked his head through a small hole to

King Tutankhamen

look inside the chamber. Asked what he could see, he replied, "wonderful things." The tomb was indeed filled with many magnificent treasures that were being uncovered for the first time in thousands of years. Two trumpets, one silver and one gilded bronze, were found—the world's oldest surviving musical instruments. In 1939, the BBC arranged for an extraordinary recording: military bandsman James Tappern was selected to play the ancient horns. They produced a somewhat shrill but haunting sound, as the presenter announced, "And so, after a silence of over three thousand years, these two voices out of Egypt's glorious past have gone echoing across the world." After the broadcast, the horns were placed on exhibit at the Museum of Egyptian Antiquities in Cairo. Fast forward to 2011. A popular uprising deposed Egyptian president Hosni Mubarak after weeks of protests; during the unrest, the museum was broken into and the bronze horn vanished. Fortunately for posterity, the trumpet was recovered in good condition and is once again on display.

APRIL 17 | Public Service

These U.S. presidents also served in both the House of Representatives and the Senate:

John Quincy Adams
Andrew Jackson
William Henry Harrison
John Tyler
Franklin Pierce
James Buchanan
Andrew Johnson
John F. Kennedy
Lyndon Johnson
Richard Nixon

James Garfield represented Ohio in the House for nine terms; he was then elected to the Senate in 1880 but declined the seat because he had also been elected president. Though he never served in either house of Congress, President William Howard Taft did become Chief Justice of the United States after he left office; he was nominated to the court by President Warren Harding in 1921. In that capacity, Taft administered the oath of office to two of his successors in the White House: Calvin Coolidge and Herbert Hoover.

APRIL 18 | Houses of Stone

The Great Zimbabwe was a major city a thousand years ago, the largest stone construction in southern Africa, and the center of a commercial empire built on gold and cattle. It was created by Bantu-speaking ancestors of the Shona people, from local granite blocks assembled without mortar, and covered an area of about eighteen hundred acres. The vast stone ruins of undulating walls, some more than thirty feet tall, indicate that there were three sections of the complex, Hill and Valley dwellings and a Grand Enclosure, which were built and occupied over several centuries. The racist attitudes of European travelers and colonizers since the sixteenth century caused them to deny Zimbabwe's African origin and assume the structures had been designed and built by Phoenicians, Arabs, or another foreign culture; some identified it as the home of the biblical Queen of Sheba. Serious archaeological study in the twentieth century confirmed that black Africans were responsible for this remarkable architectural achievement.

APRIL 19 | The Tie Is the Man

Men have long liked the idea of tying a piece of cloth around their necks, for practical or decorative purposes. When the terracotta army of the Emperor of China (third century BCE) was unearthed, many of the figures were wearing what looked like ties as part of

A tie

their uniforms. Roman orators wrapped their throats to protect the voice. The birth of the modern tie came in the seventeenth century. Croatian soldiers wore a neck adornment that resembled a bow tie, which caught the eye of King Louis XIV of France. He called them *cravats* (from the French word for "Croat"), and they soon became a fashion accessory in his domain. The style spread to the rest of Europe and eventually to the United States. It was in New York that tailor Jesse Langsdorf gave us the modern necktie. He figured out that cutting the cloth on the bias would cause it to hang straight down from the knot. He also discovered that sewing the tie from three pieces of cloth, rather than just two, allowed the tie to keep its shape. He patented his methods, and ties have remained more or less the same since, though they have gotten longer or shorter, wider or skinnier, sedate or garish, according to the taste of the time. As Oscar Wilde once wrote, "A well-tied tie is the first serious step in life."

APRIL 20 | Continent or Island?

Why is Australia considered a continent, but Greenland is an island? On most standard maps, Greenland actually appears larger than Australia (it even appears to be larger than Africa), but that's due to the distortion created by trying to depict the curved surface of the Earth on a flat map. Australia is actually larger (2,941,300 square miles to Greenland's 836,330 square miles), but the distinction between continent and island is not about size. Continents are "areas of geologically stable crust tectonically independent from other continents; with biological distinctiveness; cultural uniqueness; and local belief in separate continental status," as the World Island Info website explains it. Greenland is considered part of North America in the first three criteria, and the local opinion is that they live on an island, not a continent.

APRIL 21 | "The Master of the Monstrous"

Almost nothing is known about the life of Hieronymus Bosch (1450?–1516). He left no diaries, letters, or essays about his fantastical art. We know only a few details from the records of his hometown, Hertogenbosch in the Netherlands (whence he took his pseudonym). His real name was Jeroen van Aken; he was a deeply religious but pessimistic man, and the art he produced was unlike any other. He seemed obsessed with the devil and human folly, and his paintings are full of sinners punished by grotesque demons and beasts in surreal landscapes. *The Garden of Earthly Delights* is perhaps his most famous work. It is a triptych, a large three-paneled painting. On the left section are Adam and Eve with Christ, surrounded by all manner of birds and animals, some realistic and some wholly imaginative. More of those distorted creatures inhabit the center panel, with nude men and women, large pieces of fruit, and birds and other creatures engaged in odd activities. The right panel shows hell in its full horror, with sinners being tortured in a dark, foreboding atmosphere. Perhaps psychoanalyst Carl Jung best described Bosch when he called him "The master of the monstrous . . . the discoverer of the unconscious."

APRIL 22 | Gandy Dancing with Wild Cat Roughnecks and Grease Monkeys

Some occupational titles go out of fashion, or their meaning is modified. Blue-collar jobs seem to get the most colorful nicknames. *Gandy dancer* is a good example. Originally, it referred to the railroad men who straightened and tamped the tracks, a difficult daily job they accompanied with songs and chants. The source of the name is obscure and may come from the way the crews moved while working on the tracks or—less likely—from a manufacturer of railroad equipment. The term came to be applied to any railroad worker but is rarely used today. A *roughneck* was a carnival worker, similar to a roustabout, and not a term of endearment, because roughnecks were often vagrants with no connection to the community who were regarded with suspicion. Over time, the word came to be used for oil field workers, which is the meaning it retains today (another term for oil prospectors is *wildcatter*, someone who is willing to engage in risky or dangerous behavior). A *grease monkey* was originally a child worker, who in the early period of the Industrial Revolution would climb over and scramble into the machinery to keep the gears greased. Eventually, the term was applied to anyone who works with engines but primarily to auto mechanics.

APRIL 23 | From Lepidoptery to Lolita

Famed Russian novelist Vladimir Nabokov (1899–1977), the author of *Lolita* and *Pale Fire*, had a passion that he valued even above writing—butterflies. A self-taught lepidopterist, Nabokov was for a time in charge of the butterfly collection of the Museum of Comparative Zoology at Harvard University. He wrote numerous scientific papers and traveled across North America collecting specimens. In 1945, he postulated an unusual thesis: he claimed that the group of butterflies called Polyommatus blues had come from Asia in a series of five migrations, beginning about eleven million years ago; they had traveled over the Bering Strait and then flew all the way down to South America. His peers were not impressed, and his theory was dismissed and then forgotten. But recent DNA studies indicate that Nabokov was completely correct. Naomi Pierce, the coauthor of the study that vindicated Nabokov's theory, was amazed. "What's the probability of predicting the exact sequence of five evolutionary events?" she asked. "He had extraordinary insight, and for 65 years, nobody really paid much attention."

APRIL 24 | The First to Die in Space

The first person officially acknowledged to have died in space was Soviet cosmonaut Vladimir Komarov. On April 23, 1967, he went into orbit in the *Soyuz-1*, on a mission to rendezvous with a second craft that was to be launched the next day. Komarov started experiencing problems with communications, power, and navigation soon after achieving orbit, and the second launch was canceled. On April 24, at reentry, the parachutes did not deploy properly and *Soyuz-1* hurtled to the ground; Komarov was incinerated on impact. From the official TASS communiqué:

> After completing all the operations connected with the transition to landing regime, the spacecraft went happily through the most difficult and responsible portion of deceleration and braking in dense atmosphere layers. . . . However, during opening of the main parachute dome at seven kilometer altitude, the spacecraft descended with high speed, which, according to preliminary data, was the result of shroud line twisting, and this was the cause of loss of V. M. Komarov.

An American listening station in Turkey had monitored the *Soyuz*, and one analyst claims he heard the cosmonaut screaming in rage and cursing "this devil ship!" but official Soviet transcripts of the final transmissions do not confirm that account. Various stories have come out since the crash, but this flight, like most of the Soviet space program, was shrouded in such secrecy that we may never know exactly what happened.

APRIL 25 | A Female Midnight Rider

A rider sets out in the night, galloping hard from town to town, warning the populace about the incursion of British forces. Not Paul Revere, but a young woman named Sybil Ludington; her ride served a similar purpose and was at least as difficult as Revere's earlier trip. Sybil's father, Colonel Henry Ludington, was in charge of the local militia near his home of Fredericksburgh (now Kent), New York, close to the Connecticut border. On April 25, 1777, British forces under General William Tryon landed in Connecticut and marched toward Danbury, planning to destroy the Continental Army's supplies there. The next day, a messenger arrived at Ludington's home to tell him of the invasion. Ludington's regiment was scattered over the area, and with no one else available, he sent his daughter on a mission to get them on the march. Sybil had just turned sixteen, but she rode alone through the night to Carmel, Mahopac, and Stormville before returning home, a total of forty miles—twice as long as Paul Revere's ride. She was successful; her father's regiment was assembled and marched out to meet the enemy. After the battle near Ridgefield forced the British to retreat, a visitor came to the Ludington home to thank young Sybil for her extraordinary service. It was George Washington. A statue now stands in Carmel, New York, to commemorate her ride, and a postage stamp was issued in her honor in 1975.

APRIL 26 | Shrieking Agony

In 1937, Pablo Picasso created one of his most famous paintings, *Guernica*, to commemorate the terrible bombing of that Basque town by Nazi planes during the Spanish Civil War and the subsequent occupation of the area by troops of General Francisco Franco. Picasso later described the work to a reporter for the BBC: "My painting *Guernica* is strictly a personal reflection. . . . All living creatures in that town, human and animal, were converted into tortured objects, decomposed, distorted and shrieking their agony to the sky. The painting is simply a symbolic representation of the horror as seen in my own mind—that is all." After an international tour, the monumental mural resided primarily at the Museum of Modern Art in New York, because Picasso refused to have it exhibited in Spain under fascism. Not until 1981, on the one-hundredth anniversary of Picasso's birth and eight years after his death, was *Guernica* presented to the Spanish people.

APRIL 27 | The Crown Palace

The Taj Mahal is a mausoleum but also an expression of deep and abiding love. It is India's most popular tourist site, hosting some three million visitors a year. Anyone who tours the complex can't help but be inspired by the graceful architecture that manages to harmonize Islamic, Indian, Hindu, Persian, and European styles. It was built in the city of Agra by the Mughal emperor Shah Jahan in the seventeenth century, after the death of his beloved wife Mumtaz Mahal. Construction took more than fifteen years and twenty thousand laborers, and when it was completed, Shah Jahan had erected a monument he hoped would last until the end of time. It may not. Preservationists are concerned about pollution deteriorating the brilliant white marble and the red sandstone that cover the brick structure, and fears are growing that the foundations may be affected by the instability of the adjacent Yamuna River. Though activists have had some success controlling pollution-producing factories in the area, automobile exhaust and foot traffic continue to take a toll.

American missionary Arthur Judson Brown wrote about the Taj Mahal in 1915 that it was "a tomb before which the artists and architects of the twentieth century stand in wonder, delight, and awe, a dream in marble and precious stones, the most beautiful structure the world has ever seen—the glorious Taj Mahal."

The Taj Mahal

APRIL 28 | Counting the Living and the Dead

Demographers at the Population Reference Bureau wrestle with a perennial question: how many people have lived in the entire history of the Earth? Complicating the issue is the fact that somebody somewhere once claimed that 75 percent of all humans who have ever lived are alive today. Senior PRB scholar Carl Haub tackled the problem in October 2011, pointing out that "Any such exercise can be only a highly speculative enterprise. . . . Nonetheless, it is a somewhat intriguing idea that can be approached on at least a semi-scientific basis. And semi-scientific it must be, because there are, of course, absolutely no demographic data available for 99 percent of the span of the human stay on Earth." Starting with a population of two in 50,000 BCE, Haub calculated that a total of approximately 108 billion human beings have been born during that span of time. With our current world population at about 7 billion, that means that fewer than 7 percent of all humans who have ever existed are living today. Based on predicted population trends, it seems unlikely that the number of the dead will be surpassed by the number of living people.

APRIL 29 | Modern Design in America

The 1925 Paris Exposition des arts decoratifs et industriels modernes was to be the definitive show of modern design, but the United States was not represented at the exhibition. Although we had been invited and offered a prime space, Herbert Hoover (then secretary of commerce), after consulting with various cultural leaders, declined to participate, saying that America had no original modern design. He wasn't wrong; most Americans were still attached to old-fashioned design and decorative art. The *Chicago Daily Tribune* reported, "[A]pparently there is not enough modern decorative and industrial art in the United States to justify a place in the Paris exposition. Secretary Hoover . . . has chosen a committee of 100 representative business men to visit the exposition, examine its exhibits, and report back to American industry why we have nothing to show and why other nations have." Hoover's commission of experts—architects, artists, designers, curators, and representatives of design trades—returned from the exposition and, inspired by what they had seen, encouraged a surge of art deco and other modern design forms in the United States.

APRIL 30 | God Bless Vespucciland

To Western geographers in the fifteenth century, the world was divided into three regions: Europe, Asia, and Africa. That didn't change when Christopher Columbus returned from his first voyage

in 1493; he thought he had discovered the eastern
edge of Asia, not a new continent. When Amerigo
Vespucci wrote about his 1502–1503 voyages,
however, he seemed to indicate that he had found
an actual new land, a fourth part of the Earth. In
1507, *Cosmographiae Introductio* was published in
France, incorporating Vespucci's discoveries and
naming the new region: "Since both Asia and
Africa received their names from women, I do not

Amerigo Vespucci

see why anyone should rightly prevent this [new part] from being
called Amerigen—the land of Amerigo, as it were—or America, after
its discoverer, Americus, a man of perceptive character." The text
referred to a map made in conjunction with the book, but no copies
of the map were known until 1901, when a Jesuit historian discovered
one in Germany. There, on the left side of the huge map, was the first
depiction of a new land mass with the name *America*. The cartogra-
pher was Martin Waldseemüller, and he was given credit for naming
the new continent. But recent studies indicate that although the map
is Waldseemüller's work, the *Cosmographiae Introductio* was probably
written by his collaborator, Matthias Ringmann. It therefore seems
likely that Ringmann is the man responsible for giving the Americas
their name. The 1507 Waldseemüller map was acquired by the Library
of Congress for ten million dollars, and on April 30, 2007, it was
formally transferred to the United States. It is on permanent display
at the library.

MAY

MAY 1 | A Storm of Strikes

May 1, 1886, was an exceptional day in U.S. labor history. Unions and their sympathizers had been agitating for an eight-hour workday, and passions were intense on both sides of the worker-management divide, nowhere more so than in Chicago, which had become the hub of the country's labor struggle. A national strike had been called for Saturday, May 1, and it was remarkably successful, with hundreds of thousands of workers across the country joining in. The following Monday a scuffle broke out at the McCormick Harvesting Machine Company in Chicago, where workers had been locked out. Police fired on the crowd, killing two. Enraged labor leaders called for a mass meeting at Haymarket Square the following evening. The rally was peaceful, but as the last speaker was concluding, police marched on the crowd to disperse it. Then someone threw a bomb. The explosion killed one policeman, and the rest of the force opened fire. Panic ensued; six more officers were killed, some by friendly fire. An unknown number of workers were killed and wounded as well. Eight of the organizers were brought to trial on charges of murder. All were found guilty and seven were sentenced to death; four were hanged. The event enshrined forever the image of the "bomb-throwing anarchist," although the identity of the perpetrator was never discovered, and it established May 1 as a day for international celebration of workers' struggles.

MAY 2 | Our Ancient Ancestor

The oldest mammal fossil discovered so far is the *Adelobasileus cromptoni* (from Greek *adelos*, "obscure," and *basiliskos*, "king"), a tiny, scansorial (climbing), insect-eating shrewlike creature, unearthed by a team of paleontologists from the New Mexico Museum of Natural History and Science who were working in the Texas desert in 1989. The fossil is a dime-size section of the rodent's skull. The *Adelobasileus* lived in the late Triassic forests about 225 million years ago and is probably the common ancestor of all mammals, including humans.

MAY 3 | The Figure of the Earth

The true shape of the world is a question that has intrigued humans since the ancient Greek philosophers and astronomers; they knew that it is round, not flat. Exactly how round is it, though? By the time of the Enlightenment, Isaac Newton believed the Earth was flattened at the poles and bulged at the equator. Other scientists thought it was elongated at the poles, like an egg. In 1735, two geodesic missions set out from Europe to find the answer, one team to the equator in Peru and the other to the Arctic Circle at Lapland. Their purpose was to precisely measure one degree of latitude in each location, compare their findings, and thus properly describe the shape of the Earth. It was a perilous slog for both groups. Weather, disease, politics, and their own egos caused the South American team to spend four years at the task. Members of the Lapland expedition had to contend with near shipwrecks and extreme cold, but they completed their survey first. When the final calculations were made, they demonstrated that Newton was correct; the Earth is indeed oblate. The discovery satisfied their intellectual curiosity but was also crucial for global navigation and trade. Later geodesic missions made additional surveys and calculations, and a more accurate understanding of the curve of the planet emerged.

MAY 4 | Red Gold

Humans have been cultivating it for at least thirty-five hundred years; Minoan frescoes depict it being gathered; it's mentioned in the Song of Solomon in the Bible; and it is the most expensive spice in the world. Saffron comes from the *Crocus sativus*, a fall-blooming plant with gorgeous purple flowers and a sweet fragrance. Yet it's not the beautiful petals that supply the pungent flavor; it's the stigmas, the female parts of the flower, which collect the pollen. There are only three stigmas per plant, and they are thin and just a few inches long. Originally used medicinally, saffron has been considered a stimulant, a painkiller, a cure for measles, and even an aphrodisiac. It is also used

 as a dye, imparting a vivid reddish-yellow color, but it is as a spice that it is so popular today. In cooking, saffron adds a pleasant haylike flavor and a golden color to any preparation (as in paella or bouillabaisse). The reason for its high cost ($3,200 per pound retail, from a California source in 2011) is the labor-intensive harvesting: once the flowers open they are collected and the stigmas are plucked by hand, and then dried into threads. It takes about 75,000

Saffron   flowers (225,000 stigmas) to make a pound of saffron.

MAY 5 | Flopsy, Mopsy, and Tipsy

The Aztecs worshipped an astounding array of gods that covered all aspects of life. They even had gods for drunkenness—four hundred of them. The *Centzon Totochtin*, or "Four Hundred Rabbits," are linked to pulque (also known as *octli*), a milky alcoholic beverage made by fermenting the sap of the maguey or century plant and combining it with acacia root. Each rabbit represented a different level of intoxication and had a numerical name such as Ometotchtli ("two rabbit"). They were known to throw wild parties, and were also tricksters, an aspect of rabbits that appears in the stories and the myths of many cultures (in the United States, think Brer Rabbit and Bugs Bunny). Pulque was used in religious rituals, but "the image of a rabbit symbolized uninhibited, drunken conduct, something the Aztecs frowned upon. The *Codex Mendoza*, an Aztec pictorial manuscript dating from about 1541, shows three young people being stoned to death for drunkenness," explains Patricia Anawalt of the Fowler Museum at the University of California at Los Angeles. It was said that if you were born on Ometotchtli's festival day, you would likely become a drunkard. Although pulque is still made and consumed in Mexico, it has largely been replaced by beer.

MAY 6 | A Hill in Jerusalem

There is a hill in Jerusalem that is sacred to Jews, Christians, and Muslims. Tradition says it was originally called Mount Moriah, the site where Adam was created and Abraham almost sacrificed his son. King Solomon built the first Jewish temple there three thousand years ago. Nebuchadnezzar, the Babylonian king, conquered Jerusalem in 587 BCE, destroyed the temple, and exiled most of the Jews. When they returned from captivity, they built a second temple, and this was the place where Jesus cast out the money changers. The Romans sacked Jerusalem and destroyed the second temple in 70 CE. The remaining part of its western wall is now the holiest site in Judaism. Muslim tradition says that this is the spot where the Prophet Muhammed ascended to heaven on a winged horse. After Caliph Omar conquered Jerusalem in the seventh century, the Dome of the Rock and the al-Aqsa mosque were constructed on the mount. Muslims call it Haram al-Sharif or "Noble Sanctuary," and it's their third holiest site. Passions run high between Jewish and Muslim groups concerning the site and its history, and numerous clashes have started there, including the second Palestinian Intifada in 2000. Although Israel controls Jerusalem, Haram al-Sharif is under the authority of a

Muslim council known as the Waqf, which forbids any major archaeological excavation there.

MAY 7 | A River Unbridged

The Amazon is the second-longest river in the world, running about
four thousand miles, but it is the largest in terms of volume. It dis-
charges more water than the next seven longest rivers combined. Yet
not a single bridge crosses it. For most of its course, from its source in
the Peruvian Andes until it enters the Atlantic Ocean in northern
Brazil, the Amazon runs through the lightly populated rainforest, and
there are very few roads. The Amazon itself is the main "road," and
most destinations are reached by boat, rather than overland. For those
who need to get from one side to the other, ferries are adequate. With
its hundreds of tributaries, the Amazon has the largest drainage basin
in the world, about 2,700,000 square miles, or almost half of the
entire continent. One-third of all of the world's species live in the
Amazon rainforest.

MAY 8 | The Father of American Golf

He was a working-class kid, but Francis Ouimet (1893–1967) aspired
to play golf with the rich folks he watched across the street from his
boyhood home. They were playing at the Country Club (TCC) in
Brookline, Massachusetts, one of the most esteemed courses in the
United States. Francis and his brother created a few rough holes in
their backyard and taught themselves to play. Francis began caddying
at TCC at age eleven and in a few years was competing in small tournaments. In 1913, he won the state amateur championship and
decided to enter the U.S. Open. He was only twenty years old and was
playing against some of the premier names in golf, including the Eng-
lishmen Harry Vardon and Ted Ray, both British Open champions.
His caddy, Eddie Lowery, was only ten years old. After botching his
opening shot, Ouimet hit his stride and kept up with the two Britons.
The sportswriters took note and soon the crowds swelled, sensing

something special was happening. At the end of four rounds, Vardon, Ray, and Ouimet were tied. At the next day's playoff, Ray folded early, Vardon ran into a little bunker trouble, and Francis Ouimet became the champion. American golf would never be the same; within ten years there were two million active golfers and many thousands of spectators. Ouimet never turned pro, continuing to play for the love of the game. And his caddy? Eddie Lowery became a successful car dealer, and he and Ouimet remained lifelong friends.

MAY 9 | Hollywood East

The motion picture business did not start in Hollywood. It was born in the laboratory of Thomas Edison in West Orange, New Jersey, in 1888 with the development of the kinetoscope. A few years later, he built a production studio there but soon moved it to New York City. By the turn of the century, competitors had also established themselves in the area. Fort Lee, New Jersey, became the home of numerous film studios in the early years of the century, including Biograph and its brilliant young director, D. W. Griffith, who shot several films there. Movie pioneers from Oscar Micheaux to the Marx Brothers made pictures in Fort Lee. In 1910, Griffith began to make annual journeys to the West Coast to take advantage of the warm winter weather and the cheaper nonunion labor and to avoid Edison's licensing fees; that was the beginning of the end for New York film production. It didn't disappear entirely, however. In 1920, the Famous Players/Lasky Studio (soon to become Paramount Pictures) was built in Astoria, Queens, and numerous films were made there, both silent and sound. The facility still exists today as the Kaufman/Astoria Studios, where movies, television shows, and commercials are shot.

MAY 10 | A Green Capital

Stockholm, known as "the Venice of the North" or "the Green and Blue City," is built on fourteen islands connected by fifty-seven bridges, between the Baltic Sea and Lake Mälaren. It is part of the

Stockholm Archipelago (*Stockholms skärgård*), twenty-four thousand islands and rocks that follow the coastline, north and south of the city. They were formed not by falling sea levels, but by land elevation, or postglacial rebound following the last Ice Age, when land masses in northern regions were no longer depressed by the enormous weight of the ice sheets, and the land began to rise slowly. In 2010, Stockholm was named the first "Green Capital" by the European Commission for its environmentally friendly urban living and for the city's plan to be independent of fossil fuels by the year 2050.

MAY 11 | The Star of the Columbian Exposition

In 1890, architect Daniel Burnham was appointed director of works for the upcoming World's Columbian Exposition in Chicago. He wanted to outdo the French, who had impressed the world a year earlier with the construction of the Eiffel Tower for their Exposition Universelle. Burnham challenged the nation's civil engineers with a taunting speech, complaining that they "had contributed little or nothing either in the way of originating novel features or of showing the possibilities of modern engineering practice in America." He didn't want another Eiffel Tower but "something novel, original, daring and unique must be designed and built if American engineers are to retain their prestige and standing." At least one person in the audience was spurred to action. Pittsburgh engineer George Washington Gale Ferris Jr. submitted a plan for a structure that would "out-Eiffel Eiffel"—a

giant rotating wheel with thirty-six cars, capable of carrying more than two thousand people at a time. Two hundred sixty-four feet high, the Ferris Wheel became the hit of the fair, with thousands lining up every day to ride it. When the fair ended, the wheel was moved to new locations but didn't achieve commercial success and was blown up with two hundred pounds of dynamite on May 11, 1906.

The Ferris Wheel

MAY 12 | An Acquired Taste

The pioneering German agricultural chemist Justus von Liebig (1803–1873) started a company in 1865 to sell the beef extract he had perfected as an inexpensive replacement for meat, and he later discovered that brewer's yeast could be concentrated as a food product. Some thirty years later, the Marmite Food Extract Company was founded. Its eponymous substance was a mix of the yeast extract with plenty of salt, celery, and some spices (vitamins were added later), producing a thick paste that could be spread on bread or otherwise consumed. Described as "industrial lubricant," "stolid, mucky, stubborn, salty," or "oil-slick gloop"—even by people who like it—it's a polarizing product. The strong flavor provokes such extreme reactions that "Love it or hate it" became the company's marketing slogan (its website directs you in one direction or the other). Yet it became so popular in the United Kingdom that Marmite was a staple in British backpacks during the world wars. There are other yeast extract products available today, including Vegemite in Australia and Cenovis in Switzerland.

MAY 13 | Gross Anatomy

The National Museum of Health and Medicine of the Armed Forces Institute of Pathology is one of the country's more obscure, fascinating, and cringe-inducing museums. Founded in 1862 as the Army Medical Museum to collect pathological specimens and case histories from Civil War soldiers, its exhibits formed the basis for one of the first studies of wartime injuries. Among its twenty-five million artifacts—skeletons, preserved organs, medical equipment, and documents—are Paul Revere's dental tools; the leg bones of Civil War general Daniel Sickles (who visited his leg for many years, on the anniversary of its amputation); the mummified body of Cleveland gangster Andy "Dutch" Kapler; and the Lincoln assassination artifacts, including the bullet that ended the president's life. Many a father has taught his sons about the dangers of sexually transmitted diseases by taking them to the museum's syphilis exhibit.

MAY 14 | The Gladiatrix

Intensely violent, gory, cruel, and exciting—we're all familiar with the enormously popular gladiatorial games of ancient Rome's Colosseum (official name, the Flavian Amphitheater) and other arenas. You might be surprised to learn that, as stated by scholar David S. Potter, "There were female gladiators. They were regarded as absolutely a special treat. They were sufficiently rare that you would advertise them up front as something spectacular that you were going to have in the show." References to their existence can be found in the works of Roman writers, who described their participation ("gladiatorial shows by torchlight in which women as well as men took part") and the efforts to ban them. Like their male counterparts, most female gladiators were slaves, but a few volunteered to take the oath, "to be burnt with fire, shackled with chains, whipped with rods, and killed with steel." A marble relief from Halicarnassus, now in the British Museum, provides some physical proof: it depicts two armed women in gladiatorial combat, with the noms de guerre Amazon and Achillia.

MAY 15 | Runaway Train

On May 15, 2001, a thirty-five-year railroad veteran made a rookie mistake. He was moving a forty-seven-car freight train from one track to another at the Stanley Yard in Toledo, Ohio. Seeing that a switch just ahead was lined improperly, he applied the braking systems, jumped out of the cab, and ran to the switch. He intended to hop back on the train, but he had mis-set one of the brake switches and, instead of slowing, the train was picking up speed. The worker tried to jump aboard but missed and was dragged for eighty feet before he let go. CSX 8888 was now a runaway train, and its consist included two tanker cars of molten phenol, a dangerous chemical. An attempt was made to stop the train by using portable derailers, but it was moving too fast and blew right through them. Police then tried to shoot the fuel cut-off button on the side of the locomotive as it sped past, but they missed. Barreling along at nearly fifty miles per hour, the train seemed unstoppable until another locomotive on the line, Q63615, began to chase it, going in reverse. Its two crew members managed to catch up to the runaway, couple with its rear car, and hit their brakes, soon slowing CSX 8888 to around eleven miles per hour. That allowed another rail employee to leap aboard and finally bring the train to a stop. It had traveled a total of sixty-six miles, unmanned. The incident inspired the 2010 movie *Unstoppable*. The identity of the engineer who made the error has not been revealed.

MAY 16 | A Carrot of a Different Color

Carrots, slightly sweet, orange-colored root vegetables, were not originally so sweet nor were they orange. The historic wild carrot, originally from Afghanistan, was rather bitter and tough and was usually purple or yellow. For the most part, the root wasn't eaten, but the seeds and the leaves were used medicinally; the Romans thought carrots were an aphrodisiac and cultivated them for that purpose. The purple carrot gradually worked its way west, where an orange-colored mutant variety appeared. Dutch growers began to experiment with them in the seventeenth century and produced a much sweeter vegetable that was orange, perhaps as a tribute to their royal House of Orange. Wild and domesticated carrots are not the same species; they coexist today. When left untended for a few generations, the garden carrot reverts to its ancestral type.

Carrots

MAY 17 | The Derby Founder

Churchill Downs racetrack and its most famous event, the Kentucky Derby, were founded by Meriwether Lewis Clark Jr. (1846–1899), a grandson of the famed explorer William Clark. Horse racing—both thoroughbred and harness—had been very popular in Kentucky since the late eighteenth century. Clark, inspired by a visit to the courses of

England and France, leased eighty acres of land from his uncles, John and Henry Churchill, to create what was originally called the Louisville Jockey Club and Driving Park Association. The track officially opened on May 17, 1875, with more than twelve thousand people attending. The winner of that first Kentucky Derby was a horse called Aristides, ridden by an African American jockey named Oliver Lewis. Colonel Clark, beset by illness and financial difficulties, committed suicide in 1899. The *New York Tribune* reported that he "was one of the most notable figures of the American turf. Over twenty-five years of his life were devoted to it, during all of which no breath of scandal has ever assailed his name. He was the author of a majority of the turf rules or laws of the present day and the founder of the first American Turf Congress."

MAY 18 | The Egyptian Cinderella

Rhodopis (meaning "roselike" or "rosy-cheeked"), whose real name may have been Doricha, was a Thracian *hetaira*, or courtesan, one of the earliest named prostitutes in history. In the fifth century BCE, the Greek historian Herodotus mentioned a woman named Rhodopis, who had been kidnapped and taken to Egypt, where she became acquainted with Aesop, a fellow slave and a great storyteller. Known for her beauty, she was treated harshly by envious fellow serving girls. By the time another Greek historian wrote of her four hundred years later, the outlines of a charming story mixing fact and fable—perhaps coming from Aesop—had taken hold. As Rhodopis was washing in the river, she removed her slippers, and an eagle swooped down and snatched one of them. The bird flew to the pharaoh and dropped it in his lap. Fascinated, the pharaoh searched for the one whose foot had worn the slipper, forcing every woman in his kingdom to try it on. Eventually, Rhodopis was found and the shoe fit, and the pharaoh married her. Hundreds of other variations evolved over the centuries, until 1697, when Frenchman Charles Perrault published the story "Cinderella" that we are familiar with today, in a collection called *Tales of Mother Goose*.

MAY 19 | **The Fastest Woman on Earth**

Betty Skelton (1926–2011) is in eleven halls of fame, for her flying and driving acumen. She learned to fly an airplane when she was a preteen and became renowned for her aerobatic skills. She was the first woman to perform the "inverted ribbon cut"—she flew upside down ten feet off the ground, cutting a ribbon with the plane's propeller. In 1951, she set a light plane altitude record at 29,050 feet. On the ground, she became the first female test driver for the auto industry and set numerous speed records at racetracks and the Bonneville Salt Flats. She once jumped a boat over a Dodge convertible. "I just like to go fast. I enjoy it, I really do," Skelton once told an interviewer. In 1959, *Look* magazine asked her to undergo the same rigorous testing the astronauts did, and she performed so well that the original *Mercury Seven* astronauts nicknamed her "No. 7½." Her Pitts Special biplane now hangs in the National Air and Space Museum's Udvar-Hazy Center.

MAY 20 | **The First Black Republic**

The French Revolution caused reverberations throughout Europe and overseas as well, nowhere more dramatically than in the French colony then known as Saint Domingue. The Caribbean island was very profitable for the French, because it produced half of the world's sugar and coffee. It was a harsh plantation economy that ran on the backs of slaves. By 1789, there were at least half a million enslaved workers and only about sixty-thousand white and free black citizens. When word of the rebellion in France reached the island, the slaves were inspired to throw off their shackles. Uprisings began in the early 1790s that became full-scale civil war. The slaves killed many whites, burned the plantations, and attacked the towns; atrocities were committed by both sides. From 1791 to 1804, mostly led by former slave François-Dominique Toussaint L'Ouverture, the people fought and defeated troops from France, Great Britain, and

Spain. In 1804, the independent republic of Haiti was declared (named for Ayiti, "mountainous land," as the indigenous people called it). It was the first successful slave revolt in history and the first black republic. France demanded reparations of 150 million francs (about $20 billion in today's money) and the debt, though reduced, was not paid until 1947.

MAY 21 | The Dean of American Engineers

Gustav Lindenthal (1850–1935) was born in what is now the Czech Republic, studied engineering in Europe, and worked for railroad companies in Austria and Switzerland. He immigrated to the United States and in 1881 set himself up as a consulting engineer in Pittsburgh and worked on several important bridge projects in the area. He had a brief term as New York City bridge commissioner, starting in 1902. He designed the Queensboro Bridge (better known as the 59th Street Bridge, thanks to Simon and Garfunkel) which opened in 1909 and carried trains, trolleys, cars, bicycles, and pedestrians. One of Lindenthal's greatest achievements was the Hell Gate Bridge (1917), a spandrel arch across the East River between Queens and the Bronx—for a time, the longest and heaviest railroad bridge in the world. It provided connections for several train lines, allowing uninterrupted service from New England to the South. From 1885 until his death, Lindenthal was involved in several unrealized projects to build a bridge across the Hudson River from New Jersey to mid-town Manhattan. Ground was broken and a cornerstone laid in Hoboken in 1895, but political, financial, and legal problems prevented its completion (the stone remained in a Hoboken backyard until a few years ago). In 1931, the Hudson was finally crossed by the George Washington Bridge, from Fort Lee to West 179th Street; it was designed by Lindenthal's assistant, Othmar Ammann. When Lindenthal died in 1935, the *New York Times* called him "one of the leading bridge builders in the United States, the dean of his profession in this country."

MAY 22 | An Early Gender-Neutral Weapon System

The spear-thrower, called *atlatl* by the Aztecs, was one of humankind's first weapons systems, and it represented a huge technological advance in hunting and warfare technique. The World Atlatl Association provides this definition: "An atlatl is essentially a stick with a handle on one end and a hook or socket that engages a light spear or dart on the other. The flipping motion of the atlatl propels a light spear much faster and farther than it could be thrown by hand alone." Using an atlatl gives the hunter ten times the distance and force of a hand-thrown spear or dart. Atlatls have been found on every continent (except Antarctica), and their history is estimated to go back twenty-five thousand to forty thousand years. Successful use of the atlatl required skill, rather than arm strength, so it allowed women to hunt and fight as well as men. Some indige-nous peoples in Australia and New Guinea still use the atlatl for hunting, and it's now a competitive sport, with organizations that promote atlatl con-tests of distance and accuracy.

An atlatl

MAY 23 | Animal Magnetism

Franz Anton Mesmer (1734–1815) was an Austrian physician who began to study theology and law, then turned to medicine. In his doc-toral thesis, he theorized that the fluids of the body were influenced by the alignment of the planets, causing a gravitational "tidal" effect that he called "animal magnetism." He experimented with ways to use this force to heal a variety of conditions and ailments. Here's a description of his process from an academic journal: "patients gathered in a room surrounding a large enclosed wooden tub with iron wands protruding out of it. The patients would hold the wands and touch them to their afflicted parts. The animal magnetism would flow from the tub through the wands to the patient. Patients were convinced they were cured." It wasn't animal magnetism, however; Mesmer had used the power of suggestion in his apparent cures, which made him immensely popular. Yet his work was not well-accepted by the medical community, which saw no scientific validity in his theory. In 1784, King Louis XVI appointed a commission that included Benjamin Franklin and chemist Antoine Levoisier to investigate Mesmer's claims. They found no evidence of animal magnetism and concluded that Mesmer was a charlatan. His reputation never recovered.

MAY 24 | The Singing What?

The *Micronecta scholtzi*, also known as the "water boatman" and the "singing penis," is considered the loudest creature on earth, relative to body size. These insects are tiny—two millimeters, or a little more than one-sixteenth of an inch—but the sound they produce reaches seventy-nine decibels on average and can approach one hundred decibels (city traffic is around eighty decibels). This process is called stridulation, rubbing body parts together to make a noise. The water boatman rubs its penis against its abdomen to produce a mating call. Scientists still aren't sure how the tiny insect can project such a loud sound. "There are no obvious body or external resonating systems that could amplify the sound, as observed in insects, amphibians, mammals and birds," according to the team of biologists and engineers who published a report in 2011. *Micronecta scholtzi* is an aquatic insect, so its sound is made underwater, but it is still loud enough for humans to hear. "Remarkably, even though 99 percent of sound is lost when transferring from water to air, the song is so loud that a person walking along the bank can actually hear these tiny creatures singing from the bottom of the river," one of the scientists explained.

MAY 25 | Home Party Pioneer

Plastics were still a new phenomenon in post–World War II America, and maybe that's why Earl Tupper's airtight polyethylene food storage containers weren't flying off store shelves. Then he met Brownie

Wise, who was doing quite well selling a range of products, including Tupperware, at home party demonstrations. In 1951, Tupper hired the charismatic, ambitious woman, who proved to be a marketing genius, and sales skyrocketed. Wise tapped into the dreams of American housewives, who had entered the workforce during the war in great numbers but were now being pushed aside. Home party Tupperware sales allowed them to travel, earn money, and be part of a successful organization. Wise pulled out all the stops, starting Tupperware Jubilees, elaborate (and expensive) sales meetings that included big prize giveaways and other awards to motivate the sellers. She became the public face of Tupperware, appearing on talk shows and in newspapers; she was the first woman featured on the cover of *Business Week*. But that level of fame can also engender jealousy, which is what many people believe was behind Earl Tupper's sudden and unceremonious firing of Wise in 1958. He soon sold his company and bought an island in Central America. Wise, left with only a $30,000 severance payment, started a few different cosmetics sales companies, but they were not successful. She died in 1992. Tupper wrote her out of the company history, and today there is barely a mention of Brownie Wise on Tupperware's website.

MAY 26 | The World's Most Perfect Town

There had been other company towns before, but none quite like this. Pullman, Illinois, was the creation of George Pullman (1831–1897), the founder of the railroad sleeping car company, and it represented a new type of community. In 1880, a few miles south of downtown Chicago, construction began of a quintessential planned community, with tidy brick shops, schools, a library, a hospital, and a hotel, but no saloons. There were different levels of housing, from the grandest for the executives to small block houses for single men and young families. The homes were comfortable, with gas and indoor plumbing, unusual for worker housing at the time. Appearances aside, though, it was a confining community, with Pullman controlling almost every aspect of the workers' lives. "We are born in a Pullman house, fed from

George Pullman

the Pullman shops, taught in the Pullman school, catechized in the Pullman Church, and when we die we shall go to the Pullman hell," one resident complained. Economist Richard Ely said, "[T]he idea of Pullman is un-American. . . . It is benevolent, well wishing feudalism." Paternalistic officials could inspect the residents' homes at any time and evict them if the premises weren't maintained to Pullman's standards. He expected his town to be profitable, so rents were not cheap. When the economy faltered in 1893, Pullman laid off many workers, cut wages for the rest, yet refused to lower the rents. Workers went on strike in 1894, and that was the beginning of the end for the company town. Pullman died in 1897, and the following year Pullman, Illinois, was incorporated into the city of Chicago.

MAY 27 | Golden Gate

Why is the Golden Gate Bridge orange? When construction began in 1933 on the span to cross San Francisco's Golden Gate strait, orange wasn't the first idea. There were plenty of suggestions, however. Othmar Ammann, a consulting engineer, preferred the gray he had used for the George Washington Bridge in New York; others thought black would be better. The navy suggested yellow with black stripes, which would stand out in the fog, making it easier for ships to see. The Army Air Corps preferred red and white, which would make it visible to airplanes. Consulting architect Irving Morrow wrote in a 1935 report, "Its unprecedented size and scale, along with its grace of form and independence of conception, all call for unique and unconventional treatment from every point of view. What has been thus played up in form should not be let down in color." The bridge had already been painted with a primer coat of red lead, and Morrow began to think that color looked just fine, was harmonious with the surroundings, and made the bridge easier to see in the frequent fog. The decision was made; the bridge would be an orange vermilion color, dubbed

"International Orange." In case you want to duplicate it for your own bridge, the staff has provided some options: PMS Code 173, Pantone 180, or CMYK formula of cyan, 0 percent; magenta, 69 percent; yellow, 100 percent; and black, 6 percent. Touchup painting of the ten million square feet of steel is continuous, and it's the primary maintenance task for the Golden Gate Bridge, which opened to pedestrians on May 27, 1937, and to vehicular traffic the next day.

MAY 28 | The First Lady of the Black Press

It was a presidential press conference in July 1954, and Dwight D. Eisenhower looked annoyed. A feisty African American reporter named Ethel Payne had just asked him a tough question, about whether his administration would support the banning of segregation in interstate transit. "The administration is trying to do what it thinks and believes to be decent and just in this country," the president said testily, "and is not in the effort to support any particular or special group of any kind." The president's curt reply drew headlines, and Payne was satisfied that she had done her job—raising serious questions about thorny problems that the administration would prefer not to answer. It was the kind of thing she had been doing for the *Chicago Defender* since 1951 and would continue to do there and for other news organizations until her death in 1991. That attitude earned her the title of "First Lady of the Black Press." Payne's rise in journalism had been rapid and marked by solid and sometimes cheeky reportage that pulled no punches. "You are either acquiescent, which I think is wrong," she explained, "or else you just rebel, and you kick against it. I wanted to constantly, constantly, constantly hammer away, raise the questions that needed to be raised."

MAY 29 | Tiny Golf

Long before miniature golf links were populated with windmills, pirates, dinosaurs, and other exotic obstacles, they were exactly what the name implies: a true golf course built small. Two clubs—a putter and a short driver—were needed, because the holes were often fifty to one hundred yards long. The first miniature golf course was probably the Ladies' Putting Club (known as the Himalayas) at St. Andrews in Scotland, the ancestral home of golf. Its eighteen-hole putting green was opened in 1867, at a time when it was considered improper for a lady to robustly swing a club, and it's still in operation. The first modern miniature golf course, the kind we're familiar with, was the Thistle Dhu in Pinehurst, North Carolina, in 1916. It was much more geometric and formalized than the previous courses, and only a putter was required. Then came the invention of dyed cottonseed hull carpet that replaced grass (and its expensive upkeep), and the craze really took off; there were even rooftop miniature golf courses all over Manhattan. In 1955, Al Lomma started a company that developed trick obstacles and hazards that required not only good putting, but accurate timing. Today there are professional minigolf competitions in the United States and around the world.

MAY 30 | The Maid of Orleans

Joan of Arc, or *Jehanne Darc* in medieval French (1412?–1431), might have escaped being burned at the stake if she hadn't insisted on wearing men's clothing. Cross-dressing was a violation of biblical and Church law, but Joan had received permission to adopt the soldier's doublet and hosen as she led the French into battle against the pro-English Burgundians during the Hundred Years' War. Captured and tried for heresy by a partisan tribunal, she was held in a secular prison guarded by English soldiers (rather than the ecclesiastical imprisonment overseen by nuns, which was the norm), where male attire also provided her with some protection from molestation. Joan was tricked into repudiating the heavenly voices she claimed had been guiding her actions, and agreed to put on women's clothes again. Yet because only a relapsed heretic was subject to execution, her English guards set a trap: during the night, they stole her female garb and left her only men's clothing to put on in the morning. A witness in her posthumous retrial about twenty years later testified, "[I]nduced by bodily

necessity, she put on the male clothing; nor was
she able to obtain any other clothing from the
guards during all the rest of the day, so that she
was seen in this male clothing by many people,
and judged relapsed as a result." Joan was burned
to death on May 30, 1431.

Joan's signature

MAY 31 | A Room of Amber

It is one of the great lost treasures of the modern age. The Amber
Room was commissioned by Friedrich I of Prussia in 1701; it was a
small room in the castle of Charlottenberg that was covered with
sheets of amber and decorated with jewels and semiprecious stones,
worth about $150 million in today's money. Friedrich's successor pre-
sented the room to Peter the Great of Russia, and it was shipped to
St. Petersburg. When Adolf Hitler invaded the Soviet Union in 1941,
officials there tried to disassemble the room so that it could be hidden, but the dried-out amber began to crumble, so they covered the
room with wallpaper. That didn't fool the Nazis, who stripped the
room and shipped the panels to Königsberg (now Kaliningrad). That's
where it was last seen before the Allies attacked the city in 1944.
There are a variety of stories about what happened to the Amber
Room. Most historians believe it was destroyed in the bombings or
that it was in a ship that was sunk in the Baltic, and some think the
Germans did manage to hide it in Kaliningrad. A replica of the
Amber Room was constructed for the three hundredth anniversary of
St. Petersburg and opened on May 31, 2003. Perhaps the original is
stored with the Ark of the Covenant in the vast warehouse depicted
in the Indiana Jones movies.

JUNE

JUNE 1 | Beasts of a Feather

What did dinosaurs really look like? Did they have the scaly, drab reptile skin that has been depicted so often? A group of Canadian scientists are rethinking the appearance of some nonflying dinosaurs. Ryan McKellar of the University of Alberta and his team examined a cache of amber found near Grassy Lake, Alberta, that contained feathers and protofeathers from birds and nonavian dinosaurs that lived at the same time, seventy-eight million years ago. Amber is fossilized tree resin that often trapped insects and other small objects and kept them nicely preserved when it hardened (remember the *Jurassic Park* films?). "We've got feathers that look to be little filamentous hair-like feathers, we've got the same filaments bound together in clumps, and then we've got a series that are for all intents and purposes identical to modern feathers," McKellar said. "We're catching some that look to be dinosaur feathers and another set that are pretty much dead ringers for modern birds." What color were these ancient feathers? That is harder to say, because the melanin that causes coloring in feathers tends to deteriorate over time. New techniques are emerging, however, that could provide more information. One researcher stated, "We're getting more and more evidence . . . that these animals were also brightly coloured, just like birds are today."

JUNE 2 | Our Feathered Friends

Since the extinction of the dinosaurs, birds are the only animals that have feathers, and all birds have them. Feathers are made of keratin, a strong but lightweight protein that's also found in human hair and nails and in the scales on fish and reptiles. There are several types of feathers, and not all birds have all types. Contour feathers are the ones we're most used to seeing, with a hollow center spine called a rachis and barbs growing out from it to form vanes. There are two types of contour feathers: symmetrical body feathers and flight feathers, which provide lift. Down feathers are the soft, fluffy kind on young birds and beneath the contour feathers of adults, especially water birds. They are good for insulation and waterproofing. Semiplumes are halfway between contour and downy feathers and are also helpful for maintaining body temperature. Filoplumes have a long spine with a tuft of feathers on the top. They serve as sensors of a sort, letting the bird know about the positions of the other feathers and when they need to be maintained. Bristle feathers have a stiff rachis, usually with no barbs. They're mostly around the eyes and the beaks and not only protect those areas, but may also provide tactile feedback that helps the bird find food. All birds molt—lose and replace their feathers—completely or partially, once or twice per year.

A contour feather

JUNE 3 | Tornado Technology

The American Meteorological Society defines a tornado as "a violently rotating column of air, pendant from a cumuliform cloud or underneath a cumuliform cloud, and often (but not always) visible as a funnel cloud." Saving lives and property in a tornado is dependent on predicting its formation and movement. Great strides in weather technology have been made in the last thirty-five years. NEXRAD Doppler radar is a network of sites that can provide an average fifteen minutes' advance warning of impending tornadoes. That technology has spawned many offshoots, including CASA (Collaborative Adaptive Sensing of the Atmosphere), which updates the radar image every minute, instead of every five, allowing much better tracking of fast-moving weather systems. Other developing technologies include phased radar arrays, lightning data assimilation, and acoustic measuring devices to pick up the low-frequency sounds (fifty decibels and lower) emitted by severe storms and tornadoes. If Dorothy had gotten more warning of the tornado that hit her Kansas farm, maybe she never would have visited Oz.

JUNE 4 | Geek to Geek

It's always interesting to trace a word's evolution, and the *Oxford English Dictionary* is a great source. In sixteenth-century Germany, a *geck* was apparently a fool or a simpleton, someone who was easily duped. By the 1800s, that had become *geek* in English, with the same meaning. In the United States by the early decades of the twentieth century, the definition of *geek* had been broadened to include carnival performers, especially those involved in grotesque acts, such as biting the heads off live chickens or snakes. A few more decades passed and the definition had morphed again, now referring to an overly studious and not particularly friendly person, someone who obsessed over an endeavor. By the 1980s, that obsessive person was focused on new technology, and *geek* began to take on its current meaning of someone who is a whiz with computers. *Geek* has now lost some of its pejorative connotations—geeks do run the world, after all—becoming fully glamorized in such phrases as *geek chic*.

JUNE 5 | A Seat at the Table

In the last few years, a number of new elements have joined the Periodic Table. Elements 114 and 116, added in June 2011, were products of experiments by a joint Russian-American collaboration. The intriguing thing about them is their extremely short life span. Element 116 lasted only a few milliseconds before it shed two protons and two neutrons and decayed into element 114, which also lasted barely half a second before decaying into 112, Copernicium (itself a new member of the table). Both new elements are so small and short-lived that their behavior could not be measured or described. The Joint Working Party on the Discovery of Elements made the decision to acknowledge 114 and 116 after three years of review by scientists from the International Union of Pure and Applied Chemistry and the International Union of Pure and Applied Physics. Six months after their acceptance, the new elements were named: 114 is Flerovium (for Russian physicist Georgiy Flerov), and 116 is Livermorium (after Lawrence Livermore National Laboratory). Still waiting for official acceptance and naming is another group of lab-created elements: numbers 113, 115, 117, and 118.

JUNE 6 | Elements Named

Some of the elements on the Periodic Table are named for countries or cities or for mythological figures. In addition to the newly named Flerovium, a few were named for real people, including two women:

096 Curium—Marie and Pierre Curie, who discovered polonium and radium

099 Einsteinium—Albert Einstein, who developed the theory of general relativity

100 Fermium—Enrico Fermi, who helped develop the first nuclear reactor

101 Mendelevium—Dmitri Ivanovitch Mendeleyev, who created the Periodic Table of the Elements

102 Nobelium—Alfred Nobel, the inventor of dynamite and the founder of the Nobel Prizes

103 Lawrencium—American physicist Ernest Lawrence, who invented the cyclotron

104 Rutherfordium—New Zealand chemist Ernest Rutherford, the father of nuclear physics

Nicolaus Copernicus

106 Seaborgium—Glenn T. Seaborg, who discovered transuranium elements
107 Bohrium—Niels Bohr, a pioneer of quantum physics
109 Meitnerium—Lise Meitner, Austrian physicist and a discoverer of nuclear fission
111 Roentgenium—Wilhelm Roentgen, the discoverer of X-rays
112 Copernicium—Nicolaus Copernicus, who proposed the heliocentric view of the solar system

JUNE 7 | The Field of Cloth of Gold

In the spring of 1520, the kings of England and France engaged in a pointless political exercise; one author has called it "national peacockery." It's difficult to imagine a more ostentatious display than what occurred during eighteen days in June near Calais, France, a town that was then under English control. Henry VIII of England and François I of France—and about ten thousand of their closest and most important relatives and retainers—met in support of peace and mutual friendship, despite their nations' long history of animosity. Henry's temporary palace, three hundred- by three hundred-feet in size and two levels high, was part painted brick and timber, part canvas, with real glass windows. Outside, there were fountains that poured out wine and water. Other structures were erected—brightly colored, highly decorated tented pavilions made of cloth of gold (silk woven with gold threads), velvet, damask, and other fine fabrics, and all the men and the women dressed in their most sumptuous and extravagant attire. They feasted, jousted, danced, and were thoroughly entertained with sports, music, and fireworks, but little of diplomatic importance was accomplished on the Field of Cloth of Gold (or Camp du Drap d'Or in French). Henry soon signed an alliance with Charles V, the Holy Roman Emperor, and in 1522, England declared war on France.

JUNE 8 | "The Second Legion Augusta Built This"

The Roman Empire was no longer expanding when Hadrian became emperor in the second century CE. The farthest northern extent of the empire was in Britannia, close to the boundary with modern Scotland. Hadrian decided to build a wall in order to guard against raids from the "barbarians" in the north. In the year 122, Roman soldiers began construction of a seventy-three-mile barrier, stretching across the entire width of the island, from the mouth of the Tyne River in the east to the Solway Firth in the west. The wall was about fifteen feet high and varied from six to ten feet wide, faced in stone with an infill of rubble. Small forts (milecastles) were placed at one-mile intervals, with twin turrets that housed from eight to thirty-two men; eventually, a few larger forts were built. A trench and an earthwork called a vallum on the south side of the wall, and another trench dug on the north side added further protection. Altogether it was, for its time, an efficient, state-of-the-art defensive system. Remnants of the wall remain today, and you can walk its entire length along the National Trail and stop at a number of museums or observe archaeological excavations along the way.

JUNE 9 | A Composer's Painful Life

Cole Porter (1891–1964), one of America's greatest songwriters, was as prolific as they come. During his college life at Yale, he wrote the music and the lyrics for more than three hundred songs and six full musicals. In the 1920s and the early 1930s, he composed some of his most famous hits: *Night and Day, Let's Do It, Anything Goes, You're the Top, Begin the Beguine*, and many others. Then in 1937, he was struck by a tragic accident. While he was out riding, his horse reared and threw him, then fell on top of him. Both of Porter's thigh bones were crushed, and for the next two decades he lived with chronic osteomyelitis and substantial pain, undergoing dozens of operations. That kind of continuous agony might have ended Porter's creative life, but it didn't. He continued to compose his suave and sophisticated tunes. The Broadway shows from this period include *Can-Can*, *Silk Stockings*, and *Kiss Me Kate*, his most successful show, which ran on Broadway for 1,077 performances. Bone infections finally caught up with him, and in 1958, his right leg was amputated. "I am only half a man now," he told friends, and his creative output all but disappeared. Porter died on October 15, 1964.

JUNE 10 | Un Grande Escargot

"It's us against the snails," said one agricultural expert in 2011. He was talking about *Achatina fulica*, the giant African land snail. The *Achatina* can grow up to ten inches long and, like all snails, leaves a slime trail wherever it goes. It also provides a home for the rat lungworm, which can cause meningitis in humans. Giant African land snails are not picky eaters, consuming at least five hundred different types of plants, including beans, cucumbers, and peanuts, and they will occasionally eat concrete or the stucco from your house to obtain calcium for their shells. They're also very prolific; they can lay hundreds of eggs per year, starting when they're only six months old. The U.S. Department of Agriculture considers *Achatina* a serious invasive pest. One infestation in Florida (they've had several) occurred in the mid-1960s, when a young Miami boy returned from a trip to Hawaii with three giant snails in his pockets. His grandmother released them into her garden, and soon there were eighteen thousand. It took the state ten years and a million dollars to get rid of them. A native of east Africa, the snail has been introduced—accidentally or illegally as pets or food—into ecosystems around the world.

A giant snail

JUNE 11 | Fuzzy Urban Art

In the last few years, a new form of graffiti or street art has emerged and is spreading quickly around the world: yarn bombing or yarn storming. The motto of these (mostly female) guerrilla artists:

"Improving the urban landscape one stitch at a time." A wide range of projects has been reported: the *Charging Bull* bronze sculpture near Wall Street was covered in a pink-and-purple crocheted body suit; the Philadelphia Museum's statue of *Rocky* wore a fuchsia vest; there are leg-warmers for stop signs and utility poles; and cars and buses have found themselves suddenly clothed in nicely knitted sweaters. Technically, it's littering or vandalism, but so far incidents seem to be ignored or tolerated by police. The first Yarn Bombing Day was observed on June 11, 2011.

JUNE 12 | Houses by Rail and Mail

It was the ultimate do-it-yourself project: build your own home from a kit. In the early decades of the twentieth century, prefabricated houses were all the rage and saved many a would-be homeowner considerable time and expense. There were a number of manufacturers of these prefab homes, but as soon as Sears & Roebuck entered the field, that company dominated it. Already well-established as the king of mail-order, Sears marketed almost five hundred different home styles to fit a wide variety of tastes and budgets. These were solid, attractive houses that were fairly easy for the owner to assemble. All of the elements—pre-cut lumber, nails, shingles, paint, plumbing, light fixtures, and even a couple of trees for the yard—were delivered by train to practically any part of the nation. Sears estimates that it sold around seventy-five thousand kit houses between 1908 and 1940; many are still in existence and are often considered collector's items. Today they sell for considerably more than the $650–$2,500 prices from the first catalog.

JUNE 13 | Runway Turtles

Many things can delay flights at airports: weather, traffic, security concerns. An unusual cause of passenger angst is wildlife on the runway. Turtles—more precisely, diamondback terrapins (*Malaclemys terrapin*)—have delayed travelers at New York's John F. Kennedy

International Airport. Scores of the tiny reptiles crawl out of nearby Jamaica Bay and cross the tarmac in search of a good place to lay their eggs. "The sandy spot on the other side of Runway 4L is ideal for egg laying. It is a naturally provided turtle maternity ward," explained a Port Authority spokesman. Airport staff and local researchers collect the turtles, tag them with microchips, and move them to a safe location. The Federal Aviation Administration tracks encounters between civilian aircraft and wildlife; they reported eighteen "collisions" with diamondback terrapins from 1990 to 2007. The JFK traffic controllers heard this exchange from two approaching pilots in 2011:

> JetBlue pilot: JetBlue 102. We got a couple turtles storming the access road here off our right.
>
> Unidentified pilot: Can we really use the word *storming* about a turtle?

JUNE 14 | Not a Sweet Sound

There is no harp in Sacred Harp singing, nor any accompanying instruments or even an audience. There is harmony and verve and volume, and a performance can be a haunting and totally absorbing experience. Sacred Harp is a type of shape-note singing that evolved in the early American singing schools. The system was developed as an aid to sight-reading for people who didn't know standard music notation. Each printed note has a distinctive shape: triangle, circle, rectangle, or diamond; and a name: fa, sol, la, or mi. At a "singing," the group is divided into four sections—treble, alto, tenor, and bass—and participants sit in a hollow square, facing one another. The leader stands in the center and beats out the rhythm. The singers don't hold anything back; they sing at full volume. As NPR host Melissa Block remarked while covering a Sacred Harp convention, "This is full-body, shout-it-out singing. The harmonies are stark and haunting—raw, even. In Sacred Harp, you don't want a sweet sound." The name comes from the title of an early hymnal; the Sacred Harp is the human voice.

JUNE 15 | Literary Monsters

Almost everyone knows the story of the writing of the novel *Frankenstein, or the Modern Prometheus*; that on a June evening in 1816, Lord Byron and Percy Bysshe Shelley and his fiancée, Mary Godwin, were entertaining one another with ghost stories when Byron suggested they each attempt to write one. The novel that Godwin produced has resonated through the centuries; Shelley wrote a very short poem called "Fragment of a Ghost Story," and Byron came up with only a brief bit of prose he called "A Fragment." Yet there was another member of the party that night, John Polidori, Byron's young physician. He wrote *The Vampyre: A Tale*, the first English-language story "of the dead rising from their graves, and feeding upon the blood of the young and beautiful." The main character was based on Lord Byron, who was also assumed to be the author when it was first published in a magazine in 1819. This annoyed Byron, who denied writing the story and published his own "Fragment" as proof. The image of the aristocratic, elegant, and attractive but sinister vampire was now established, however, and it became the model for the many literary vampires that followed—in novels, plays, operas, and eventually in films—especially Bram Stoker's *Dracula*.

JUNE 16 | The Threefold Knowledge

The Vedas (from the Sanskrit root *vid*, "to know") are the oldest texts in Hindu literature and are the foundation of the religion. According to tradition, they were revealed at the dawn of creation, as a system of "threefold knowledge," the Rig Veda, the Sama Veda, and the Yajur Veda. A fourth, the Atharva Veda, was added at a later time. They are considered *apaurusheya* ("not made by man") and *nitya* ("eternal"). The oldest, the Rig Veda, was probably composed around 1500 BCE. Passed along by oral tradition, the Vedas were eventually written down using a form of archaic Sanskrit, one of the oldest surviving examples of an Indo-European language. They consist of hymns, incantations, and rituals that provide guidance in all aspects of life.

The first three Vedas deal with public ceremonies and common beliefs; the Atharva Veda is simpler and more personal, with spells to control disease or bring success. Together, they not only form a philosophical base for Hinduism, but offer insight into the daily life of India thousands of years ago.

JUNE 17 | "Wake Up the Conscience"

James Weldon Johnson (1871–1938) played a crucial role in the movement for African American rights in the early years of the twentieth century. A true Renaissance man, Johnson was a poet, a diplomat, a novelist, a songwriter, a politician, an educator, a lawyer, and a journalist; he was an important figure in the Harlem Renaissance and one of the driving forces behind the NAACP (National Association for the Advancement of Colored People). Johnson carved a lasting place for himself during what he called the "Red Summer" of 1919, when in response to multiple lynchings and race riots, he toured the country delivering eloquent, impassioned speeches about the evils of racial violence and the need for African Americans to stand up for their rights. "We've got to wake up the conscience of the American people," he said to a Boston crowd that year, "to hold the mirror before the people and

let the Nation see itself—a sinning Nation—for the American spirit is not dead. We need an organization of the white people and the black people to save America from mob violence." Sometimes overshadowed by his contemporaries W. E. B. Du Bois and Booker T. Washington, Johnson believed that promoting African American artistic and literary work, in addition to political activism, would help

James Weldon Johnson   overcome racial barriers in society.

JUNE 18 | Tibetan Sky Burial

Humans have practiced burial rites for tens of thousands of years. Remains are interred—often with decoration or personal or symbolic objects—or they are burned or placed in water. Religious and cultural mores, as well as practical considerations, guide the process. In Tibet, the Roof of the World, there are few trees and the ground is rocky and frozen, so cremation or earth graves are difficult. Buddhists in Tibet perform a ritual called *jhator* ("giving alms to the birds"), or sky burial. A few days after death, the body is brought to a large flat rock in a sacred place where monks dismember it and crush the bones. Vultures swoop down and consume the entire corpse, while the family sits out of sight nearby. As one Western witness to the ceremony explained,

> Tibetans believe that the soul and spirit of each person just borrows the body, and therefore death is just another phase in the circle of reincarnation. The sky burial is not full of mourning, for the tears and mourning are completed earlier during the three days of prayers and chants after one dies . . . death for a Tibetan is not the end, merely the beginning for a new stage in a soul's existence.

Sky burial is considered the deceased person's final act of generosity.

JUNE 19 | Five-Cent Theater

A revolution took place on June 19, 1905. On that day in downtown Pittsburgh, Pennsylvania, an entrepreneur named Harry Davis opened the world's first nickelodeon. His storefront was, according to a later newspaper account, "the first theater devoted exclusively to exhibition of moving picture spectacles." It had only ninety-six seats and charged a nickel admission (which, along with the Greek word for *theater*, gave the place its name). The moving picture "spectacles" that Davis and other nickelodeon owners exhibited were short films, sometimes only a minute or two in length. They included clips of famous people or news events (called "actualities"), exotic locations and other travel views ("scenics"), a plethora of performers, and scenes of leisure and sport activities. Motion pictures had been shown in theaters earlier, but usually as short breaks between live vaudeville acts, not as the featured entertainment. Nickelodeons returned the favor, occasionally inserting vaudeville acts between films. The new venues were instantly popular and proliferated rapidly across the country, with perhaps as many as ten thousand by 1910. Yet their era was short-lived. As films became longer, larger theaters were built, and soon the storefront nickelodeon died out. Still, their effect was enormous, making movies an important part of daily American life.

JUNE 20 | Urban Arcadia

Frederick Law Olmsted Sr. (1822–1903) began his career as a journalist but ended it as "the father of American landscape architecture." Although he and his partner, Calvert Vaux, designed hundreds of public spaces, their crowning achievement remains Central Park—an 843-acre oasis in the middle of Manhattan. Influenced by both the "City Beautiful" movement and the societal stresses brought on by the emergence of a new urban culture, Olmsted envisioned the park as a tranquil respite from city noise and bustle and a way to teach social and cultural lessons to average (that is, nonwealthy) New Yorkers. In 1870, he said, "No one who has closely observed the conduct of the people who visit the Park, can doubt that it exercises a distinctly harmonizing and refining influence upon the most unfortunate and most lawless classes of the city—an influence favorable to courtesy, self-control, and temperance." It was his urban Arcadia. Central Park—home to 24,000 trees (including 1,700 American elms); 7 bodies of water; 9,000 benches; 36 bridges; and 21 playgrounds—is now visited by 35 million people each year.

JUNE 21 | "Sodom by the Sea"

In the second half of the nineteenth century, mass culture was forming in America, as leisure time and spending power increased along with city populations. Frederick Law Olmsted and the other urban reformers of the time considered strolls through the verdant landscape of Central Park to be the ideal recreation, but members of the working class were also looking for something a little less genteel. They found it at Coney Island in Brooklyn. The wealthy had journeyed there first in the early 1800s, seeing it as a haven of seclusion from the city, but it also attracted a rowdier element. By mid-century, the section called Norton's Point at the western end of the island had gained notoriety as a den of gamblers, thieves, and prostitutes. Nearby West Brighton Beach earned the nickname "Sodom by the Sea." In the late 1890s, Paul Boyton, George C. Tilyou, Frederick Thomson, and others sought to redeem Coney Island—and make a nice profit for themselves—by bringing family-oriented, yet thrilling, amusements to the beach. According to cultural historian John Kasson,

> [I]nstead of stressing self-control, Coney Island stresses release. Instead of entertainments that make you self-aware and self-disciplined, it offers games of make believe, of theatricality, and games of vertigo, where you're literally spun around. And I think they fill the need of people who want to forget their jobs, who want to forget their everyday lives, and in that sense, that's what modern mass culture does too.

Coney Island offered everyday New Yorkers a freedom, a casting off of inhibitions, that they couldn't find in their work lives or in the pastoral landscape of Central Park.

JUNE 22 | Saddle Up That Camel

The camel was first domesticated around 2500 BCE and over time became crucial to the development of the Middle East. Yet it was the evolution of the saddle that really changed things. Early saddles were mounted behind the hump, on the animal's hindquarters. Somewhere between 400 and 100 BCE a new saddle was developed. It used two wooden braces shaped like arches, one in front of the hump, one behind, with a padded seat on top. Not only did this permit a better distribution of heavy loads, it allowed the rider to sit

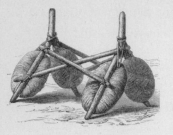

A camel saddle

up high with an unimpeded view, and therefore he could drive (and fight, when necessary) more effectively. The saddle was so advantageous that wheeled carts disappeared from some trade routes for centuries. Where camel breeders and owners had once been subservient to the buyers and the sellers who launched the caravans, suddenly they were a cultural force. "Camel-breeding nomads acquired unprecedented military, political, and economic power and were enabled thereby to achieve a degree of social and economic integration with the settled lands that their predecessors had never dreamed of," wrote historian Richard W. Bulliet.

JUNE 23 | The Call of the Universe

The didjeridu (or didgeridoo) is a musical instrument of Australia's aboriginal peoples, and it may be one of the world's oldest aerophones. It's a long hollow tube, usually at least four feet in length, but sometimes up to twenty. The didjeridu produces a low, rumbling, droning sound that can be highly rhythmic, depending on the performers' expertise in manipulating the tongue, the lips, and the throat. Playing it involves the use of circular breathing, where the performer expels a stream of air from the mouth into the end of the tube while simultaneously breathing in through the nose, thus producing a continuous sound. This technique seems to induce a relaxed or even euphoric state in the player. Bamboo was probably the original material for didjeridus, with hot coals used to burn out the diaphragms between sections. Termite-hollowed eucalyptus trees are also used, and today the instruments are made from all sorts of materials, even metal. The didjeridu developed in Arnhem Land in the north of Australia, where some of the finest players are still found, but it spread to tribes throughout the country. The word *didjeridu* (or its several other spellings) is the modern, onomatopoeic term; the various tribal groups have their own names for it—*yidaki, garnbak, djibolu, paampu,* and so on. As one researcher explains it, "To hear the Didjeridu is to hear the Universe calling. To play the Didjeridu is to answer the call."

JUNE 24 | Holy Wifi

In 2004, the Vatican's Apostolic Library—home to more than two million books, manuscripts, and other documents—began to install a radio frequency identification (RFID) tag system to manage its collections. As part of an $11.5 million renovation that also included improved climate control, fireproofing, security, and wifi for the research scholars, computer chips have been attached to about a hundred thousand volumes so far. The system stores data about each item, and ensures that anything can be instantly located—so a misshelved book is no longer a missing book. Periodic inventory checks that formerly required a month to complete can now be performed in half a day. In 2010, retail giant Walmart announced that it would institute a similar system to track store merchandise by installing microchips on individual items; previously, it had used RFID technology only on warehouse pallets and cases.

JUNE 25 | Prester John

Prester John didn't really exist, but he had an enormous effect on global exploration. He was a legendary Christian king, based in or near India, first mentioned in the *Chronicon* of Bishop Otto of Freising in 1145, who claimed the king was a descendant of one of the Three Magi. Twenty years later, a letter supposedly written by Prester (a corruption of the word *Presbyter*, or "priest") John surfaced in Europe. There were several versions of this letter over the years, addressed to the Byzantine emperor or to the pope. In it, Prester John described his glorious kingdom, with all manner of exotic beasts and fabulous riches. He was under threat from infidels and requested the help of Christian armies. With that spur, a number of expeditions journeyed to the East, exploring the region while searching for Prester John. Marco Polo looked for him, as did Vasco da Gama, and many others. When Prester John's kingdom hadn't been located by the fourteenth century, new versions of his letter indicated that he was actually in Abyssinia (Ethiopia), and explorers were sent there. Eventually, the Prester John legends died out, but not before Europeans had conducted substantial explorations of Asia and Africa.

JUNE 26 | Not Doubleday

How did the myth that Civil War general Abner Doubleday invented baseball come to be so widely believed? It was because of the Mills Commission, which was formed in 1905 to settle the question of baseball's beginning. Albert Spalding—a pitcher, a promoter of the game, and the founder of a hugely successful sporting goods company—had an ongoing debate with sportswriter Henry Chadwick about the origins of the game. Chadwick believed it had evolved from the British game called rounders. Spalding believed it was entirely an American invention. They formed a commission to decide the question, headed by Abraham Mills, the president of the National League. The commission reached out to the American public through newspaper articles (a very early version of crowdsourcing) for anyone who could provide details of the game's formation. Unfortunately, there were no historians (or librarians) on the panel, and there was no rigorous investigation of claims by a man named Abner Graves that he had witnessed Doubleday codifying the rules of "town ball" in Cooperstown, New York. Though his story was completely fictitious, the commission accepted it and issued a report naming Abner Doubleday the inventor of baseball, a claim the man himself never made.

JUNE 27 | The Flying Mammal

Although they are one of the more misunderstood groups of mammals in the world, bats (*Chiroptera*, which means "hand wing") are extraordinarily important to healthy ecosystems. Not only do they eat large numbers of insect pests, they are also major pollinators and seed spreaders for plant life. There are more than twelve hundred species of bats, at least one-fifth of all mammal species. They range in size from the giant golden crowned flying fox that weighs about 2.5 pounds to the tiny bumblebee bat, which may be the world's smallest mammal. Bats are quite long-lived, with some

A bat

species having a life span of thirty years or more. They are also the only mammals that are capable of true flight (as compared to gliding, which is what so-called flying squirrels do). Bat populations are declining globally, partly due to destruction of their habitats and other man-made dangers such as wind turbines, but also due to disease. White-nose syndrome (WNS) is caused by a fungus (*Geomyces destructans*) that interrupts the bats' winter hibernation, allowing frigid temperatures and low food supplies to take a huge toll. It is estimated that almost seven million bats have died from WNS since the disease was first discovered in 2006.

JUNE 28 | Stonewalling for Their Rights

In 1969, the Stonewall Inn on Christopher Street in New York's Greenwich Village wasn't much to look at. Technically a private club, it was a sleazy bar that catered to the city's gay community. At that time, homosexual acts were illegal in public or even in private homes, and antilewdness laws made cross-dressing and same-sex dancing dangerous activities. Police crackdowns at gay bars were common; in some weeks, a hundred people were arrested. The Stonewall was owned by organized crime, which took advantage of the customers by charging exorbitant prices for watered-down drinks. In the early hours of June 28, things came to a crisis point when police raided the Stonewall and started to make arrests. A crowd gathered, objects were tossed, and soon people were breaking windows and setting garbage on fire. Cries of "gay power" alternated with antipolice taunts, and the cops retreated into the bar. Reinforcements arrived and fought the protestors until they dispersed; violence continued the following night and during the next week. The events of those days were a turning point for the gay rights movement, propelling it in a more open direction. The first Gay Pride march occurred a year later on Christopher Street. By the fortieth anniversary of the Stonewall uprising, New York officials were promoting the city as a destination for gay and lesbian travelers. The Stonewall Inn was designated a national historic landmark in 2000.

JUNE 29 | Meet Me at the Corner of Prospect and Weyse

It doesn't have quite the same ring as Hollywood and Vine, does it? But the streets at the world's most glamorous intersection, once a lemon grove, did not get their famous names until 1910, when the small town of Hollywood was annexed to the city of Los Angeles. The area had been owned by Horace Wilcox and his wife, Daeida. The historical plaque at the intersection reads, "Hollywood was given its name by pioneers Mr. and Mrs. Horace H. Wilcox. They subdivided their ranch in 1887 and called two dirt cross-roads Prospect Avenue and Weyse Avenue. Prospect Avenue, the main artery, was renamed Hollywood Boulevard and Weyse Avenue became Vine Street. This was the origin of 'Hollywood and Vine.'" As the movie industry grew, film studios and related companies sprang up near Hollywood and Vine, giving it a cachet that was reinforced by radio broadcasts and newspaper columnists; Hedda Hopper touted it as the place to see Hollywood celebrities. The area faded in the 1960s when movie businesses relocated to other parts of town, but residential and retail development projects have been underway since the beginning of the twenty-first century.

JUNE 30 | Stunting at Niagara

They aren't the highest waterfalls in the world, but they may be the most famous. Niagara Falls for many decades was the premier honeymoon spot for newlyweds, and it also became the quintessential location for daredevils. On June 30, 1859, a funambulist (a tightrope walker) who called himself "the Great Blondin" strolled along a three-inch wide, eleven-hundred-foot-long rope over the gorge. Many other tightrope walkers followed in his well-balanced footsteps. On June 15, 2012, Nik Wallenda of the "Flying Wallenda" circus family became the first person to cross on a tightrope directly over the falls (he wore a safety harness, at the insistence of his sponsor, which some people found disappointing). The first person to go over the falls in a barrel was a woman, sixty-three-year-old Annie Edson Taylor, in 1901. She jammed herself into a four-and-a-half-foot barrel, along with pillows, a mattress, and an anvil for ballast. Mrs. Taylor survived the 170-foot drop and emerged dazed and a bit battered. Others were not so lucky. There have been five deaths from Niagara stunts, the most recent in 1995, when Robert Overacker challenged the falls on a jet ski. The plan was for a parachute to deploy and float him to earth. The chute opened but wasn't properly tethered to Overacker, who plummeted to his death. Perhaps the most amazing feat was not performed by a daredevil. In 1960, seven-year-old Roger Woodward was spilled into the upper Niagara River when the small boat he was riding in capsized. Going over the falls wearing just his bathing suit and a life jacket, the young boy survived with only some scrapes and bruises. That event has come to be known as the "Miracle at Niagara."

JULY

JULY 1 | Crossing the USA

America's first transcontinental road was the Lincoln Highway—originally 3,389 miles through thirteen states from New York City to San Francisco. In the first decade of the twentieth century, the automobile was still a novelty, and most of the country's roads were unpaved. Traveling could be a dusty or muddy endeavor, depending on the weather. Many roads had formed haphazardly and didn't provide direct connections between cities. Carl Fisher wanted to change that. An entrepreneur who got rich selling automobiles and who built the Indianapolis Motor Speedway, Fisher proposed a true transcontinental highway in 1913—the Coast to Coast Rock Highway—which he envisioned as a graveled road costing about $10 million to construct. He turned to auto manufacturers for funding, but Henry Ford said no. Henry Joy, the patriarch of Packard Motors, did pledge his support and, in fact, became the highway's most enthusiastic booster. He was the man who suggested it be named after Abraham Lincoln. Existing roads were improved and connected; there was haggling over the selected route, but the finished highway was straight and efficient. The 1916 edition of the *Official Road Guide* estimated that the cross-country trip would take twenty to thirty days, at an average speed of eighteen miles per hour. In 1925, the American Association of State Highway Officials opted for a numbered road system, which called for the major east-west routes to be numbered in multiples of ten, and the north-south routes to end in one or five. The Lincoln Highway was broken up into a variety of numbered roads, but the name lingers on, thanks in part to an eponymous 1940s NBC radio show about life along the route. Today, concrete markers for the Lincoln Highway can still be found along some roads, and a centennial tour is planned by the Lincoln Highway Association for 2013.

JULY 2 | Drift and Dream

One of the oddest fish in the sea is the *Mola mola* or ocean sunfish. It looks like a giant fish head with two fins but no body or tail. In place of a tail, it has a rudderlike lobe called the clavus. When its dorsal and ventral fins are extended, it can be as tall as it is long. It's also huge and the heaviest of all bony fish; the largest one ever found was fourteen feet long and weighed almost five thousand pounds. One oceanographer described them this way, "They're slow dreamers who peacefully drift around the seas and aren't known for lively enthusiasm." The name comes from the fish's habit of lying on its side near the surface, as if sunbathing. Fortunately for humans, *Mola mola* has a very small mouth and lives primarily on jellyfish and squid. The only danger to people comes when the fish breaches, because it can jump as high as two body lengths and has been known to land on a boat's deck. There are four known species of *Molidae*, distributed globally, and some are now consumed as a delicacy in parts of Asia.

A Mola mola

JULY 3 | The President Is a Sick Man

Unknown to the press, the American people, and possibly even to his vice president and staff, President Grover Cleveland underwent a secret surgical procedure in 1893. The cigar-smoking president had noticed a fast-growing lump on the roof of his mouth; it was diagnosed as cancer ("It's a bad looking tenant, and I would have it evicted immediately," his physician told him). Concerned that the nation would panic, and with an economic crisis already underway, Cleveland contrived to have the tumor removed on board a friend's yacht, while ostensibly taking a fishing trip to Cape Cod during the July Fourth holiday. To maintain the secret, the surgery had to be performed without scarring his face or damaging his mustache. Sections of Cleveland's jaw and hard palate and some teeth were excised through his mouth; a rubber prosthetic was inserted soon after the operation, and the president recovered in a few weeks. One journalist's effort to uncover the story was suppressed, and the truth was not revealed until twenty-four years later.

JULY 4 | The Firelands

During the American Revolution, the city of Norwalk, Connecticut (established in 1651), and several surrounding towns were attacked, burned, and almost completely destroyed by the forces of British general William Tryon. "Connecticut was . . . the victim of terrorization! To harry, ravage and burn became the British policy after 1778 when the campaigns for control of the Hudson had miscarried. . . . But little could England realize that the invasion of Connecticut towns would serve to push westward the frontiers of the very colonies it was struggling to stifle," according to a 1935 article in the *Ohio Archaeological and Historical Quarterly*. After the war, the people who had lost their homes were offered land in the Connecticut Western Reserve, which is now called Ohio. (The Western Reserve was the land the colony had claimed, from its western border to the Mississippi River.) The area, half a million acres near Lake Erie, became known as the Fire

Sufferers Land, then just Firelands. The "sufferers," or their descendants or agents, established Norwalk, Ohio, and other municipalities and townships.

JULY 5 | The Sun Goddess of Japan

As with all myths, there are a number of variations of the story, but this seems to be the general outline of the legend of the Shinto sun goddess, Amaterasu. She was so radiant that her father, Izanagi, elevated her to rule heaven, where she tended a beautiful garden; birds sang in her presence and flowers bloomed. She had a brother named Susanoo, a storm god with a mischievous streak. Like many younger brothers, he was loud, annoying, and destructive. One day he created a gale that wrecked her garden. Feeling depressed and disheartened, Amaterasu retreated to a cave and shut herself in behind a door of stone. With her absence, the Earth became cold and dark, demons ruled, and the rice fields withered. The other gods tried to lure her out, but she refused, until Uzume performed a provocative dance outside the cave. It was so outrageous that the other gods began laughing. Curious, Amaterasu peeked out, and one of the gods grabbed her and pulled her outside, returning light to the world. Her great-grandson, Jimmu, became the first emperor of Japan, and Amaterasu is the ancestor deity of the imperial family.

JULY 6 | An Artist for Peace

Manu Dibango (full name, Emmanuel N'Djoké Dibango)—a pioneer of world music—is a Cameroonian musician, born in 1933, who was influenced by many genres, from jazz and soul to reggae and techno. He studied piano and saxophone in France, where he attended concerts by such jazz greats as Duke Ellington and Louis Armstrong, and began his performing career in Parisian cabarets. He was soon traveling and playing concerts in Africa, Europe, and the Caribbean. In the early 1970s, his single "Soul Makossa" was the first international Afrobeat hit and one of the first disco tunes on the charts;

it's been sampled or covered by dozens of performers (a couple of whom were sued for using the refrain without permission). The song "was a bridge connecting America with the motherland in the early '70s, during the 'black is beautiful' period," he told the *Los Angeles Times*. Dibango has been designated a UNESCO Artist for Peace, "in recognition of his exceptional contribution to the development of the arts, of peace, and to dialogue among the world's cultures."

JULY 7 | The Greatest Thing Since

It is the event to which every other achievement is compared. The invention of sliced bread was trumpeted with an advertisement that hailed it as "the greatest forward step in the baking industry since bread was wrapped." Otto Rohwedder, an Iowa jeweler, invented a crude prototype of the bread slicer in 1912, but a series of problems prevented its refinement and distribution until 1928, when he installed the first commercial bread-slicing machine at the Chillicothe Baking Company in Missouri. On July 7 of that year, customers were able to buy presliced bread for the first time. The *Chillicothe Constitution-Tribune* waxed ecstatic: "So neat and precise are the slices, and so definitely better than anyone could possibly slice by hand with a bread knife that one realizes instantly that here is a refinement that will receive a hearty and permanent welcome." It was an immediate success, and demand for the slicing machine rose steadily, despite the onset of the Depression. In 1930, Wonder Bread began distributing presliced bread nationally, using its own bread-slicing equipment. The trend coincided nicely with the release a few years earlier of a home pop-up toaster, which required evenly sliced bread to work efficiently. Chillicothe calls itself "The Home of Sliced Bread."

JULY 8 | In a Galaxy Far, Far Away

The Big Bang, the event that formed the universe we live in, occurred about 13.7 billion years ago. In 2011, astronomers analyzing data from the Hubble Space Telescope's Ultra Deep Field announced that they had identified one of the oldest and most distant galaxies yet known. At 13.2 billion years, this proto-galaxy, called UDFj-39546284, was formed just 480 million years after the Big Bang. It is a small, dim galaxy of blue stars—one-hundredth the size of the Milky Way—and detecting such a distant object pushed the Hubble telescope to its limits. To further explore the formative years of the universe, astronomers will have to wait for NASA's James Webb Space Telescope, slated for launch later this decade. One of the scientists on the team points out, "We're moving into a regime where there are big changes afoot. Another couple of hundred million years toward the Big Bang, that will be the time where the first galaxies really are starting to get built up."

JULY 9 | To Delight the Inhabitants

The oldest municipal park in New York City is a small, tear-shaped acre of land in Manhattan's financial district. It was originally a Native American council ground and the site where Peter Minuit "purchased" the island in 1626. In 1733, the city leased the plot to three prominent New Yorkers, who agreed to build a bowling green and walkways there, for "the Recreation & delight of the Inhabitants of this City." It became one of the city's most fashionable areas. In 1765, when the hated Stamp Act was imposed, angry inhabitants burned the governor in effigy at Bowling Green. When the act was repealed, forgiving New Yorkers erected a gilded lead statue of King George III on his horse, and later they built a fence around the park to protect the statue. The fence didn't help on July 9, 1776, the day that the Declaration of Independence was read at City Hall. A crowd, led by the Sons of Liberty, marched down Broadway to Bowling Green Park and pulled down the statue of the king. They cut off its head and put it on a pike, then broke the rest up into pieces and sent them off to a foundry to be turned into bullets for the coming Revolution. They also tore the crowns from the posts of the fence, which still stands today, now a city landmark.

JULY 10 | "Forced to Write for Bread"

Aphra Johnson Behn (1640–1689) was the first Englishwoman to earn her living as a writer of poetry, plays, and fiction. Details of her early life are sketchy: she was probably born near Canterbury and spent time in Surinam and was briefly married to a completely unknown (and possibly fictional) merchant named Behn. She was hired as a spy by King Charles II during the second Anglo-Dutch War and spent time in debtor's prison when he failed to provide her with compensation. In the preface to her play *Sir Patient Fancy*, Behn described herself as "forced to write for Bread and not ashamed to owne it." The female characters she created had strong personalities and were realistic, autonomous, and intelligent. Her most famous

works are probably the play *The Rover* (a sophisticated comedy set during carnival in Naples) and *Oroonoka, or the Royal Slave* (a novel about a slave revolt in South America that Behn claimed to have witnessed herself). Virginia Woolf, in *A Room of One's Own*, suggested that "All women together ought to let flowers fall upon the tomb of Aphra Behn . . . for it was she who earned them the right to speak their minds."

Aphra Johnson Behn

JULY 11 | Carnivores Triumphant

Scientists have long speculated that eating meat was a crucial factor in human evolution. Surviving on nuts, leaves, tubers, and berries requires a large amount of time and effort and a big gut to digest it all. Once our human ancestors began to eat meat, they were able to absorb energy more efficiently and didn't require such a large digestive system. Richard Wrangham of Harvard University agrees that meat was important, but he thinks cooking was the real evolutionary advance. In his book *Catching Fire: How Cooking Made Us Human*, Wrangham says, "Cooking increased the value of our food. It changed our bodies, our brains, our use of time and our social lives. It made us into consumers of external energy and thereby created an organism with a new relationship to nature, dependent on fuel." The cooking process breaks down the long protein chains and the collagen in meat and softens the starches in vegetables, making them much easier to digest. Wrangham thinks humans may have started cooking their food about two million years ago, although other anthropologists posit more recent dates. Still, cooking food not only made digestion easier, it gave us a fire to sit around and talk over dinner, and that, too, was a big part of what made us human.

JULY 12 | The Prince of Soups

In early America, there were no establishments called "restaurants." There were certainly taverns and public houses, but their primary draw was alcohol. The food was secondary, and it usually tasted that way. One of the earliest true restaurants opened in Boston in 1793. Called "Julien's Restorator," it was owned by Jean Baptiste Gilbert Payplat dis Julien, who had come to the United States to escape the French Revolution. He marketed his dining establishment as a place to restore health: "a Resort, where the infirm in health, the convalescent, and those whose attention to studious business occasions a lassitude of nature; can obtain the most suitable nourishment," as one advertisement in a local paper described it. He became famous for his soups, particularly turtle soup and a potage composed of finely slivered vegetables he called Julien soup. The soup and the method of cutting the vegetables still bear his name (now usually spelled *julienne*).

JULY 13 | The Blue Stone

The brilliant blue pigment used by Egyptians and others in the ancient world came from a stone called lapis lazuli (primarily made of the mineral lazurite). It was relatively rare and therefore very expensive. One of the main sources for lapis is the Kochka River valley in Afghanistan, where mines have existed for perhaps six thousand years. Lapis lazuli was coveted throughout the ancient world; it was used in jewelry-making and was also ground up and mixed with oil to make paint. It was mentioned in the Bible and in the Epic of Gilgamesh, and Cleopatra is said to have used powdered lapis as eye shadow. The Romans called it *ultramarinum*, which means "beyond the sea." In addition to its beauty, lapis lazuli was thought to have a variety of magical and medicinal powers.

JULY 14 | *Nettoyage à Sec*

Jean Baptiste Jolly, the owner of a dye-works in France, is often credited with inventing the process of dry cleaning. In the mid-1800s (some sources say as early as 1825; others, 1840s or later), he came up with the idea after his maid spilled kerosene or turpentine on a dirty tablecloth. When the cloth dried, it was clean, leading Jolly to experiment with different substances and refine the process, which he called *nettoyage à sec* or "dry cleaning." In 1821, however, Thomas Jennings (1791–1859), a free black tailor in New York City, had received a patent for a "dry scouring" process that used petroleum-based solvents. He was the first African American to be awarded a patent. Dry cleaning is not actually "dry"; it uses liquid solvents, but it doesn't use water, which could harm delicate fabrics. Over the years, various solvents have been tested; some were toxic or flammable and had to be abandoned. The current primary chemical used is the chlorocarbon perchloroethylene (also called tetrachloroethylene). Jennings became a rich man and was an active abolitionist. When Jennings died in 1859, Frederick Douglass described him as "Born in a slave state, and of a race held in slavery, living in the midst of all the crushing influences which human prejudice and caste could heap upon him, he yet fulfilled all the purposes of an upright man, a useful citizen, and a devoted Christian."

JULY 15 | A Nineteenth-Century Rosa Parks

The tailor Thomas Jennings had a daughter named Elizabeth (1830–1901), who earned a special place in African American history. She was a schoolteacher who was on her way to play the organ at her church in July 1845 and was running late. She and a friend took the first horse-drawn streetcar that came along, not wanting to wait for one marked "Negro Persons Allowed in This Car." The conductor tried to throw them off, but Jennings fought back, first arguing with him, then hanging onto a window frame when he attempted to forcibly eject her. The conductor called a policeman to come aboard and remove Jennings. She wrote a statement about the incident that was read for her at a church

Elizabeth Jennings

meeting (she was too "sore and stiff from the treatment I received from those monsters in human form" to attend) and then was published in the *New York Tribune* and in *Frederick Douglass's Paper*. She sued the Third Avenue Railroad Company and won her case in 1855. The judge ruled that "Colored persons if sober, well behaved and free from disease, had the same rights as others and could neither be excluded by any rules of the Company, nor by force or violence." Jennings received about $225 in compensation, and her case helped open New York's public transportation to all people, regardless of color.

JULY 16 | The First Commercial Hijacking

A Chinese national named Wong (or Huang) Yu and three accomplices boarded a Cathay Pacific seaplane on July 16, 1948. The flight, on its regular forty-mile run from Macau to Hong Kong, was known to regularly carry rich passengers and large amounts of cash and gold. Once the plane was airborne, the men drew their guns and demanded that the pilot turn the controls over to them. One of the passengers tried to intervene, and the copilot struck one of the hijackers with an iron bar. In the confusion, the pirates started shooting, and the pilot and the copilot were killed. The plane fell into the sea, killing everyone aboard except for Wong. The plan had been to hold the passengers for ransom, Wong revealed while in custody. This was the world's first act of air piracy on a commercial flight—the term *hijacking* was in use but primarily for bootleggers—and there were jurisdictional issues between Portuguese Macau and British Hong Kong. Wong remained in prison for three years until he was deported to China, where he disappeared from history. Passengers in the region were soon being subjected to screening by a device previously used primarily in prisons—a metal detector.

JULY 17 | The Smartest Man Ever

It may be difficult to understand in today's celebrity-obsessed culture, but some people do not desire or pursue fame. William James Sidis (1898–1944) would have preferred anonymity, but that was not his destiny. Born in Boston to a psychologist father and a physician mother, Sidis was a prodigy whose parents pushed him to excel, and he exhibited an early love of knowledge and learning. It is said he was able to read the *New York Times* before age two and spoke eight languages by the time he was six. He graduated from Harvard University with honors at age sixteen. Sidis taught mathematics for a time but then was arrested at a May Day demonstration in 1919 that had turned violent. To avoid jail, his parents placed him in a sanitarium for a year. Estranged from his family and tired of the media attention that had dogged him since childhood, Sidis went into seclusion, working a variety of menial jobs in a number of cities. He wrote books, often under a pseudonym and sometimes self-published, on a range of subjects from cosmology to the collecting of streetcar transfers. Then, in 1937, *New Yorker* magazine published an unflattering portrait of Sidis under the title "Where Are They Now? April Fool." He sued the magazine for libel and invasion of privacy but was only partly successful. Sidis died from a cerebral hemorrhage on July 17, 1944.

JULY 18 | Wrong Way Corrigan

Douglas Corrigan (1907–1995) was enamored with flying, learned to fly at age eighteen, and soon got a job as an airplane mechanic in San Diego. There he met Charles Lindbergh and helped build his *Spirit of St. Louis.* Inspired by Lindbergh's 1927 transatlantic flight, Corrigan bought a used Curtiss Robin monoplane for $325 a few years later and began to make modifications that would allow it to fly across the ocean. He applied for permission to fly from New York to Ireland but was denied because officials said the plane wasn't sound enough. Corrigan made additional changes and applied again. He was again denied. More modifications. Denied. Feeling frustrated, in 1938, Corrigan flew from California to New York and filed a flight plan for a return trip. On July 17, he took off from Floyd Bennet Field in Brooklyn, and twenty-eight hours later, he landed in Baldonnel Airport in Dublin, Ireland. Officials questioned him, and he said he got mixed up in the clouds and the fog, his compass wasn't working properly, and he thought he had been heading west to California. Skeptical, they pressed him further. "That's my story," he replied. His pilot's license was suspended but only for a few days, and when he returned to New York (via steamship), he was lionized. Amused with this unorthodox hero, the city threw him a ticker-tape parade that drew a bigger crowd than the one for Lindbergh. Corrigan led a quiet life after his famous flight, never admitting that he had intentionally flown across the Atlantic. Thanks to that exploit, he will forever be remembered as "Wrong Way Corrigan."

JULY 19 | Just Out of Reach

Tantalus was the wealthy king of Sipylus and a son of Zeus. As a demigod, he was admitted to the table of the deities, and something happened there to provoke their anger. Maybe he stole some of their sacred food or revealed to mortals a divine secret. Some versions of the story say he killed his son Pelops, then cooked and served him to the gods to test their ability to detect forbidden food. Whatever occurred, Tantalus became one of the "archetypal violators of the laws laid down by Zeus for the conduct of human society, criminals whose exemplary punishment stands as a moral landmark for posterity," as the *Oxford Dictionary of Classical Myth and Religion* explains it. The punishment of Tantalus was severe

Tantalus

and eternal. He was submerged in water, but each time he tried to drink, the water receded; branches of apples and pomegranates hung above him, but as he reached for them, the wind blew them beyond his grasp. A large rock may also have been balanced threateningly above him. In Book 11 of Homer's *Odyssey*, Tantalus is observed still suffering in Hades. His agony is preserved forever in our word *tantalize.*

JULY 20 | For All Mankind

As *Apollo 11* astronauts Neil Armstrong and Buzz Aldrin were descending to the surface of the moon on July 20, 1969, few of the millions watching the coverage on television were aware of how close they came to aborting the mission. The men realized they had overshot their original landing site, and the area where they were coming down was strewn with boulders and craters. They were running out of fuel; Armstrong took manual control, and with Aldrin calling out velocity and altitude figures, Armstrong carefully guided the lunar module down to the surface. No wonder the Capcom (capsule communicator) at mission control reacted, "You got a bunch of guys about to turn blue. We're breathing again." The next day, as they ended their visit to the moon, the two astronauts left behind a few mementos: a gold olive branch signifying peace; an *Apollo 1* patch to honor the three astronauts who had died in the 1967 launch pad fire (Gus Grissom, Ed White, and Roger Chaffee); and two Soviet medals commemorating Vladimir Komarov, who died upon reentry of his *Soyuz 1* capsule, and Yuri Gagarin, the first man in space, who had been killed in a plane crash.

JULY 21 | "The Abyss of the Deep Laid Open"

Egyptians called it "the day of horror." On July 21, 365 CE, an earthquake struck near the island of Crete and caused a tsunami that devastated the Egyptian coastline, especially the city of Alexandria.

I could not hope to provide a more vivid description of this event than that given by Roman historian Ammianus Marcellinus:

> Day had just dawned when, after a thunderstorm of exceptional violence, the solid frame of the earth shuddered and trembled, and the sea was removed from its bed and went rolling back. The abyss of the deep was laid open; various types of marine creatures could be seen stuck in the slime, and huge mountains and valleys which had been hidden since the creation in the depths of the waves then, one must suppose, saw the light of the sun for the first time. Many ships were stranded on what was now dry land, and a host of people roamed at large in the shallows that were left to pick up fish and similar objects. Then, however, the roaring sea . . . turned back, and rushed over the seething shoals to burst in fury upon islands and wide tracts of the mainland. Innumerable buildings in towns or wherever they were standing were leveled to the ground, and the whole face of the earth was changed by this mad conflict of the elements. . . . The sudden return of the vast sea when it was least expected drowned many thousands; when the watery element again subsided many ships had been destroyed by the force of the tidal wave.

JULY 22 | A Plague of Locusts

Locusts are a type of grasshopper (family *Acrididae*) that can alter their behavior in crowded conditions and enter a swarming phase, where they are able to migrate over long distances in huge numbers, devastating crops wherever they land. Like the biblical plague in Egypt, there have been and continue to be periods of major destruction by locusts around the world. A swarm can contain tens of millions of insects per square mile. In the 1870s on the American prairie, there were swarms of Rocky Mountain locusts that darkened the sky as they passed overhead, consumed every bit of vegetation, and even ate the wool from live sheep and the clothes off people's backs. The *New York Times* described the scene in Nebraska in 1874: "When the train attempted to move on

A locust

it was prevented by the numbers [of locusts] crushed by the wheels, as they made the track so slippery. . . . When they rise in the air they are so dense as to oftentimes obscure the sun, and the noise they make is somewhat like the rush of a wind-storm at sea, except that it seems duller and heavier."

JULY 23 | The Conqueror of the Air

In the early years of the twentieth century, the race to build and fly the first heavier-than-air craft riveted the world. Of all the personalities involved, none was more colorful than Alberto Santos-Dumont (1873–1932), a wealthy Brazilian who lived in France. In the late 1890s, he began to design powered dirigibles, small one-person balloons, and he flew them around the rooftops of Paris, even circling the Eiffel Tower. A short but always elegantly dressed man, he would sometimes host "aerial dinners," with guests sitting at elevated tables and chairs to simulate the experience of being in the air. Turning his attention to heavier-than-air craft, he designed a number of fixed-wing airplanes, including the *14-bis*, which he flew for approximately sixty meters on October 23, 1906. Because word of the Wright Brothers' 1903 flight had not yet spread to the general populace, Europe hailed Santos-Dumont as the "Conqueror of the Air." In 1910, he became seriously ill and was diagnosed with multiple sclerosis. Horrified at the damage that airplanes were able to inflict during World War I, Alberto Santos-Dumont moved back to Brazil and, struggling with mental illness, became more and more eccentric until, on July 23, 1932, he took his own life. At the moment of his burial, thousands of pilots around the world tipped their wings in his honor.

JULY 24 | It's about Time

At the time of Alberto Santos-Dumont's pioneering flights around Paris, most men carried pocket watches. Because his hands were fully occupied operating the controls while flying, Santos-Dumont longed for a timepiece that didn't require him to dig into his pockets. Wrist-watches had been available for some time, but in the 1800s, they were mostly worn by women as jewelry. Santos-Dumont's friend, watch-maker Louis Cartier, designed a wristwatch for him with a square bezel and a leather band, and he never flew again without it. Thanks to the fame of Santos-Dumont, wristwatches soon became a fashion essential for men. Cartier still sells a line of watches named for Santos-Dumont.

JULY 25 | QWERTY

Anyone who looks at the layout of a standard computer or type-writer keyboard must wonder why the letters are arranged the way they are. It all has to do with mechanics. Christopher Sholes (1815–1891) patented the first commercially successful typewriter in 1868. Sholes had originally designed the keyboard with the let-ters in alphabetical order, but key-jamming proved to be a major problem. He thought that if he moved the most-used letters to the edges of the board, there would be less chance of the key levers sticking. He experimented with a few different layouts until the patent was sold to E. Remington & Sons in 1873, and the com-pany's mechanics tweaked it further to the QWERTY layout we are familiar with today. There were other typing machines with different keyboards in development, and on July 25, 1888, a typing contest was held in Cincinnati. Frank McGurrin, a court stenog-rapher, had memorized the Remington's QWERTY keyboard and so could use what we call touch typing. His opponent, Louis Traub, had a Caligraph machine, with separate keys for upper and lower cases. A local newspaper reported the scene: "The clicking of the two machines made a metallic chorus, the tinkling bell on each machine doing a solo before a line was finished." McGurrin won the $500 prize, averaging ninety-seven words per minute, and went on to a number of similar contests and demonstrations, becoming a minor celebrity and helping to ensure the staying power of the QWERTY layout.

JULY 26 | Candy from the Marshes

The candy we call marshmallow originated in ancient Egypt thousands of years ago, as a treat made from the sweet sap of the marsh mallow plant (*Althaea officinalis*). French candy makers in the nineteenth century hand-whipped the sap and created molded candies in the now-traditional shape. They were hugely popular, so manufacturers looked for cheaper and less labor-intensive production methods and started to

use gelatin or egg whites, instead of mallow root extract. The National Confectioners Association tells us that Americans consume about ninety million pounds of marshmallows in a year, and 50 percent of those sold during the summer are toasted over a fire. The world's largest supplier of novelty marshmallow treats is the Just Born Company of Bethlehem, Pennsylvania—the maker of Peeps.

A marsh mallow plant

JULY 27 | From Bill-Posters to Pop Hits

Billboard magazine—the primary trade journal for the music industry—is also one of the oldest. It was founded in 1894, not to gauge the popularity of music, but for bill-posting businesses that produced advertising posters, and it was originally called *Billboard Advertising*. According to the first issue, it was "devoted to the interests of advertisers, poster printers, bill posters, advertising agents and secretaries of fairs." Entertainment news was quickly added, and the editor realized that show business was the future of the publication, so the magazine began to focus on carnivals and outdoor amusements. *Billboard*'s significant role in tracking popular music was initiated in 1936, when it started Chart Line, a listing of the tunes played most often on the radio. The Best Selling Retail Records chart—the ancestor of today's Hot 100—premiered on July 27, 1940; the first national number one song was "I'll Never Smile Again," performed by the Tommy Dorsey Orchestra, with a young vocalist named Frank Sinatra.

JULY 28 | Black Blizzards

In 2011, heat and drought conditions plagued many areas of the Great Plains. Suffering farmers took some comfort in the fact that they didn't also experience dust storms similar to those in the 1930s, which had given the name "Dust Bowl" to the southern plains. That drought was a natural disaster, but the condition of the soil was a man-made problem. Great numbers of people had migrated to the region since the nineteenth century, and most were running small farms or raising cattle. Dry-land farming and over-grazing had stripped the plains of prairie grasses, so when the drought hit, one hundred million acres of topsoil dried out and blew with the winds, sometimes so thick the storms blocked out the sun and were called "black blizzards." Farms were devastated, and hundreds of thousands of poor, hungry Americans moved west out of the plains states in a great exodus. Lessons were learned from the dust bowl tragedy; farming techniques evolved, and although droughts remain a constant threat, the land is less vulnerable than it once was.

JULY 29 | Adaptable Gulls

Black-legged kittiwakes (small members of the gull family, *Laridae*) on Alaska's Prince William Sound do not breed very well, but they can live for twenty years, a relatively long time. Decades ago, a British researcher studying the same birds in England found just the opposite: they bred successfully but had only ten-year life spans. The difference seems to be their adaptability. "It's kind of a strategy, it's a game," says U.S. Geological Survey biologist Scott Hatch. "Do I put all my eggs into—no pun intended—do I put my effort into breeding, and therefore not live as long, or do I sit it out, live a long time and hope that I'll have adequate reproduction over the long term?" Hatch believes that the adaptability of wildlife may help some species overcome changes that humans have wrought in their habitat and climate.

JULY 30 | **Extended Family in Heaven**

Catholics don't worship the saints (sometimes referred to as "your extended family in heaven"), but they do venerate them and ask for their intercession through prayer. The Vatican has an office called the Congregation for the Causes of Saints. Patron saints and angels have been designated as special protectors for specific countries, diseases, occupations, conditions, and so on. Sometimes the choices are obvious: Matthew, a tax collector, is the patron saint of accountants. Some selections are rather clever:

- Joseph of Cupertino is the patron saint of aviators and astronauts, because it was said that he levitated at prayer (he's called "the flying friar").
- Archangel Gabriel—the announcer, an instrument of revelation—is the patron for broadcasters and telecommunications.
- Isidore of Seville was named the protector of the Internet, because he compiled the Christian world's first encyclopedia.
- Lawrence, a martyr who was roasted alive on a grill, is the patron of cooks.
- Fiacre is the guardian saint of taxi cab drivers, because in the seventeenth century the Hotel de Saint Fiacre in Paris was the first to rent out coaches, which therefore became known as fiacres. The Church chose to follow the popular designation.

JULY 31 | **Our Father's Home**

Mount Vernon, the plantation home of George Washington, was part of an estate originally called Little Hunting Creek that had been granted to his great-grandfather in 1674. Our first president lived there for more than forty-five years, expanding the acreage and dividing it into five working farms and enlarging and improving the house. After Washington's death in 1799, the property passed to several relatives, but by the 1850s, it had fallen into disrepair, and the family could not afford to maintain it. In 1853, the Mount Vernon Ladies Association (MVLA) was formed by Ann Pamela Cunningham of

South Carolina, to save, restore, and preserve the home and the grounds. The MVLA acquired Mount Vernon in 1860 and began to repair the dilapidated mansion. With the start of the Civil War, however, the estate found itself dangerously situated between the

Mount Vernon

opposing armies, and the regents feared occupation and devastation. The two staff members in charge—one Northerner (Sarah Tracy) and one Southerner (Upton Herbert)—persuaded generals of the Union and the Confederacy to respect Mount Vernon as neutral ground and to forbid any soldiers from entering the estate while armed. On July 31, 1861, Union general Winfield Scott issued General Order No. 13, which stated, "It has been the prayer of every patriot that the tramp and din of civil war might, at least, spare the precincts within which repose the sacred remains of the Father of His Country."

AUGUST

AUGUST 1 | The Unicorn Whale

The narwhal (*Monodon monoceros*, "one tooth, one horn") is a toothed whale that has no teeth in its mouth. Instead, the male narwhal has a large tusk that grows in a counter-clockwise spiral from its upper jaw and extends as much as six to ten feet. The tusks were highly valued by medieval kings and probably are the source of the myth of the unicorn. Because female narwhals don't have tusks, it must be a sexual trait, rather than a requirement for survival. There are somewhere between forty thousand and eighty thousand narwhals worldwide, and they're found in the Canadian arctic, around Greenland, and sometimes as far east as Svalbard. Herman Melville wrote a chapter in *Moby Dick* describing a number of whales, including the unicorn whale:

> From certain cloistered old authors I have gathered that this same sea-unicorn's horn was in ancient days regarded as the great antidote against poison, and as such, preparations of it brought immense prices. It was also distilled to a volatile salts

for fainting ladies. . . . The Narwhale has a very picturesque, leopard-like look, being of a milk-white ground colour, dotted with round and oblong spots of black. His oil is very superior, clear and fine; but there is little of it, and he is seldom hunted.

A narwhal

AUGUST 2 | The Center of the Nation

Here's a tricky question: where is the exact center of the United States? Just outside Lebanon, Kansas, is a marker announcing it as the geographical center of the forty-eight contiguous states, based on data supplied by the U.S. Coast and Geodetic Survey (USCGS). That 1918 survey, however, described a point that is three-quarters of a mile away. When the marker was placed in 1940, the actual center was on a privately owned hog farm, and the owner did not want his place to become a tourist attraction, so the nearby spot was chosen. The USCGS calculations weren't very precise, anyway. A cardboard cutout of the United States was balanced on a point, and its center of gravity became the center of the country. When you include all fifty states, then the center is twenty miles north of Belle Fourche, South Dakota. As one USCGS mathematician pointed out, "Since there is no definite way to locate such a point, it would be best to ignore it entirely . . . there is no such thing as the geographical center of any state, country, or continent." There is one more center to consider; every ten years, the U.S. Census Bureau calculates the population center of the country. The results from the 2010 census show that mark is now in Plato, Missouri.

AUGUST 3 | The Cathedral of Learning

The tallest educational building in the western hemisphere is the University of Pittsburgh's Cathedral of Learning, a Gothic Revival tower that stands forty-two stories (535 feet) tall and has 2,529 windows. After several years of discussion and planning, construction began in 1926, supported by contributions from local businesses, organizations, and ninety-seven thousand school children. The cathedral houses the university library, classrooms, administrative offices, a café, and the Nationality Rooms, which represent and celebrate the many cultures of Pittsburgh. A proposal to clean the building's limestone façade in 2003 was met with objections from some faculty and historians, who thought the city's grimy industrial history should be preserved. In 2007, the university did approve and carry out a $5 million restoration project. John Gabbert Bowman, the visionary chancellor who proposed and developed the cathedral, had predicted that "[t]hey shall find wisdom here and faith—in steel and stone, in character and thought—they shall find beauty, adventure, and moments of high victory."

AUGUST 4 | A Moving Experience

The escalator was first patented in 1859 by Nathan Ames; he called it "revolving stairs." He died the next year, and his rather impractical design was never built. It took more than thirty years for the first working escalator to be developed. That was Jesse Reno's "endless conveyor or elevator," which he patented in 1892. It was primitive, a kind of segmented belt with iron cleats for steps, comblike structures at the top and the bottom, and a moving handrail. Installed at Coney Island as a novelty ride three years later, it rose only seven feet with an incline of twenty-five degrees, but seventy-five thousand people enjoyed it. In 1898, a Reno escalator was purchased by Harrod's department store in London. Attendants with brandy and smelling salts were posted at the top for shoppers who were overcome by the exciting ride. Reno's machine did have some competition. G. A. Wheeler had patented a similar moving stairway in 1899, but it was never produced. Charles Seeberger bought that patent and then began working for the Otis Elevator Company, where he developed a wooden escalator that won a prize at the 1900 Paris Exposition. He also came up with the name *escalator* (from the Latin word for "steps"), which Otis trademarked. After competing for a few years, Otis bought the patents from both Seeberger and Reno and became the country's leading manufacturer. In 1950, however, Otis lost the trademark name, after the patent office decided that *escalator* had become the generic name for moving stairways.

AUGUST 5 | The Shogun

Taikun is the Japanese term of respect for a great lord or prince and was used as a formal title for the shogun or military governor. The word—usually spelled *tycoon* in English—was introduced to Americans by Commodore Matthew C. Perry when he returned in 1854 from his journey to open Japan to the West, an early example of gunboat diplomacy. Abraham Lincoln's secretary John Hay was one of those who used the term as a nickname for the president, in his diaries and letters ("the Tycoon is grieved silently but deeply about the escape of Lee"). *Tycoon* later came to be used to describe a wealthy and powerful business magnate or mogul. (*Magnate* comes from the Latin word for "great person," and *mogul* refers to the Mughal or Mongol emperors who ruled India from the sixteenth to nineteenth centuries.)

AUGUST 6 | Work Begun by Nero

The Peloponnese is an area of Greece attached to the mainland by a four-mile wide strip of land, the Isthmus of Corinth. Ancients long envisioned a canal there, because without it, ships had a long and dangerous journey between the Aegean and the Ionian seas. Periander of Corinth was the first to actually consider constructing a canal, in 602 BCE, but such an engineering feat was not yet feasible, so he built the *diolkos* (from the words meaning "transportation from the other side"). It was a deep stone-lined track with a huge wheeled platform onto which boats or their cargo could be lifted and hauled overland. In 67 CE, the Roman emperor Nero actually started the canal-digging project (supposedly, he personally began the work using a golden pickaxe or trowel). After his death, the idea of the canal languished for more than eighteen hundred years, until it was revived in the late nineteenth century by King George I of Greece. On August 6, 1893, opening ceremonies were held, with the king sailing through the canal on his royal yacht *Sphacteria* and thanking those involved for finishing the work that Nero had begun.

AUGUST 7 | The First Family of Human Paleontology

Five family members over three generations made groundbreaking discoveries in their field. That is the story of the Leakey family: the patriarch was Louis Leakey (1903–1972), and the field is the study of human origins. Fellow paleoanthropologist Donald Johanson described them as a "family that dominated anthropology as no family has dominated a scientific field before or since." Louis was born in Kenya, the son of missionaries; he attended Cambridge University and became convinced that humans not only first evolved in Africa, but did so much earlier than was believed at the time. Both ideas met considerable resistance, but Louis was a persistent man, lecturing and writing as he continued his explorations and becoming internationally famous. He and his team unearthed bones and tools at Olduvai Gorge in Tanzania, one of the most significant sites for early hominid evolution. His second wife, Mary (1913–1996), also became a leading paleoanthropologist, and some of her discoveries—such as the fossilized footprints of early hominids—outshone those of her husband. One of their sons, Richard, continued the tradition of fossil hunting, making many important finds on his own, including a 1.6 million-year-old skeleton. His wife, Meave, also is a respected paleoanthropologist, and their daughter, Louise, has joined the "family business" and now heads the Koobi Fora research project in Kenya. "It is only by the study and understanding of the past," Louis Leakey once wrote, "that we can hope to foretell, and perhaps control, the future."

AUGUST 8 | "Very Loud and Noisy"

"The 1812 Overture" (complete title: *The Year 1812*, Festival Overture in E flat major, Op. 49) by Pyotr Ilyich Tchaikovsky (1840–1893) is one of the world's favorite pieces of classical music, though scholars don't consider it among his greatest works—and neither did he. The piece was commissioned for the opening of a Moscow exhibition to commemorate Napoleon's retreat from Russia in 1812 (and not the U.S.-British War of 1812, as many Americans assume). Tchaikovsky took only about a week to write the piece. "The Overture will be very loud and noisy—but I wrote it without any warm and loving feelings, and consequently it will probably be lacking in artistic merit," he wrote to a friend. To another, he said, "I'm undecided as to whether my overture is good or bad, but it is probably (without any false modesty) the latter." The original instrumentation called for the dramatic ending with bells and cannon that fans have come to expect, along with fireworks displays at July Fourth celebrations in recent decades. Its first performance was indoors, however, in August 1882, with conventional orchestration. Tchaikovsky probably never heard it performed as it was intended.

Pyotr Tchaikovsky

AUGUST 9 | Nixon and McDonald's

In 1974, the Judiciary Committee of the U.S. House of Representatives passed three Articles of Impeachment against President Richard M. Nixon for abuse of power and obstruction of justice. Two other articles were rejected. The specifications in support of the articles identified some interesting details, for example:

> Solicited and obtained for the reelection campaign . . . in June, July and August, 1972, from Ray A. Kroc, Chairman of the Board of McDonald's, Inc., contributions of $200,000, in exchange for permission from the Price Commission, first

denied on May 21, 1972, then granted on September 8, 1972, to raise the price of the McDonald's quarter pounder cheeseburger, in violation of article II, section 4 of the Constitution and Section 201, 372, 872 and 1505 of the Criminal Code.

(In an attempt to stabilize the economy, Nixon had established the Price Commission in 1971—along with a Wage Board—to set guidelines and oversee increases in prices and salaries.) Nixon resigned on August 9, 1974, rather than face trial by the Senate.

AUGUST 10 | Lines Seen Only by the Gods

What was the purpose of the ancient lines that cover four hundred square miles of the desert around Nasca (or Nazca), near the southern coast of Peru? The hundreds of long straight lines, trapezoids, spirals, and gigantic figures of animals and humans were discovered by the outside world when airplanes first flew over the area in the 1920s, and scientists and others have pondered their meaning ever since. Were they ancient roadways? Astronomical aids? Maps to water sources? Landing strips for alien spacecraft? They were created by the Nasca people between fifteen hundred and two thousand years ago. On the ground, they don't look very impressive, and the animal figures especially are difficult, if not impossible, to discern. These geoglyphs were made by turning over the dark rocky ground surface to expose the white or pinkish sand beneath. The lack of rain in the region—this is one of the driest areas on earth—has helped preserve them over the centuries. Yet their function is still a mystery. Anthony Aveni of Colgate University is one of the scientists who has studied the lines for decades. He believes they were made to walk on, as pathways, and were connected to rituals that included water, astronomy, and social interaction: "The maze of lines and figures etched across the desert floor in a seemingly confusing manner is neither whimsical nor chaotic. . . . There is order—a pattern and a system behind the geoglyphs—and it tells us about the people who lived there."

AUGUST 11 | Time Shift

In August 2010, the largest clock on earth—more than six times bigger than the famous clock of Big Ben in London—began keeping time in Mecca (Makkah), Saudi Arabia, Islam's holiest city. Atop the world's second tallest skyscraper and largest hotel, and adjacent to the Grand Mosque, the Mecca Clock was intended to be the official time-keeper for the world's 1.5 billion Muslims. Its tower is decorated with ninety million pieces of colored glass, and two million LED lights illuminate its four faces (each 151 feet in diameter). This clock doesn't run on Greenwich Mean Time, now known as Universal Coordinated Time, which has been the norm for 125 years. It sets Mecca as the prime meridian and deviates from GMT-based time by about twenty-one minutes; however, Adam Barrows of Carleton University in Ottawa points out, "In an online poll by an Arabian business news site, only 15 percent of respondents stated they would change their watches to Mecca Time, while more than 57 percent affirmed their belief that Greenwich should remain the standard."

AUGUST 12 | Early American Idol

The oldest choral ensemble in continuous existence in the United States is the Old Stoughton Musical Society of Stoughton, Massachusetts. The original group was formed in 1786, under the leadership of Elijah Dunbar. Because its members often met in homes and taverns where alcohol was served, women were not allowed to join until 1844. The group sang psalms and hymns from William Billings, America's choral music master, and many other composers. In 1790, they participated in what must have been one of the first singing contests in America. Having heard of the Stoughton Musical Society's vocal prowess, the First Parish Choir of Dorchester challenged the group to a sing-off. The First Parish choristers, male and female, were accompanied by a bass viol; the twenty men of the Stoughton Society performed a capella. Each group performed in turn, but when the Stoughton men sang the "Hallelujah Chorus" from Handel's *Messiah*, "the Dorchestrians gave up the contest, and gracefully acknowledged defeat." A century later, the Stoughton Society sang at the World's Columbian Exposition in Chicago. They continue to perform today, giving two concerts a year.

AUGUST 13 | A Boyhood Dream Accomplished

Before the Panama Canal was constructed, the only way to sail between the Atlantic and the Pacific oceans was to travel around the southern tip of South America. It was a long, arduous journey, and it inspired many to seek a northerly route. Thus began the search for the Northwest Passage, a way through the icebound islands of the Canadian arctic to open new shipping lanes from Europe to Asia. The British sent out the first expedition, under John Cabot in 1497. He experienced the two things that would vex all of those looking for the Northwest Passage—ice and shallow waters. Cabot did not succeed, nor did Martin Frobisher, Henry Hudson, William Baffin, James Cook, John Franklin, and many others who made the attempt over the centuries. The first successful passage was not made until 1903, when Norwegian explorer Roald Amundsen sailed from Baffin Bay to Nome, Alaska, albeit in a converted herring boat, not a full-size shipping vessel. He stopped at King William Island, where he stayed for more than a year, then continued westward. On August 13, 1905, he met a whaling ship that was sailing east, so he knew the transit was possible. In his diary, Amundsen wrote, "The North West Passage was done. My boyhood dream—at that moment was accomplished. . . . I felt tears in my eyes. 'Vessel in sight. . . . Vessel in sight.'" Now that climate change is melting the arctic ice, the passage is navigable for longer and longer periods each year.

AUGUST 14 | A Riot Like a Cyclone

In Springfield, Illinois, on August 14, 1908, two African American men sat in the city jail. Joe James was accused of murdering a white mining engineer, and George Richardson had just been arrested after Mabel Hallam, a young married white woman, claimed he had raped her. A crowd of angry white residents gathered outside, demanding that the prisoners be released to them. Instead, in an effort to defuse tensions, the sheriff surreptitiously moved the men out of town. Enraged, the mob—now estimated at five thousand to ten thousand—set off on a spree of violence, ripping apart the storefronts of black businesses and their sympathizers and burning many of them. The black residents did not stand by helplessly, though; some had guns and were able to protect their stores and homes. The rioting lasted for two days, and the local newspaper likened the damage to that caused by a cyclone. When it was over, seven people were dead—two African Americans who had been lynched, and five white townspeople. A subsequent grand jury handed out 117 indictments, and 85 arrests were made, but in the end, no one was really held accountable. Two weeks after the riot, Hallam admitted she had concocted the entire story of the assault, Richardson was released, but James was convicted of murder and hanged. The country was horrified by the violence, particularly a group of white liberals in New York City, who met to seek a solution to racial injustice. The group called for a conference to take place in Springfield on February 12, 1909, and invited many prominent people, including W. E. B. Du Bois and Ida B. Wells. That meeting was the birth of the NAACP.

AUGUST 15 | Most Fearless

A honey badger, or ratel (*Mellivora capensis*), is the "most fearless animal in the world," according to the *Guinness Book of World Records*. No other animal seems as willing to attack a hive of bees or pounce on a king cobra and devour it. Honey badgers eat bee larvae and consider snakes to be a tasty treat. Bee stings have no effect on them, and snake venom merely puts the badger into a temporary coma. The honey badger has skin that is rubbery, thick, and loose, so that most predators find it difficult to grip or penetrate. If a leopard or a lion does attack, the badger's powerful jaws and sharp claws make it a formidable opponent. Despite the name, honey is not its main source of food; badgers are carnivores that consume a wide range

A honey badger

of mammals, reptiles, and amphibians. Resembling a skunk but more closely related to wolverines and ferrets, they range in size from about fifteen pounds for females to double that for males. Honey badgers can be found throughout much of sub-Saharan Africa and in parts of Asia.

AUGUST 16 | America's Prima Ballerina

Somehow, she made the most difficult moves look easy. Maria Tallchief was born in 1925 and grew up on the Osage reservation in Oklahoma; she didn't seem destined to be America's first prima ballerina. Yet her grace and determination helped her blaze a path to the pinnacle of the dance world. When the family moved to Los Angeles, she began to take lessons with Bronislava Nijinska, the sister of famed dancer Vaslav Nijinsky. Tallchief danced her first solo performance at the age of fifteen and soon joined the Ballet Russe de Monte Carlo. There she met George Balanchine; they fell in love and were married in 1946. The next year, Balanchine invited her to join his Ballet Society, soon to become the New York City Ballet, and there her career really blossomed. She was known not just for her talent, but also for her intense dedication; she danced as many as eight performances a week. Tallchief wowed the critics with her signature role in *Firebird*, created for her by Balanchine. Dance critic Walter Terry wrote, "[S]he was truly a flaming figure—she soared through the air in effortless flight, she preened, she shimmered, she gloried in speed and airy freedom." She was the prima ballerina at the New York City Ballet for eighteen years. Tallchief left the company and retired from performing in 1966 and was awarded the National Medal of Arts in 1999.

AUGUST 17 | "Look to Africa"

The Rastafari movement was inspired by the teachings of Marcus Garvey, a Jamaican journalist and orator, who founded the Universal Negro Improvement Association in 1914. He espoused black nationalism and pan-Africanism and told his followers to "Look to Africa, for the crowning of a black king; he shall be the redeemer." When

Prince Ras Tafari Makonnen was named emperor of Ethiopia in 1930 and became Haile Selassie I, many people felt that the prophecy had been fulfilled, and the Rasta movement began to grow in Jamaica, particularly among the poorer classes. Rastafarians believe Haile Selassie was the Messiah, the living god for the black race, and that Garvey was his prophet. They also believe that the Western, white-dominated world (called Babylon) is corrupt; that Ethiopia (Zion) is the true home of black people; and that the Bible is actually the story of the African race that was misinterpreted by white evangelists. Rastafarians wear their hair in dreadlocks, in part to symbolize the lion's mane, and some smoke marijuana (*ganja* or "wisdom weed") for spiritual, rather than recreational, purposes. It is not a tightly organized religion with a clearly defined leader, and its beliefs have spread informally, especially through reggae music, thanks to Bob Marley, Peter Tosh, and other Jamaican musicians.

AUGUST 18 | Sun Writing

Joseph Nicéphore Niépce (1765–1833) was a man of many fascinations. Born into a well-to-do French family, he was able to indulge his passion for scientific research and invention. He was interested in the new art of lithography but didn't have a talent for drawing, so he began to experiment with ways of permanently fixing an image on a surface. In 1826, he succeeded, using polished pewter plates coated with bitumen of Judea, a petroleum derivative. The bitumen hardens in light but requires a long exposure time to create an image. So Niépce mounted a pewter plate on a camera obscura (a box with a hole in it that projects an inverted image, used as an aid to drawing), pointed it out his rear window, and exposed it for eight to ten hours. He then washed the plate in oil of turpentine to dissolve the unexposed areas, and there, visible only when held at certain angles, was the image of the trees and the structures in his backyard. It was the world's first permanent photograph, which he called a heliograph ("sun writing"). Soon after that, Niépce teamed up with fellow Frenchman Louis Daguerre, who was experimenting in a similar vein. They worked together for four years, until Niépce's sudden death in 1833. That first photograph was thought to have been lost for many decades but was rediscovered in 1952 and is now at the University of Texas at Austin.

AUGUST 19 | A Gift to the World

In the early 1820s in Paris, one of the most popular theatrical venues was the Diorama, which exhibited huge paintings of historical and allegorical scenes, with special lighting effects. It was run by painter, showman, and entrepreneur Louis Jacques Mandé Daguerre (1787–1851). He created the paintings himself using a camera obscura to get accurate details and perspective. He wanted something that would fix the image permanently and began to look for a new process. Daguerre heard about another Frenchman, Joseph Nicéphore Niépce, who was doing similar work, and in 1829 the two began to collaborate. When Niépce died four years later, Daguerre continued to experiment and finally discovered a successful process. It involved exposing a sheet of silver-plated copper sensitized with iodine vapors, then developing it in mercury fumes and fixing it with sodium thiosulphate. He called the resulting image a "Daguerrotype." At first, he tried to market his process by subscription, but that failed. But he did find a champion at the Academie des Sciences, who argued that it was "indispensable that the

Government should compensate M. Daguerre direct, and that France should then nobly give to the whole world this discovery which could contribute so much to the progress of art and science." The French government agreed and purchased Daguerre's patent in exchange for a lifetime pension. On August 19, 1839, the process was put in the public domain as a gift to the world.

Louis Daguerre

AUGUST 20 | War's End

The dates of the American Civil War are generally given as 1861 to 1865, but when did the war actually end? Was it when Robert E. Lee surrendered his Army of Northern Virginia to Ulysses S. Grant at Appomattox on April 9, 1865? Was it when the last soldier died in battle, on May 13? Was it June 23, when Stand Watie, the last Confederate general in the field, signed a cease-fire? There was no formal peace treaty between the Federal and the Confederate governments, so the official end of the war was decided in court. Nelson Anderson, a free black man who had lived in Charleston, South Carolina, during the war, filed a claim in 1868 under the Captured and Abandoned Property Act for payment of about $7,000 due him for bales of cotton that had been confiscated by Union soldiers. Government lawyers argued that the act stated that all claims must be made within two years of the cessation of hostilities, and because the war had ended in 1865, Anderson had filed too late. Anderson's lawyers countered that there was no formal legislation ending the war in that year. They pointed to a proclamation that President Andrew Johnson issued on August 20, 1866, which concluded, "And I do further proclaim that the said insurrection is at an end, and that peace, order, tranquility and civil authority now exist in and throughout the whole of the United States." The Supreme Court agreed that the proclamation marked the formal end of the Civil War, and Nelson Anderson won his case.

AUGUST 21 | Stolen Mona

Leonardo da Vinci's *Mona Lisa* is arguably the most famous painting in the world. But it wasn't always that way. A century ago, the *Mona Lisa* was certainly known but not well-known to the general public, and it was far from the most famous or popular work of art at the Louvre in Paris. Art critics and curators were aware of its significance, which is why the museum arranged for it and a number of other important paintings to be put under protective glass. One of the glaziers on the project was an Italian workman named Vincenzo Perugia. He and two friends, the Lancelotti brothers, hid in a Louvre storeroom one Sunday night. The next morning, August 21, 1911, they took the *Mona Lisa* out of its case and frame, Perugia hid it under his clothes, and they slipped out. When the theft was revealed, it caused no small embarrassment to the museum and the French police. The story was a media sensation, and people crowded the Louvre to look at the empty space on the wall. The bumbling police talked to Perugia but let him go, and instead they arrested Pablo Picasso and the poet Guillaume Apollinaire, because they were acquainted with a man who had stolen some small sculptures from the museum. They were quickly released. Twenty-eight months later, Perugia tried to sell the *Mona Lisa* to an art dealer in Florence. The dealer called the police, Perugia was arrested, and the painting returned to Paris. One hundred thousand people came to see it in the first two days after it was reinstalled. Its fame was assured, and today the *Mona Lisa* is viewed by eight million people a year.

AUGUST 22 | Confused Fruit

The strawberry is not really a berry, and the banana doesn't grow on a tree. The strawberry is the only fruit with its seeds on the outside, causing botanists to classify it with the rose family (*Fragaria*). The strawberry is an accessory fruit, or pseudocarp—it does not develop

from the plant's ovaries but from the tissue surrounding them. Each of the seeds on the outside is considered a separate fruit, which makes the flesh, well, a vegetable. The banana plant is actually the world's largest herb. It looks like a tree and is commonly referred to that way, but its trunk does not contain woody tissue. It's actually a member of the lily family. And the banana itself? It's technically a berry.

A strawberry plant

AUGUST 23 | "A Scene Truly Horrible"

On August 23, 2011, a magnitude 5.8 earthquake, centered in Mineral, Virginia, struck the East Coast, rattling people from South Carolina to Massachusetts. Although no severe damage was done, it did remind us that quakes are not restricted to the West Coast. That was no surprise to people who reside around New Madrid (pronounced MAD-rid), Missouri, and the adjacent states of Arkansas, Tennessee, Kentucky, and Illinois. They live in the most active seismic area east of the Rockies. Known as the New Madrid Seismic Zone (NMSZ), the region experiences about two hundred microshocks—tremors under magnitude 2.0 that are not felt by humans—every year. In 1811–1812 there was a series of major earthquakes in the area, likely magnitude 7.0 or greater, perhaps even 8.0. This was sparsely populated territory at the time, but about a thousand people were killed. Eliza Bryan was an eyewitness: "The screams of the affrighted inhabitants running to and fro, not knowing where to go, or what to do— the cries of the fowls and beasts of every species—the cracking of trees falling . . . formed a scene truly horrible." The Mississippi River briefly ran backward, due to the shifting ground. Church bells rang in Boston, thirteen hundred miles away. Earthquakes in this region and farther east tend to affect an area twenty times the size affected by a similar earthquake on the West Coast because the rock is older, harder, and drier. The last large earthquake in the NMSZ was in 1895, and the region appears overdue for one of magnitude 6 or larger.

AUGUST 24 | A Cosmic Classic

Twenty-one million years ago, a star exploded and became a supernova. Astronomers on Earth, thanks to a robotic telescope, were able to see the dying star within hours of the light first reaching Earth in 2011. PTF 11kly, as the supernova was dubbed, is in the Pinwheel Galaxy, which is visible near the constellation called the Big Dipper (*Ursa Major*). Supercomputers at the National Energy Research Scientific Computing Center (NERSC) at the Lawrence Berkeley National Laboratory picked up the stellar event on August 24 and relayed the information to telescopes around the world, which captured additional data. It is a Type 1a supernova, which astronomers study to measure the expansion of the universe. "Seeing one explode so close by allows us to study these events in unprecedented detail," said one of the scientists. Another called it "an instant cosmic classic."

AUGUST 25 | Not Jimmy's Night

The Chicago Cubs faced the Philadelphia Phillies and their pitcher Jimmy Ring in a home game on August 25, 1922. It was a tough outing. Trailing 3–1 in the second inning, the Cubs pounded Ring for ten runs, but Phillies manager Irvin "Kaiser" Wilhelm didn't pull him. He should have; the Cubs scored fourteen more runs in the fourth inning, bringing the score to 25–6. But the Phillies didn't give up, battling back against Chicago relief pitchers in the last two innings. It wasn't quite enough, however, and the Cubs won by a final score of 26–23 (with a total of fifty-one hits, ninety-eight at-bats, twenty-one walks, nine strike-outs, and nine errors)—it remains the highest scoring game in Major League Baseball history.

AUGUST 26 | A Filk State of Being

It's like folk music, but with a twist. *Filk* is the music of the science fiction and fantasy fan community, and it is laced with humor, cheekiness, and often ribaldry. The term began with a typographical error in a paper about the influence of science fiction on folk music, where *folk* was misspelled *filk*, and the name stuck. Attendees at science fiction conventions in the 1950s sometimes gathered to sing parodies of folk songs with lyrics rewritten to reflect SF interests—monsters, space travel, wizards, computers, and so on. After a time, people began to write original tunes as well, and informal filk hootenannies became a regular feature at the cons. One newspaper article defined filkers as "a vibrant, if niche, global community of nerds devoted to making music in a fun and freeing environment. For them, filk's not so much a genre as a state of being." There are groups around the world devoted to filk music, with annual gatherings of filk aficionados, where songs and ideas are exchanged. A look through the titles on a filk archive can reveal some rather funny parodies: "Elvish Girls" (based on the Beach Boys' "California Girls"), a computer lament called "Boot It" (sung to Michael Jackson's "Beat It"), or "The Ballad of Darth Vader" to the tune of "Mack the Knife."

AUGUST 27 | The Fury of Vulcan

The eruption of Krakatoa (or Krakatau) on August 27, 1883, was devastating; it killed forty thousand people, primarily from tsunamis created by the volcanic explosion. But the giant waves weren't the only cause of fatalities. A pyroclastic flow—a superheated mixture of gas, ash, and debris that surges down from erupting volcanoes—killed about forty-five hundred. The flow traveled twenty-four miles over the ocean to Sumatra, where two thousand people were scorched to death and whole villages were incinerated. As it moved over the open water, the heat of the pyroclastic debris converted the surface water to steam, which allowed it to travel such a distance. One survivor recalled the experience:

> Suddenly, it became pitch dark. The last thing I saw was the ash being pushed up through the cracks in the floorboards, like a fountain. . . . I felt a heavy pressure, throwing me to the ground. Then it seemed as if all the air was being sucked away and I could not breathe. . . . I realized the ash was hot and I tried to protect my face with my hands. The hot bite of the pumice pricked like needles. . . . I noticed for the first time that [my] skin was hanging off everywhere, thick and moist from the ash stuck to it. . . . I did not know I had been burnt.

Krakatoa

AUGUST 28 | An Essential Element

Iron is one of the most common elements on the planet; it's all around us. You don't find it just lying about in pure form, however; it's mixed in with rocks and other material in iron ore. Iron is also found in meteorites, which is probably how ancient humans first discovered and used it to make ornaments and tools by 4000 BCE. Extracting iron from ore by smelting took a few thousand years longer to develop. Iron is always mixed with another element in an alloy, the main one being carbon. The earliest iron workers heated the ore in a charcoal fire, using a bellows to provide sufficient oxygen. The result was a spongy mass of close to pure iron mixed with some carbon from the charcoal. This was called the bloom. The amount of carbon determines what type of iron is produced. Pig iron is the crudest form, containing 3 to 4 percent carbon. It got its name from the molds it was poured into, which looked like baby pigs gathered around their mother. Cast iron contains about 2 percent carbon, and it's so hard that it can't be worked or welded, but it can be poured into molds to make such things as your favorite frying pan. Wrought iron is nearly pure, with very little carbon in it. It can be shaped and rolled, and that's why it became the main industrial metal used in everything from fences to bridges, until the development of mass-produced steel in the mid-1800s.

AUGUST 29 | "Ye Noble Tons of Soil"

William Archibald Spooner (1844–1930) attended New College at Oxford University and then remained there for more than sixty years as a scholar and a chaplain, eventually rising to the position of warden or head of the college. Though known at the time for his translations of Tacitus, he is remembered today for the verbal gaffes known as "spoonerisms," where the initial sounds of two or more words are accidentally transposed. The very image of a kindly Oxford don, Spooner could be absent-minded but admitted to uttering only one spoonerism: instead of announcing the hymn "Conquering Kings" from the pulpit, he once called it "Kinkering Congs." Nonetheless, hundreds of verbal miscues have been attributed to him, ensuring his lasting fame. Here are a few slips-of-the-tongue, credited to Spooner but likely created by others:

"A blushing crow" for "a crushing blow"
"Our queer old Dean" for "our dear old queen"
"Is the bean dizzy?" rather than "is the Dean busy?"

"A nosey little cook," for "a cozy little nook"

"I believe you are occupewing my pie," instead of "occupying my pew"

AUGUST 30 | The White Mouse

Nancy Wake (1912–2011), one of the most decorated Allied service-women in World War II, was an important leader of the French Resistance. She was called "the white mouse" by the Nazi Gestapo, who put a bounty on her head, because she eluded all of their attempts to capture her. As a member of the Resistance and later as an agent for the British Special Operations Executive, she hid stranded soldiers, bribed prison guards, organized the Maquis bands of the Resistance, trained thousands of partisan fighters and led them on sabotage raids, and once killed a German soldier with her bare hands. She smoked cigars and was a hard drinker, but a French colleague described her as "the most feminine woman I know until the fighting starts—then she is like five men." After her death, her body was cremated and her ashes were scattered over the hills of central France, where she had fought so courageously.

AUGUST 31 | "Completely Free"

Slave narratives—autobiographical accounts of the lives of Africans in bondage—were an important tool for abolitionists who wanted to expose the horrors of the slavery system. One of the earliest and most powerful was *The Interesting Narrative of the Life of Olaudah Equiano, or Gustavus Vassa, the African, Written by Himself*, published in 1789. Writing with sophistication and style, Olaudah Equiano (1745–1797) told the story of his life: born in what is now Nigeria, kidnapped at age eleven, surviving the Middle Passage, and being sold to a Royal Navy officer in Virginia. He learned to read and write, was sold twice more, and eventually earned enough money by trading on the side to purchase his freedom. He traveled much of the world during the next two decades and joined an abolitionist group in London called the Sons of Africa. In his autobiography, he recalled the day of his manumission:

Olaudah Equiano

"[B]efore night, I who had been a slave in the morning, trembling at the will of another, was become my own master, and completely free." Equiano's book was immensely popular, and he became a leading spokesmen for abolition in Britain. Ten years after his death, the British slave trade was outlawed by Parliament.

SEPTEMBER

SEPTEMBER 1 | The Battle That Stopped Rome

It was one of the most unexpected and far-reaching defeats in military history. In September of the year 9 CE, three Roman legions marched into the woods of the Teutoburg Forest near what is now Kalkriese, Germany. Under the command of Publius Quinctilius Varus, the Romans intended to subdue the Germanic tribes just as Julius Caesar had conquered the Gauls. Varus was operating on information he had received from a man they called Arminius, a German chieftain working with the Romans. Varus should not have trusted him; Arminius led the Romans into a trap, and they were soon surrounded by Germanic warriors in the tight confines of the forest. Trained to fight on open ground and unable to maneuver effectively, the Romans were massacred, losing fifteen thousand to twenty thousand men, with only a few surviving. Humiliated, Varus committed suicide. Roman historian Suetonius wrote that Caesar Augustus, who had ordered the

Publius Quinctilius Varus

campaign, "would dash his head against a door, crying 'Quinctilius Varus, give me back my legions!' And he observed the day of the disaster each year as one of sorrow and mourning." Stunned by the unprecedented defeat, the Romans never again threatened Germania, and the course of European civilization was forever changed.

SEPTEMBER 2 | "I Will Harm"

An ailing person is given a placebo, a sugar pill, and is told it will have a beneficial effect on the condition. That beneficial effect often occurs psychosomatically, because the patient believes it will. The opposite can also be true, where the person is prescribed an inert compound but told the treatment may have a negative side effect, and the mind produces that effect. The idea of *nocebo* ("I will harm" in Latin) has proved a difficult concept for physicians, who focus on physical causes for medical problems. Even the expectation of illness or pain can be self-fulfilling. In the 1980s, an experiment was performed by hooking up college students to a device they were told would send an electric current through their heads that might cause a headache. No current was actually transmitted, yet more than two-thirds of the subjects reported a headache. Medical students sometimes manifest symptoms of a condition they're studying. The nocebo effect can also be an issue with a doctor's bedside manner. "A cold, uncaring, disinterested and emotionless doctor will encourage a nocebo response," says Dr. Brian Olshansky of the University of Iowa. "In contrast, a caring, empathetic physician fosters trust, strengthens beneficent patient expectations and elicits a strong placebo response." The power of suggestion is a potent force.

SEPTEMBER 3 | The Ancient Land of Liberty

The Most Serene Republic of San Marino, on the Italian peninsula, is one of the world's smallest countries; it's only twenty-four square miles—about one-third the size of Washington, D.C.—and has about thirty-two thousand residents. San Marino claims to be the world's oldest republic; it was founded in 301 CE, by a stonecutter named Marinus. According to tradition, he may have been escaping religious persecution by the Roman emperor Diocletian. Marinus formed a Christian community on Mount Titano that eventually became a city-state that has managed to survive as a sovereign entity through wars, poverty, and even the unification of the rest of Italy in the nineteenth century. San Marino served as a safe haven for many pro-unification partisans, including Giuseppe Garibaldi, the hero of the Risorgimento. He took refuge there for a short while, managed to evade his enemies, and, in appreciation, later allowed San Marino to remain independent of the newly formed Kingdom of Italy. San Marino is one of the most stable European countries, with a strong economy (half of it based on tourism), very little debt, and one of the lowest unemployment rates in Europe.

SEPTEMBER 4 | The City of the Angels

On September 4, 1781, forty-four settlers—a diverse group of people of Spanish, Native American, and African descent known as Los Pobladores ("the townspeople")—founded the city now known as Los Angeles. Its precise original name has been a source of contention ever since. It was called El Pueblo de Nuestra Señora la Reyna de los Ángeles del Río de Porciúncula—"the Town of Our Lady the Queen of the Angels of the River Porciuncula" (the river was named Porciún-cula, "small portion," by the Franciscan friars to honor a favorite site in Italy). Maybe the name did not include the words Nuestra Señora ("Our Lady") or Reyna ("queen") or the reference to the river. There were as many as eleven versions of the name in its early days, depending on which books, papers, plaques, maps, or old documents you consult. Even the historical markers around Olvera Street, the center of old Los Angeles, do not agree. Whatever its original formal name, we do know that the city, which had only 315 residents in 1800, grew by 3,000 percent between 1890 and 1940. Today, the population of the Los Angeles–Long Beach–Riverside Combined Statistical Area is about eighteen million.

SEPTEMBER 5 | A Day for Laborers

It was either McGuire or Maguire. Peter McGuire and Matthew Maguire have both been given credit for founding Labor Day in the United States. Both were involved in the labor movement—McGuire as the cofounder of the American Federation of Labor, and Maguire as secretary of the Central Labor Union in New York. But the records are unclear as to who first suggested a holiday to commemorate those "who from rude nature have delved and carved all the grandeur we behold." What is known is that the Central Labor Union approved the idea, and the first celebration was held on Tuesday, September 5, 1882, in New York. Numerous states enacted Labor Day legislation in the years following, but it wasn't until 1894 that it became a federal holiday on the first Monday in September—and that only thanks to political pressure. President Grover Cleveland pushed the bill through Congress as a way to ease tensions after his suppression of the Pullman strike, in which thirteen railroad workers had been killed. Started as a day to think about and discuss issues of the working class, the holiday has become more a day for relaxing and discussing whether to have hot dogs or hamburgers at the cookout.

SEPTEMBER 6 | Horns of Dilemma

Many people think tusks, horns, and antlers are the same thing, just shaped differently, but that's not correct. Tusks are teeth, made of dentin. Antlers are bone; they have branches, are shed and regrown every year, and exist almost exclusively on male animals. Horns have a bony core covered with keratin (the same material as hair and fingernails); they are never shed, are unbranched, and usually grow throughout an animal's life. Then there's the rhinoceros. It has a horn without a bony core but instead made up entirely of keratin. The rhino horn is denser in the center, and the softer outer part can be worn away, much like a sharpened pencil, making it pointy. Unfortunately for the rhinos, their horns are used to make carved dagger handles and other decorative items in the Middle East.

More damaging, powdered rhino horn has been used in traditional Asian medicine for centuries to combat rheumatism, gout, snake bites, and even possession by demons—though it is not used as an aphrodisiac, as popularly believed. The

A rhinoceros

demand for rhino horn is pushing the five species of *Rhinocerotidae* toward extinction.

SEPTEMBER 7 | "There Is No Second"

Tennis has the Davis Cup, there's the Walker Cup for golf, hockey's Stanley Cup, and the World Cup in soccer, but none of them has been around longer than the America's Cup, yachting's crown jewel and the oldest trophy in sport. In 1851, the United States was invited to participate in a yacht race in England that was part of the Great Exhibition of the Works of Industry of All Nations, the first world's fair. The United States sent a schooner called *America*, built by George Steers for the New York Yacht Club, to sail around the Isle of Wight against fifteen boats of the Royal Yacht Squadron in what was then called the "100 Guinea Cup." One famous story of that day has Queen Victoria awaiting the end of the race on her yacht and asking the signalmaster, "Are the yachts in sight?" He replied, "Only the *America*." "Which is second?" she asked. "Ah, your majesty, there is no second." With that victory, the cup was renamed the America's Cup—after the boat, not the nation—and the United States held onto it for 132 years, until the Australians triumphed in 1983. The America's Cup, also called the Auld Mug, is not actually a cup but a ewer, more like a pitcher or a jug. The 2013 race will be held in San Francisco.

SEPTEMBER 8 | Room to Read

Former Microsoft executive John Wood left the company because he wanted to do for the developing world what Andrew Carnegie had done for the United States in the nineteenth century: build libraries.

In 2000, Wood founded Room to Read (RTR), a nonprofit organization that has worked with local communities to construct school and library buildings, provide books, and establish literacy programs and local-language publishing projects. It also focuses on gender neutrality in education, because so many girls in developing nations lack opportunities to learn. In its first decade, RTR has distributed more than ten million books to six million children; twelve thousand libraries have opened, and about six new ones start providing services every day. As Wood told *New York Times* columnist Nicholas Kristof, "I get frustrated that there are 793 million illiterate people, when the solution is so inexpensive.... In 20 years, I'd like to have 100,000 libraries, reaching 50 million kids." Room to Read was a recipient of UNESCO's 2011 Confucius Prize for Literacy.

SEPTEMBER 9 | Grog St. Laurent

When did human beings first begin to wear clothing? The exact date seems unknowable, lost in the dimness of prehistory. Yet scientists have recently discovered a clue that might provide an answer. A team of researchers led by Andrew Kitchen of Pennsylvania State University conducted a study of the DNA of lice in 2010. They traced the divergence of body lice from the variety that lives on our heads. Body lice (*Pediculus humanus humanus*) evolved tiny claws that seem perfectly designed to cling to clothing, something head lice do not have. The scientists estimate that this split occurred about 190,000 years ago, and that could indicate that humans had started clothing themselves by that time. This period also coincides with the point at which anthropologists believe we hairless apes first began to settle in cooler climates.

SEPTEMBER 10 | Naked Is the Best Disguise

Soon after humans started to wear clothes, they began to look for socially acceptable ways to take them off. Public nudity has been a part of many different cultures throughout history—Greek athletic games, Roman baths, Scandinavian saunas—but the movement known as naturism is a more recent development. Around the turn of the twentieth century, naturism began to sprout in Germany. In 1903, the first nude club, *Freilichtpark* ("free light park"), opened near the town of Klingberg. The idea spread across Europe and to the United States, where Kurt Barthel enlisted other German Americans and founded the American League for Physical Culture in 1929, which eventually evolved into today's American Association for Nude Recreation. Barthel opened Sky Farm, America's first official nudist camp, in New Jersey in 1932; it's still in operation. Antinudity laws in New York State made New Jersey the go-to place for naked New Yorkers. As defined by the International Naturist Federation, "Naturism is a way of life in harmony with nature, characterised by the practice of communal nudity, with the intention of encouraging respect for oneself, respect for others and respect for the environment." Today, recreational nudity is a $400 million global industry.

SEPTEMBER 11 | Chile's "Dark and Bitter Moment"

When Salvador Allende assumed the presidency of Chile in November 1970, he was the first democratically elected Marxist head of state in the world. Yet his administration was not long-lived. The United States, worried about "another Cuba" in the western hemisphere, had attempted to prevent his election by giving broad support, both overtly and covertly, to his opponents. After the election, the Nixon administration continued its opposition, with economic pressure and propaganda designed to hamper Allende's presidency and encourage a coup d'état against him. Those actions, along with the Allende government's own economic policies of nationalization and collectivization, did lead to a coup. On September 11, 1973, Chile's armed forces, with the support of the Chilean congress and the U.S. government, surrounded the presidential palace and fired on it. Allende made one last broadcast to the nation, in which he said, "I have faith in Chile and its destiny. Other men will overcome this dark and bitter moment when treason seeks to prevail. Go forward knowing that, sooner rather than later, the great avenues will open again where free men will walk to build a better society." Allende died during the coup from a self-administered gunshot wound. He was replaced by General Augusto Pinochet, who led a seventeen-year military dictatorship known for its brutality and the forced disappearance (*desaparecidos*) of some three thousand opponents.

SEPTEMBER 12 | A Stylish Style

Imagine being among the artists who flourished in the generation *after* Leonardo, Raphael, and the early work of Michelangelo. They were tough acts to follow. The plague, the Reformation, and the Sack of Rome—the end of the High Renaissance—were part of the societal upheaval in which artists searched for a new reality. Before the art world arrived at the grand scale and the elaborate, emotional decoration of Baroque and Rococo, there was Mannerism (from the Italian word *maniera*, "style"). The work of such artists as Cellini, Tintoretto, Bronzino, and El Greco was, as the *Encyclopædia Britannica* explains it,

> characterized by artificiality and artiness, by a thoroughly self-conscious cultivation of elegance and technical facility, and by a sophisticated indulgence in the bizarre. The figures in Mannerist works frequently have graceful but queerly elongated limbs, small heads, and stylized facial features, while their poses seem difficult or contrived. The deep, linear perspectival space of High Renaissance painting is flattened and obscured. . . . Mannerists sought a continuous refinement of form and concept, pushing exaggeration and contrast to great limits.

Mannerism was long disparaged as decadent and illogical, but more recent critics have found that its experimentation and intellectual aestheticism resonate with modern artistic expression.

SEPTEMBER 13 | "Pursuite & Carnage"

The Plains of Abraham—sounds biblical, doesn't it? Actually, it's a grassy plateau near Quebec City, named for a farmer in the early seventeenth century who grazed his animals there. It was the scene of a pivotal battle in the French and Indian War—the American part of the conflict known as the Seven Years' War in Europe. France and the British colonies had fought for a decade for control of Canada, then called New France. In the early hours of September 13, 1759, British regiments climbed the steep cliffs to the plain and surprised the French troops. A British admiral wrote this in his report:

> Then commenced the Battle which hardly lasted a quarter of an Hour. Lascelles's Regiment was the first that broke in upon them, with fixed Bayonets, and the Highlanders flanked them at the same time: The Body opposed to them was instantly turned & routed; & their whole Army gave way and fled to the Town; The rest was Pursuite & Carnage; in which the Highlanders broad Swords did great Execution. Gen'r Wolfe fell early in the action, & only lived long enough to know that his Troops were victorious; On learning of which, he said– "Since I have conquered I dye satisfied."

The commanding generals on both sides, James Wolfe and Louis de Montcalm, died of their wounds. A year later, the British captured Montreal, and New France fell. When the Treaty of Paris was signed in 1763, France ceded almost all of its colonial empire in North America. Bitterness over this loss influenced the decision of the French to support the patriots in the American Revolution fifteen years later.

SEPTEMBER 14 | What So Proudly We Hailed

Mary Pickersgill had been a successful flag maker for a while, but she had never gotten an order for one so large. When Major George Armistead was appointed commander of Fort McHenry in Baltimore harbor in 1813, he wanted a garrison flag grand enough to signal to the British—whose warships were then in Chesapeake Bay—that they should think twice about attacking the city. Because her house was too small to accommodate a thirty- by forty-two-foot flag, Mrs. Pickersgill and four teenagers worked at Clagett's Brewery to piece together the banner from more than three hundred yards of English (the irony!) worsted wool bunting. She was paid about $400 for the completed flag and presented it to Major Armistead. The British didn't attack at that time, but a year later they launched a bombardment against the fort. They attacked throughout the night, but at the light of dawn on September 14, 1814, the flag was still flying, inspiring Francis Scott Key to compose the poem that became the national anthem. The flag itself remained in the possession of Armistead's family until 1907, when it was given to the Smithsonian Institution. It hung in the National Museum of American History until 1998, when the flag, which had suffered the ravages of time and gravity, was taken down for a full restoration. The Star-Spangled Banner is now displayed in its own temperature- and humidity-controlled room, with a waterless fire-suppression system and dim lighting.

SEPTEMBER 15 | The Crash at Crush

Americans have always liked to do things in a big way, sometimes really big, especially in Texas. It was just north of Waco in September 1896 that the first prearranged head-on crash between two trains occurred. William Crush, an agent for the Missouri, Kansas, and Texas Railway Company, thought it would be a good way to get some publicity for the railroad and turn a profit. He spent months making arrangements and publicizing the event. Forty thousand people came to the place that had been dubbed "Crush, Texas, City for a Day," where four miles of track had been laid. The two old locomotives, each pulling seven boxcars, rumbled toward each other at about forty-five miles per hour. The engineers leaped out just before the impact. Boxcars flew into the air; the boilers exploded, sending shards of metal everywhere. Smoke and steam billowed out over the crowd, where three people were killed by debris and many more injured. Despite the harm it caused, William Crush had started a fad that would last for decades. A man named Joe Connolly was inspired by the event and made a career of staging train crashes at state fairs, some seventy-three wrecks in all. Perhaps his most famous crash was at the 1932 Iowa State Fair, where one train named "Hoover" sped toward another named "Roosevelt" (it was an election year), meeting in a gigantic explosion that was captured on film.

A march by Scott Joplin for the Crash at Crush

His life's work earned Connolly the nickname "Head-on Joe." Connolly's biographer explains the attraction: "I guess the train wrecks appealed to the more primitive side of man—the thrill of seeing something destroyed. Nowadays people go to demolition derbies."

SEPTEMBER 16 | Godfather of Gangsta

It started as a bar fight and evolved into one of the more enduring songs of the twentieth century. "Stagolee" (about a man also known as Stagger Lee, Stack O' Lee, Stackerlee, Stackalee, and so on) was more than just a song. The eponymous protagonist was the archetypal bad man, and for African Americans, he became an antihero, someone who couldn't be cowed, someone to be respected. "It is a story that black America has never tired of hearing and never stopped living out, like whites with their Westerns," wrote cultural critic Greil Marcus. It was in a St. Louis tavern in 1895 that Lee Shelton, known as "Stack" Lee, shot Billy Lyons dead in an argument over a Stetson hat. Songs based on the event soon began to spread through the fields and the honky-tonks of the South, with new embellishments at each turn. The first recordings were made by white dance bands in the early 1920s, then by Ma Rainey, Mississippi John Hurt, Duke Ellington, Cab Calloway, Woody Guthrie, Bob Dylan, the Black Keys, Keb' Mo', and hundreds more, both white and black. It reached its zenith as a pop hit in 1958, when Lloyd Price recorded a brass-infused rock version that shot to number one on the charts. "Stagolee" continues to be recorded and performed today, and many consider it the progenitor of gangsta rap.

SEPTEMBER 17 | A View of Death

In September 1862, the Civil War was only a year and a half old, and many Americans in the North and the South still clung to the view that war was a noble, glorious, even romantic undertaking. That notion was shattered forever when Alexander Gardner and his assistant James Gibson, photographers for the Mathew Brady firm, arrived at the battlefield of Antietam before all of the soldiers' bodies had been buried. Up to that point, war photography had primarily depicted individual commanders and landscapes of the battlefields, taken long after the fighting was done. At Antietam, Gardner and Gibson recorded a series of "death studies" that for the very first time showed the bloated, mutilated corpses that are the true aftermath of conflict. The exhibition of those images, only a month after the battle, caused a sensation. A reporter for the *New York Times* wrote, "Mr. Brady has done something to bring home to us the terrible reality and earnestness of war. If he has not brought bodies and laid them in our dooryards and along the streets, he has done something very like it." The exhibitions were financially successful, and the pictures changed the nature of war photography.

SEPTEMBER 18 | Four Dead in Five Seconds

We all know the names of Wild Bill Hickok, Wyatt Earp, and Billy the Kid, but not many remember an equally notorious gunslinger of the Wild West, Dallas Stoudenmire (1845–1882). A gunfighter turned lawman, Stoudenmire arrived in El Paso, Texas, in 1881, where he became the sixth man in eight months to accept the job of town marshal. Just a few days after taking office, Stoudenmire was involved in the fight that would make him famous. The county constable, Gus

Krempkau, was arguing with a man named George Campbell, who was quite drunk. Campbell's friend, the equally intoxicated John Hale, grabbed a pistol and shot Krempkau. Stoudenmire ran out from a nearby café, firing his Colt revolvers. He first shot and killed an innocent Mexican bystander; his second shot hit Hale. Campbell backed away while pulling his gun, saying, "[T]his is not my fight!" It was too late, Stoudenmire shot him. The gunfight had lasted five seconds, and four men lay dead or dying. Dallas Stoudenmire became a legend but also a target. When he was killed in a shootout in El Paso on September 18, 1882, the *Los Angeles Times* described him as "a most quarrelsome and dangerous man, and most insolent towards his enemies."

SEPTEMBER 19 | Under the Jolly Roger

Many people have romantic visions of colorful pirates swigging rum and cruising the high seas in search of treasure, but how much of that image is accurate? Here's a true-or-false checklist:

- Swigging rum? Absolutely; rum was the drink of choice for all pirates.
- Buried treasure? Not so much; pirates didn't envision a long life, so they didn't save what they stole.
- Walking the plank? One or two may have done that, but probably not many; flogging, hanging, and shooting were the punishments of choice.
- Peg legs, eye patches, and hooks for hands? Undoubtedly correct, because sailing in the seventeenth and eighteenth centuries was a dangerous profession.
- Parrots and monkeys as mascots? Yes, they represented the exotic lands the pirates had visited.
- Women pirates? There were a few. Anne Bonny and Mary Read in the early eighteenth century are good examples.

Mary Read

- African pirates? Correct; many of the plundered vessels were slave ships. Pirates couldn't easily sell the slaves, so they often invited them to join the crew.
- Sailing under the skull and crossbones? True. "They wanted a better life even if for a short period," says pirate expert Marcus Rediker. "So they selected this symbol and said: 'Let us live under the flag of King Death—a merry life but a short one.'"

SEPTEMBER 20 | Millions of Fellow Life Forms

How many species of living things exist on Earth? It's an intriguing question, but one we've been unable to answer. As one researcher put it, if aliens visited Earth and asked how many distinct life forms we have, we would be embarrassed by our uncertainty. In August 2011, a group of scientists came up with the best estimate so far: the world contains approximately 8.7 million species (not counting bacteria and viruses). The scientists also estimate that 86 percent of land species and 91 percent of ocean species remain undescribed. They used a mathematical formula based on the taxonomic classification system to make their predictions, which showed there are about 7.7 million species of animals; 298,000 plants; 611,000 fungi; 36,400 species of protozoa; and 27,500 of chromists (algae). Only a small fraction of these have been identified, described, and classified. Robert May, a zoologist at Oxford University, points out that "such knowledge is important for full understanding of the ecological and evolutionary processes which created, and which are struggling to maintain, the diverse biological riches we are heir to."

SEPTEMBER 21 | "With a Helpless Expression"

In 1901, German neuropathologist Alois Alzheimer examined a fifty-one-year-old woman named Auguste Deter who was suffering from a form of dementia: memory loss, disorientation, and hallucinations. He transcribed that examination: "She sits on the bed with a helpless expression. What is your name? *Auguste.* What is your husband's name? *Auguste.* Your husband? *Ah, my husband.* She looks as if she didn't understand the question. Are you married? *To Auguste.*" When she died five years later, Dr. Alzheimer was in Munich, working with the esteemed psychiatrist Emil Kraepelin. Hearing about Deter's death, Alzheimer began to study her medical records. He noticed that her cortex was abnormally thin, and her brain contained senile plaque (deposits of protein) and tangles of neurofibers. Those tangles, which Alzheimer discovered using a new staining technique, had never before been identified. Kraepelin, in his 1910 book *Psychiatrie*, named the disease after Alzheimer, who had never claimed to have discovered this most common type of dementia. In the *2011 World Alzheimer Report*, it was estimated that there are 36 million people in the world living with dementia. September 21 is World Alzheimer's Day.

SEPTEMBER 22 | Your Own Image

Like Narcissus, who fell in love with his own image in a clear stream and was unable to turn away, we all like to look at ourselves; seeing yourself reflected on a surface demonstrates that you actually exist in the world. The first "mirror" was indeed water—in still pools or in bowls or other containers. The first known manufactured mirrors were found in Çatalhöyük, in present-day Turkey. The Neolithic city at that location dates to about 6000 BCE, and archaeologists have discovered mirrors of ground and polished obsidian, a glasslike volcanic rock. Polished copper discs used as mirrors that are five thousand years old have been found in Iraq. Mirrors appeared in Egypt and other settled areas in the Middle East; they were likely a very popular item for trade. By 2000 BCE, metal or stone mirrors were in use in China, South America, and every civilized part of the world. In the Roman era, mirrors were made by adding a layer of gold or lead to the back of a piece of glass. One Roman historian credited the artisans of Sidon (in today's Lebanon) with the invention of the glass mirror. Various backings have been used over the centuries to create a reflective surface, including tin, mercury, and antimony. The process for silver-coated mirrors, the kind we still use today, was developed by the German chemist Justus von Liebig in 1835.

SEPTEMBER 23 | Go to Jail, Go Directly to Jail

The best-selling board game in the world, Monopoly, may well be a capitalist touchstone, but its predecessor was just the opposite. Elizabeth Magie Phillips was a Quaker living in Brentwood, Maryland. She was an ardent follower of economist Henry George, who considered landlords to be leeches and espoused a single federal tax on land ownership. Hoping to spread his ideas, Phillips invented a board game in 1903 that she called the Landlord's Game. "The object of the game," she wrote for the 1924 edition, "is not only to afford amusement to the players, but to illustrate to them how under the present or prevailing system of land tenure, the landlord has an advantage over other enterprises and also how the single tax would discourage land speculation." The game had railroads, utilities, and properties with such names as "Poverty Place" and "Lord Blueblood's Estate." Instead of a "Go" square, players were awarded $100 when they passed a globe inscribed "Labor Upon Mother Earth Produces Wages." Phillips's object was to show the dangers of capitalism and the landlord system, not to enshrine them. Her game was produced and distributed in modest numbers, but it gained popularity in many localities, especially college dormitories. People began to make their own versions with local street names and changed some of the rules, dropping the Georgist aspects. A salesman named Charles Darrow took one of those games, with Atlantic City place names, added a few modifications, obtained a patent for it, and sold it to Parker Brothers as Monopoly in 1935.

SEPTEMBER 24 | "Proclaim Liberty throughout All the Land"

In 1777, as British soldiers threatened Philadelphia during the Revolutionary War, some of the residents were concerned that the enemy would capture and melt down the city's bells and recast the metal to make cannons. So the colonists secretly removed eleven bells, including the Liberty Bell (then known as the Pennsylvania State House bell), and sent them in a train of seven hundred wagons of military stores traveling to Bethlehem. After dropping off the materiel, they took the bells to Northampton Towne, now called Allentown, where they hid them under the floor of the Zion Reformed Church. When the British evacuated Philadelphia the next year, the bells were returned. The State House bell became the Liberty Bell when abolitionists adopted it as a symbol in the 1830s; the famous crack that made the bell unringable also occurred in the nineteenth century. The trek to Allentown wasn't the only time the Liberty Bell was on the move. Between 1885 and 1915, it toured the country seven times but has stayed put in Philadelphia since then. The Zion Reformed Church still exists in Allentown, and it now contains a small Liberty Bell Museum.

The Liberty Bell

SEPTEMBER 25 | Talk Like an Egyptian

Foreign accent syndrome (FAS) is an uncommon speech disorder that appears to be caused by some kind of brain injury—stroke, trauma, lesions, and possibly migraines or multiple sclerosis. The rhythm and intonation of a person's speech suddenly change, and he or she begins to sound "foreign." Only a few dozen cases have been diagnosed and described; among them, a Norwegian woman hit by shrapnel in a 1941 air raid who started talking with a German accent; a British woman who sounded Chinese following a migraine headache; and a man in South Carolina who, after a mild stroke, spoke as if he were a French or Austrian native. Unlike other speech-related disorders, aphasia or dysarthia, for example, "patients with FAS do not usually sound pathological to the average listener. Instead, they are commonly perceived as non-native English speakers," explains a researcher at the Speech Production Laboratory of the University of Texas at Dallas.

SEPTEMBER 26 | The Apple Man

John Chapman was born in Leominster, Massachusetts, on September 26 in 1774 or 1775. He didn't start making a name for himself until 1801, when he arrived on horseback at the farm of John Stedden in Licking Creek, Ohio. Stedden thought the man eccentric but put him up for a few days and listened to his plans to head west and plant apple seeds along the way for future settlers. Five years later, another Ohio settler encountered Chapman. He had lashed two canoes together and was traveling the Ohio River, with one of the canoes filled with apple seeds. He was barefoot, dressed in rags, and wore a tin pot on his head as a hat. He was doing what he had told Stedden he would, traversing the country, pushing farther west each year, planting apple seeds wherever he found a suitable spot, and teaching farmers about nurseries and orchards. Chapman was a vegetarian and, by all accounts, a caring and compassionate, if somewhat odd, man. For more than forty years, he traipsed the fields and the forests from Pennsylvania to Illinois, spreading the word about apples until his death in 1845. A memorial gravesite in Fort Wayne, Indiana, has a stone marker bearing the motto "He lived for others," and the nickname by which he is known— Johnny Appleseed.

Johnny Appleseed

SEPTEMBER 27 | Outstanding Woman Athlete

Mildred Ella Didrikson Zaharias—probably the greatest female athlete of all time—was born in 1911, in Beaumont, Texas, where she acquired the nickname Babe. Consider the number of sports she participated in: basketball, track, golf, baseball, tennis, swimming, diving, boxing, volleyball, handball, bowling, billiards, skating, and cycling. At the Amateur Athletic Union championships in July 1932 (also the qualifying games for that year's Olympics), Babe was the only member of her company's team. She competed in eight events in three hours, won six of them, and earned more points than the next team's twenty-two competitors combined. She went on to the Los Angeles Summer Olympic Games, competed in three events (the maximum allowed for women), and won two gold medals and one silver. In 1938, she married professional wrestler George Zaharias. Later she took up golf, practicing ten hours a day until she was good enough to win fourteen consecutive tournaments. Zaharias was a founding member of the Ladies Professional Golf Association. The Associated Press named her the "Outstanding Woman Athlete of the Half Century" in 1950. She contracted cancer and talked about it publicly, something that was rare at the time; she died in 1956, only forty-five years old. Sports journalist Grantland Rice wrote of Babe Didrikson Zaharias, "Then you finally understand that you are looking at the most flawless section of muscle harmony, of complete mental and physical coordination, the world of sport has ever seen."

SEPTEMBER 28 | "Do Everything"

The Woman's Christian Temperance Union (WCTU) was formed in 1873 with the primary goal of ending the sale and consumption of alcohol in the United States. It was one of the first demonstrations of the political power women could wield when they banded together. Frances Willard (1839–1898), the organization's second president, recognized the latent strength of the group, and under the motto "Do Everything," expanded its reach beyond banning alcohol to other issues of importance to women. "Let us . . . stand bravely by that blessed trinity of movements, Prohibition, Woman's Liberation and Labour's uplift," she said in 1893. By advocating for women's rights, suffrage, equal pay for equal work, and an eight-hour work day, she elevated the political power of women to heights previously unimagined. Of course, she made some enemies and not only among the ranks of men. Ida B. Wells, the African American antilynching crusader, castigated Willard for perpetuating the myth that white women were constantly under threat from drunken black men.

The WCTU still exists today, focusing on the dangers of alcohol, tobacco, illegal drugs, gambling, and pornography.

SEPTEMBER 29 | American Architect

Henry Hobson Richardson (1838–1886), was a pioneer of American urban architecture. He designed churches, civic structures, mansions, railroad stations, and libraries that initiated the Romanesque style in this country. Known as Richardsonian Romanesque, his work was massive, solid, monumental, and not pretty—like the man himself. His buildings were constructed from large blocks of granite or brownstone, with arches, gables, columns, imposing rooflines, and textured surfaces. When a journal of architecture conducted a poll in 1885, Richardson's Trinity Church in Copley Square, Boston, was selected as the "most admired building," and four other Richardson structures were in the top ten. His brief career (he died before his fiftieth birthday) had a significant impact on the development of American architecture, especially in the work of his assistant Stanford White, as well as Daniel Burnham, Louis Sullivan, and Frank Lloyd Wright. Critic Brendan Gill called H. H. Richardson "unquestionably one of the dozen or so geniuses that our culture has produced since its beginnings, and in his field he is surpassed by none." By the middle of the twentieth century, however, public taste had changed, his style was less popular, and many Richardson buildings were demolished.

SEPTEMBER 30 | Scribal Errors

Sometimes monastic scribes made errors (or textual corruptions) in their copying, and, as with all things library-related, there are names for their various mistakes:

Parablepsis—from Greek words meaning "to look beside or askance," an omission caused when the writer looks away while copying a text.

Homoeoteleuton—from "like ending," when two lines have identical endings and the scribe's eye goes to the second line and leaves
out intervening words.

Haplography—"single writing," omission of a letter/word/syllable,
usually because it appears twice in close proximity.

Dittography—"double writing," the opposite of haplography; the
accidental repetition of a letter/word/syllable.

Metathesis—"transpose," reversing letters, words, phrases.

These errors are accidental, but there can also be intentional
alterations in a text, which St. Jerome, the patron saint of librarians,
complained, "are due to the ignorance or care-
lessness of the copyists, who write down not
what they find but what they take to be the
meaning, and do but expose their own mistakes when they try to correct those of
others."

A medieval scribe at work

OCTOBER

OCTOBER 1 | Fire of the Desert

Opals—widely prized for their iridescent rainbow colors—are one of the five commonly accepted types of gemstones, along with diamonds, rubies, emeralds, and sapphires (some people add pearls to the list, but they are animal products, not minerals). An opal is actually a mineraloid (with a noncrystalline structure), made of spheres of hydrated silica that are tightly packed in layers that refract light and produce the opal's characteristic gorgeous flashes of color. The indigenous people of Australia (where opals are the national gemstone) call them "the fire of the desert," and they believe opals form where rainbows touch the ground. In ancient Arabian legend, the brilliance of opals was caused by their falling to earth in lightning strikes. Pliny the Elder, in his *Natural History*, described the opal this way: "Of all precious stones, it is opal that presents the greatest difficulties of description, it displaying at once the piercing fire of carbunculus [rubies], the purple brilliancy of amethyst, and the sea-green of smaragdus [emeralds], the whole blended together and refulgent with a brightness that is quite incredible." In 2008, NASA's *Mars Reconnaissance Orbiter* observed evidence of opal-like minerals in Martian rocks. Opal is a birthstone for people born in October.

OCTOBER 2 | A Paleozoogeographic Event

A "biotic interchange" occurs when contact is made between previously isolated species of animals. North and South America were separate land masses about three million years ago, in the Pliocene era, when the Isthmus of Panama rose from the sea, creating a volcanic land bridge between the continents. During several episodes of what is called the Great American Faunal Interchange, South American animals such as armadillos, marsupials, flightless birds, and ground sloths began to move north, and North American creatures, including bears, cats, rodents, and dogs, headed south. Many South American animals were unable to adapt to the influx of new predators and became extinct; about half of the animals there today are descended from northern families. The separation of the Atlantic and Pacific oceans caused by the isthmus also had a profound effect on currents, eventually creating the Gulf Stream, which had a significant impact on the climate in northern Europe.

OCTOBER 3 | Driving on Planks

America's earliest roads were dirt paths, most adapted from Native American or trapper trails, and they were prone to dust or mud. Early in the 1800s, people began to agitate for something more suitable for a growing country. Modern tar-based surfaces such as macadam or asphalt were still many years away, but the country had plenty of trees, so wood provided the answer. Plank roads—constructed from eight-foot boards and generally about twelve-feet wide—were a vast improvement over dirt roads, although they did require a good bit of maintenance. Many of them were still in use at the advent of the automobile in the early twentieth century, and in southern California they were still constructing plank roads to cross the desert sand dunes in Imperial County. Remnants of America's plank roads still exist, particularly in the far west. Wooden roads were certainly nothing new in civilization: the oldest known wooden causeway is the Sweet Track (named for Ray Sweet, the peat worker who uncovered it in 1970) near Glastonbury, England. It dates to around 3,800 BCE.

OCTOBER 4 | Lion-Scorpion Man

The manticore (*mantichoras* in Latin, *mantikhoras* in Greek) is a mythological beast with the body of a lion, a human face, and a tail that resembles the stinger of a scorpion. Its voice is shrill and sibilant and, according to the Roman naturalist Pliny the Elder, "resembleth the noise of a flute and trumpet sounded together." The myth probably originated in Persia, where the word means "man-eater." The manticore was certainly well-equipped to consume humans, with three rows of sharp teeth. It was agile and speedy, too. As one medieval bestiary puts it, "It is so strong in the foot, so powerful with its leaps, that not the most extensive space nor the most lofty obstacle can contain it." Illustrators have created many fright-

ening depictions of manticores over the centuries, and they can still be found today; there are references to it in J. K. Rowling's Harry Potter series, and the manticore appears in several popular video games including *Heroes of Might and Magic* and *Final Fantasy*.

A manticore

OCTOBER 5 | The Story of Canudos

An itinerant mystic named Antônio Vicente Mendes Maciel was roaming the backlands of northeastern Brazil in the late nineteenth century. His preaching attracted followers, mostly landless peasants or *jagunços*, who began to call him *Conselheiro* ("the counselor"). It was a time of social, political, and environmental disruption and turmoil, and the movement became political, opposed to slavery and the imposition of harsh taxes. Conselheiro and his followers founded the village of Canudos in 1893, intending it to be an alternative society where workers could live in equality. More and more *jagunços* came from around the country until the settlement had grown to about thirty thousand people. This worried both national and local authorities, who sent several expeditions to attempt to suppress them. In October 1897, eight thousand troops of the Brazilian army attacked the village and, after a number of battles, completely destroyed Canudos. Conselheiro had died of natural causes a few weeks earlier, and those of his followers who weren't killed in the fighting were brutally slaughtered by the government forces. In the 1960s, the Cocorobó dam was built, flooding the area where the village of Canudos once stood.

OCTOBER 6 | Germy Sponges

What's the filthiest thing in your home? It's probably the kitchen sponge, the "No. 1 source of germs in the whole house," according to WebMD.com. The warm, wet pads made of plastic or cellulose are full of crevices that provide the perfect environment for all kinds of unpleasant and dangerous microscopic creatures. As you wipe the counter or the stove with the sponge, you're spreading the germs that cause colds, flu, or food poisoning. Engineers at the University of Florida experimented with methods of sterilizing sponges and discovered that zapping them for a few minutes in your microwave oven at full power will kill more than 99 percent of the living pathogens. There are two important details of the process: the sponge must be wet when it goes into the microwave (or it could burst into flames), and don't forget how hot it will be when it comes out.

OCTOBER 7 | Writing under Constraint

Constrained writing is a literary technique that places certain restrictions on how an author creates a work. In a lipogram, for example, the use of a particular letter is completely forbidden. Perhaps the most famous lipogram is a book written by Ernest Vincent Wright in 1939 called *Gadsby: A Story of Over 50,000 Words without Using the Letter "E."* Wright wanted to show that a good author could work within such limits and still produce a worthy piece of literature. He tied down the "e" key on his typewriter so that he wouldn't accidentally use it, and then put his energy and wit to finding ways of expressing himself without relying on the most common letter in the English language. In his introduction (where he did allow himself to use e's), he admitted that there were plenty of difficulties. "The greatest of these is met in the past tense of verbs, almost all of which end with '-ed.' Therefore substitutes must be found; and they are very few." Other types of constrained writing include alliterative writing, where every word must begin with the same letter; reverse lipograms, where a certain letter is required in every word; and E-prime, where any form of the verb "to be" is outlawed.

OCTOBER 8 | The Cocktail

For many of the facts in this book, I had to sift through numerous competing claims to get to the kernel of truth. None, however, proved more contentious than facts concerning mixed drinks—specifically, the cocktail. Where did the word *cocktail* come from? There are at least six different possibilities, some reasonable, others not at all. The martini? At least four. Did Kentucky or Virginia invent bourbon? That argument has been raging since the 1800s. Alcoholic refreshment was a staple of American life from the beginning. Wine (the most popular was Madeira), beer, and rum were the favored drinks of the early colonists, and they consumed them in large quantities, beginning at daybreak. Alcohol was considered a boon to health, and water was definitely not. Yet the historic cocktail—a cold drink with alcohol, water, sugar, and bitters—could not come into its own until ice became available beyond the circles of the wealthy. That didn't happen until the mid-

nineteenth century, and that's when America's first two cocktails, the Mint Julep and the Bittered Sling, evolved. The Martini came not long afterward, followed by a blinding array of concoctions. Many of our most famous cocktails were invented during Prohibition, often as a way of disguising the taste of cheaply made alcohol. Every drink has a story, but whether they are true or not is best discussed over a nice cocktail.

Cocktails

OCTOBER 9 | It Reminded Him of the Sea

As with most mixed drinks, the exact origin of the Daiquiri is muddled. The most popular story involves an American mining engineer named Jennings Cox who had been assigned to the iron mines near Daiquiri, Cuba. One night, probably around 1896, he and some mining friends ran out of gin and decided to try mixing rum, lime juice, and sugar, calling the new drink a Daiquiri. It's more likely that he just named a preexisting local favorite. In 1908, a visiting naval officer, Admiral Lucius W. Johnson, tried it, brought it back to the United States, and introduced it to the Army and Navy Club in Washington, D.C., where it became an instant hit. You can have one there today, in the Daiquiri Lounge. Ernest Hemingway enjoyed the Daiquiri so much that a version was named for him, the Papa Doble—double size, frozen, and substituting maraschino liqueur for the sugar. He even wrote rhapsodically in *Islands in the Stream* that it "looks like the sea where the wave falls away from the bow of a ship when she is doing thirty knots." When President John F. Kennedy pronounced it his favorite predinner drink, the Daiquiri's fame was assured. The basic recipe is 1½ ounces light rum, ¾ ounce lime juice, and simple syrup to taste.

OCTOBER 10 | A Product with Some Value

Look in almost anyone's medicine cabinet, and you will find a bottle of aspirin, one of the most efficacious pain relievers and anti-inflammatories in the world. The ancient Greeks were aware of the palliative properties of willow bark, a plant that contains salicylates. By the eighteenth century, a powder made from willow bark was in use to treat malaria and other fevers. Eventually, scientists were able to isolate the compounds salicin and salicylic acid from willow bark and other plants. On October 10, 1897, a chemist working for the Bayer company in Germany described his work on acetylsalicylic acid, which made the drug easier on the stomach. He called it aspirin: *a* from acetyl, *spir* from the spirea plant (another source of salicin), plus *in*, a common medication suffix. A colleague at Bayer dismissed aspirin, however, claiming that "the product has no value." He was more interested in the other new product Bayer had synthesized that year—heroin. The company decided to forge ahead with aspirin, which became one of the wonder drugs of the twentieth century. In 1948, Dr. Lawrence Craven realized that daily doses of aspirin could help prevent heart attacks and strokes. Aspirin has become an important part of the regimen for heart patients and is one of the most widely used medicines in the world—100 billion tablets per year.

OCTOBER 11 | Primitive Painters

Scientists announced in October 2011 that they had identified a hundred-thousand-year-old toolkit for making paints. Christopher Henshilwood led the team that made the discovery in Blombos Cave in South Africa, which is the oldest artist workshop yet found; previous paint toolkits were about sixty thousand years old. Two large abalone shells were discovered, coated with red ocher, a form of iron oxide found in clay that ancient peoples used for both pigment and glue. Grinding stones, charcoal, and bits of bone were also part of the kit. The discovery shows that humans were capable of symbolic thinking and understood basic chemistry at a much earlier date than previously thought. Making the paint was a moderately complex process: bone and charcoal had to be heated and crushed to release their oils, then combined with ocher for color and gently mixed. "The recovery of these toolkits adds evidence for early technological and behavioral developments associated with humans and documents their deliberate planning, production and curation of pigmented compound," said Henshilwood.

OCTOBER 12 | Megastructure

In the 1960s, the Japanese government realized that the country needed a new international airport. Population density and noise pollution issues prevented traditional construction around any major cities, so they proposed building an artificial island in Osaka Bay. Construction of Kansai International Airport began in 1987—a man-made island 2.5 miles long and 1.6 miles wide, created from forty-eight thousand tetrahedral concrete blocks and twenty-seven million cubic yards of landfill. It required ten thousand workers and ten million work hours during a period of three years. Problems occurred immediately. The island was expected to settle gradually from the weight of the materials, but engineers were shocked to discover that it was sinking rapidly. Adjustable columns, which could be extended as needed, had to be installed to support the terminal building, and by the time it opened in 1994, Kansai had become the most expensive public works project in modern times. The terminal, which is the longest in the world, was designed by noted Italian architect Renzo Piano. In 2010, Kansai averaged 293 flights—moving more than 39,000 people and more than 2,000 tons of freight—per day. The American Society of Civil Engineers has designated Kansai a "monument of the millennium." Kansai Airport did not suffer any damage from the earthquake and resulting tsunami that struck northeastern Japan in March 2011.

OCTOBER 13 | Wandering SCOTUS

The Supreme Court of the United States didn't have its own permanent residence for its first 146 years. Created by the Judiciary Act in 1789, the court first held sessions in New York City in the Merchant's Exchange Building. When Congress moved to Philadelphia in 1790, the court met in Independence Hall, then at City Hall. When the government moved to Washington a decade later, no provision had been made for housing the Supreme Court, so the justices were given space in the Capitol. After the British burned the building in 1814, the court actually met in a private home on Pennsylvania Avenue before returning to the rebuilt Capitol, where it occupied several different chambers. It was former president William Howard Taft, then chief justice, who finally persuaded Congress to approve legislation for a permanent home. Construction of the building, designed by architect

Cass Gilbert (known for the Woolworth Building in New York) on the site of the Old Capitol Prison, began in 1932. Taft's successor, Chief Justice Charles Evans Hughes, remarked as he laid the cornerstone, "The Republic endures and this is the symbol of its faith."

OCTOBER 14 | The Living Story

Cultures that are nonliterate—that do not use writing—nonetheless develop complex language systems and often have a rich history of storytelling. African griots, Celtic shanachies, and Scandinavian skalds are examples of the traveling bards and the oral historians who create, preserve, and promulgate local traditions, myths, and epics. According to *An Introductory Dictionary of Theology and Religious Studies*,

> Since they must rely on memory, nonliterate peoples must in fact memorize a prodigious amount of material. Individual members of the community become repositories of the cultural tradition that remains vital as a living part of each person. . . . Oral cultures have sophisticated religious teachings and intellectual traditions . . . carried in the memory of their living members. In nonliterate cultures, the spoken word has creative, spiritually potent, even magical dimensions. Storytelling is central to life experience.

OCTOBER 15 | Magic Mushrooms

They're neither animal nor plant but something unique to themselves: mushrooms are the fruiting bodies of fungi that grow underground. The fruits are produced from hairlike threads known as hyphae, which spread rapidly through the soil and form networks called mycelia. These networks can be tiny or can grow to immense size— one mycelium growth in Oregon spread over two thousand acres. The mycelia sprout fruits, which push their way to the surface (except for truffles, which stay underground). Plants drop seeds to propagate, but

mushrooms drop (or shoot) spores, which form
on gills underneath the cap. There can be a lot of
them, too; a single mature mushroom may release
as many as sixteen billion spores. Unlike plants,
mushrooms don't require sunlight, because they
don't produce chlorophyll; they absorb nutrients
from living or dead organic material. Humans
have eaten mushrooms for millennia, and it's

Mushrooms

important to correctly identify the different varieties, because some
are toxic, some are psychoactive, and others have medicinal uses. A
Neolithic man found frozen in the Alps in 1991 was carrying three
different kinds of mushrooms that had antibacterial and laxative
properties, leading scientists to believe he may have been using them
to treat a stomach ailment. Cave paintings have been discovered dating back some nine thousand years that depict mushrooms that have
been identified as specimens of *Psilocybe*, a hallucinogenic variety.

OCTOBER 16 | The Death of Pain

Before 1846, surgery was always a dangerous and excruciating experience. Physicians had tried a variety of techniques to lessen the pain—
soporifics, narcotics, alcohol, hypnotism—but they weren't fully
successful. In 1845, a dentist named Horace Wells started to use nitrous
oxide during tooth extractions. He demonstrated the procedure at
Massachusetts General Hospital, but the patient cried out, and Wells
was humiliated. His colleague, fellow dentist William T. G. Morton,
consulted Harvard professor Charles Jackson about other substances
that might work. Jackson mentioned ether, a volatile, aromatic compound, which had been privately tested as an anesthetic by doctors in
the United States and England. Morton began experimenting with
ether, first on a dog, then on his dental patients. Confident of success,
he persuaded surgeon John Collins Warren to make a public presentation with him. On October 16, 1846, the demonstration was held, again
at Mass General. Using an inhaler of his own design, Morton anesthe-
tized the patient, then turned the surgery over to Dr. Warren. It was a

minor procedure, removing a vascular lesion from the patient's neck, but the man experienced no pain. Painless surgery was now possible. The Ether Monument—also known as the Good Samaritan, and the oldest statue in Boston's Public Garden—commemorates the "discovery that the inhaling of ether causes insensibility to pain."

OCTOBER 17 | Separated by a Common Language

Why do many American spellings differ from their British counterparts? It's because of Noah Webster (1758–1843) and his spellers and dictionaries. The famed lexicographer was an ardent American nationalist who championed the use of language and especially spellings that were distinct from their British forebears:

> It has been observed by all writers on the English language, that the orthography or spelling of words is very irregular. . . . The question now occurs; ought the Americans to retain these faults which produce innumerable inconveniencies in the acquisition and use of the language, or ought they at once to reform these abuses, and introduce order and regularity into the orthography of the AMERICAN TONGUE?

The several editions of Webster's blue-backed speller had a profound and long-term effect in the American classroom. Many of the spelling changes Webster advocated did catch on: *gaol* became *jail*, *honour* turned into *honor*, and *masque* became *mask*, among many others. Yet some of his proposed modifications did not work: *tongue* did not become *tung*, nor did *ache* become *ake* or *machine* turn to *masheen*, and *wimmin* did not replace *women*.

OCTOBER 18 | The State of Fire

There are four states of matter: solid, liquid, gas, and plasma. Fire is a process of transformation, a form of heat and light energy together, which changes a solid or a liquid into gas. Cecil Adams of the Straight Dope website defines it this way: "Fire is the rapid combination of oxygen with fuel in the presence of heat, typically characterized by flame, a body of incandescent gas that contains and sustains the reaction and emits light and heat." Fire is rapid oxidation, but there are slower forms as well that produce no light and far less heat—rust, for example. Plasma resembles fire because it is extremely hot and glows, but it does not actually burn, and, unlike fire, plasma can conduct electricity and is affected by magnetic forces; these are the properties that make it useful in flat-screen televisions. So fire is associated with solids, liquids, gases, and plasma but is not itself a state of matter or an element.

OCTOBER 19 | A Deadly Dish

Poisoning was a frequent cause of death in Rome from the fourth century BCE to the second century CE, and many, if not most, of the poisoners were women. Some massive deaths from outbreaks of disease were erroneously blamed on poison, but the historian Livy reported that 170 matrons were convicted in one year of poisoning their husbands. Although animal- and mineral-based poisons were known to the ancient world, botanicals were preferred by most poisoners. Hemlock, mandrake, deadly nightshade, even opium were commonly used, often delivered in food or beverages. The emperor Claudius may have been poisoned by a dish of mushrooms presented to him by his wife, Agrippina; her motive was to advance her son Nero. Poisoning was so common at the imperial court that emperors hired *praegustatores* or "tasters." Poisons were also used, less frequently, for suicide by prisoners and the terminally ill.

Claudius

OCTOBER 20 | The Most Mysterious Book

The Voynich Manuscript, named for Wilfrid Voynich, the antiquarian who found it in Europe in 1912, is a book handwritten on parchment, created about six hundred years ago in an unknown and thus far undeciphered script. It's "a magical or scientific text, nearly every page contains botanical, figurative, and scientific drawings of a provincial but lively character, drawn in ink with vibrant washes in various shades of green, brown, yellow, blue, and red," as the Beineke Library at Yale University, the current owner of the manuscript, describes it. The illustrations include unknown plants, astronomical diagrams, human figures (mostly naked females), charts or maps, and possibly even recipes. Scholars, cryptographers, and computer scientists continue to debate: "No one has worked out whether [it] is a code, an idiosyncratic translation of a known tongue, elegant gibberish or cunningly-crafted nonsense." A team of physicists at the University of Arizona determined by radiocarbon dating that the Voynich Manuscript was created in the early 1400s.

OCTOBER 21 | Top Ten New Species

The International Institute for Species Exploration at Arizona State University has a committee of taxon experts who select the Top Ten New Species from the thousands of life forms fully described and published each year. For 2010, they welcomed into the world of science a carnivorous deep-sea sponge; a fanged fish named Dracula; a small phallus-shaped mushroom; an electric fish; an orb-spinning spider; a flat-faced, psychedelic frogfish; a sea slug that eats insects instead of algae; a sea worm that can shoot out little flashes of bioluminescence; a new kind of yam from Madagascar; and an insect-eating pitcher plant that's the size of a football. In 2011, the winners were a spider that spins "the toughest biological material ever studied"; a mushroom that emits a bright green light and one that lives underwater; a large frugivorous lizard; an orchid-pollinating cricket; a West African duiker; a *T. rex* leech; the first jumping cockroach since the Late Jurassic; the Louisiana pancake batfish; and a bacterium discovered eating rust off the RMS *Titanic*.

OCTOBER 22 | An Eternal Blue Glaze

Luca della Robbia was a Florentine artist of the fifteenth century who is especially well known for glazed ceramic roundels and reliefs. He perfected the technique of enameled terra cotta that was "hard, durable, and bright," and he produced a brilliant cobalt blue glaze that became his signature. Commercially successful, Luca founded a family workshop and school that produced altarpieces and decorative sculptures for several generations. The world's first art historian, Giorgio Vasari, explained that though trained as a sculptor, Luca

> seeing that the profit was very little and the fatigue very great, resolved to let marble and bronze alone, and see if he could not earn more in some other way. And considering that working in clay was easy, he set himself to find a way by which it might be defended from the injuries of time. And after many experiments he found a way of covering it with a glaze by which it was made almost eternal. And not being satisfied at having made an invention so useful, especially for damp places, he added a method by which he could give it color, to the marvel and great pleasure of every one.

OCTOBER 23 | The Hadlyme Stone Heap

Americans have always demonstrated an affection for eccentrics, particularly rich ones and especially when they build incredible homes. It would be hard to find a more idiosyncratic house than Gillette Castle in Hadlyme, Connecticut. The brainchild of actor William Hooker Gillette (1853–1937), the fieldstone fortress, which he called his "Hadlyme stone heap," sits on top of a bluff overlooking the Connecticut River. Gillette was already a famous actor and playwright in the late 1800s when he was offered the role of Sherlock Holmes in a new play written by Sir Arthur Conan Doyle. Its success made Gillette not only a millionaire, but the personification of Holmes.

Gillette Castle

It was Gillette who popularized the consulting detective's deerstalker hat and curved pipe, and he was the model for Frederick Dorr Steele's illustrations in *Colliers* magazine. In 1913, Gillette decided to build a unique retirement home for himself. It took five years, but when it was done, Gillette had constructed an intriguing, though some would say garish, residence. Built of undressed granite, the twenty-four-room castle has a rugged facade, with turrets, a tower, and parapets. The interior is equally quirky: hand-carved oak doors and locks (each one different); secret passageways; a surveillance system that uses hidden mirrors; chairs and tables that roll on wooden tracks; and hideaway furniture. Gillette designed everything himself, including the three-mile narrow gauge railway that ran through the grounds. In his will, Gillette specified that the estate not be sold to some "blithering saphead who had no conception of where he is or with what surrounded." In 1943, the compound was purchased by the state and is now one of Connecticut's most popular tourist attractions.

OCTOBER 24 | Ghost Forests

Mild winters and warmer summers are allowing mountain pine beetles (*Dendroctonus ponderosae*) to thrive in northwestern forests at higher altitudes, where they are destroying stands of whitebark pines (*Pinus albicaulis*), a keystone species (one that provides conditions that promote biodiversity, allowing other species to flourish). The beetles, along with a fungal disease called blister rust, are transforming the landscape in the Grand Tetons and Yellowstone and other areas; 98 percent of the whitebark trees in the United States are on public lands. These pests are also endangering the local wildlife: grizzly bears, small mammals, and birds that eat the pine cones are being forced to find new food sources. Hundreds of thousands of these slow-growing, long-lived trees have died in the last decade, leaving behind ghost forests of red and gray tree snags. In July 2011, the U.S.

Fish and Wildlife Service determined that the whitebark pine warrants protection under the Endangered Species Act.

OCTOBER 25 | Radar Boxes

Some of the world's more interesting inventions were created by accident. Take the microwave oven, for example. In 1945, Percy Spencer, a self-taught engineer working for the Raytheon Company on radar technology, was testing a magnetron tube when he noticed that a candy bar in his pocket was melting. That made him curious, so he placed some dried corn by the tube. It popped. Then he tried an egg, which exploded. It didn't take long for inveterate inventor Spencer, who would eventually hold some 120 patents, to begin looking for practical applications. By the following spring, he was hard at work on a secret microwave project, naming it "Speedy Weenie" because it quickly cooked hot dogs. The first microwave oven for commercial use (called the RadarRange) was ready in 1947, but it was the size of a refrigerator and cost about $3,000. Raytheon executives wanted to develop the microwave for home use, so they teamed up with the Tappan Stove company. On October 25, 1955, the first domestic microwave was released at a still pricey $1,300. It wasn't until 1967 that Raytheon introduced a countertop model at less than $500. Spencer's radar boxes have now become ubiquitous in kitchens around the globe.

OCTOBER 26 | Your Cheatin' Voice

You might be surprised to learn that the search for petroleum led to an invention that changed the music industry. Harold "Andy" Hildebrand was a research scientist working with Exxon on seismic data interpretation in the 1980s. He realized that the digital signal technology he was using could also have applications in music recording, one of his passions. He developed software for several recording techniques before he hit it big in 1997 with something he called Auto-Tune. It enabled audio engineers to manipulate the pitch of a singer's voice so that it was always in tune. Good singers could sound better, and bad singers could be fixed. In addition, Auto-Tune could be tweaked to produce a vocal distortion effect that became immensely popular, following Cher's 1998 hit, "Believe." The process swept through the industry but also drew immediate criticism for being a kind of plastic surgery for bad singers—musical cheating, as it were. A number of major artists have publicly voiced their opposition to Auto-Tune, including Death Cab for Cutie and Jay-Z, who released a song called "D.O.A. (Death of Auto-Tune)" in 2009.

OCTOBER 27 | The President and the Piranha

The piranha (*Serrasalminae*), a little fish with big teeth, has a fearsome image. That is thanks, in large part, to Theodore Roosevelt. In 1913, after losing his bid for a third presidential term, Roosevelt decided to join an expedition to the Brazilian jungle. There his companions told him lurid tales of the piranha's bloodthirsty behavior, which he transmitted to an American audience through vivid articles he wrote for *Scribner's* magazine and eventually in his book, *Through the Brazilian Wilderness*: "The razor-edged teeth are wedge-shaped like a shark's, and the jaw muscles possess great power. The rabid, furious snaps drive the teeth through flesh and bone. The head with its short muzzle, staring malignant eyes, and gaping, cruelly armed jaws, is the embodiment of evil ferocity; and the actions of the fish exactly match its looks." Roosevelt was the first popular writer to report on the piranha, and that violent image has persisted, even though the fish is far less dangerous than Roosevelt described.

A piranha

OCTOBER 28 | Ticker-Tape in the Canyon of Heroes

A few office boys working for the big banks in New York City's financial district had an idea on October 28, 1886. That was the day the Statue of Liberty was dedicated, and a parade was planned along Broadway. The *New York Times* reported that the young men went to the windows and "began to unreel the spools of tape that record the fateful messages of the 'ticker.' In a moment the air was white with curling streamers. . . . Every window appeared to be a paper mill spouting out squirming lines of tape." Ticker-tape was the paper ribbon produced by the machines that were used to telegraph stock information. More than two hundred ticker-tape parades have marched up Manhattan's "Canyon of Heroes" between the Battery and City Hall over the years. American political and military leaders, foreign dignitaries, aviation pioneers, and even Albert Einstein (the only scientist) have been honored with ticker-tape parades. The first sports-related parade occurred in 1924 for the U.S. Olympic team. New York's local sports franchises weren't honored until much later, the first being for the 1954 New York Giants (baseball, not football). A few people have been celebrated more than once: John Glenn, Amelia Earhart, Dwight Eisenhower, and Charles DeGaulle.

OCTOBER 29 | Sharing with Your Pets

One-third of the people in the world, including sixty million Americans, are infected with the toxoplasmosis parasite, and most don't even know it. *Toxoplasma gondii* are protozoa that can reproduce only in the digestive system of cats. From cats, the parasites spread into the environment. Cleaning your cat's litter box is an easy way to pick up a few *T. gondii*. Other animals, such as pigs and sheep, can also become infected and pass the parasites along to humans who eat undercooked or raw meat (it's the third leading cause of food-related deaths). Fortunately, the human immune system is normally able to control the disease, so it is not very dangerous. Many people don't experience any symptoms, some have flu-like complaints, but serious illness can result for people with weak immune systems, or if it's passed from a pregnant woman to her fetus.

OCTOBER 30 | Weights and Measures

Before achieving independence, the American colonies used the same system of weights and measures as Great Britain. That caused problems, however, because the British standards were complicated and confusing. At one point, Americans had measures for the firkin, the kilderkin, the strike, the hogshead, the tierce, the pipe, the butt, and the puncheon. In addition, a unit of measurement wasn't necessarily consistent from one colony to another: a bushel of oats weighed twenty-eight pounds in Connecticut, but thirty-two pounds in New Jersey. That confusion was relieved somewhat in 1816 when the superintendent of the Survey of the Coast selected the English Imperial system, rather than the metric, and set standards for length, mass, and capacity for America's custom houses. In 1893, the international meter and the kilogram were adopted as the official measures of length and mass in the United States. For many years, a bar of platinum-iridium with inscribed marks was accepted as the standard for length. According to the National Institute of Standards and Technology, starting in 1960 "the meter was now defined . . . as 1,650,763.73 wavelengths of the orange-red line in the spectrum of radiation from electrically excited atoms of krypton-86. The meter as an artifact had been replaced by a definition of the meter in terms of a constant of nature." That changed again in 1983, and "the International Meter is now the distance that light travels in a vacuum in 1/299,792,458 of a second." Mass is still defined by an object, the International Prototype Kilogram.

OCTOBER 31 | A Blended Holiday

Take a pagan celebration of ancient Druidism, add some Roman festivals and a Christian feast day, and you wind up with the holiday we call Halloween. Almost everyone agrees that Halloween grew out of the Celtic festival of Samhain (SAH-wen) that marked the end of the harvest and the beginning of winter. Their priests, the Druids, believed that the spirits of the dead returned to earth on that day, and the border between life and death was blurred. They built huge bonfires to keep the spirits away and made costumes of animal skins and heads. When the Romans took over Celtic territory, they merged Samhain with the festivals of Feralia, to honor the dead, and Pomona, the goddess of fruits and trees. By 800 CE, Christianity had spread to the Celtic regions and church leaders created All Saints Day on November 1 to coincide with the ancient holiday. It was also referred to as All-Hallows Day (*hallows* means "holy" or "sanctified"), and the night before was All-Hallows Evening, eventually shortened to Halloween. All of the traditions that we associate with Halloween—trick-or-treating, wearing costumes, bobbing for apples—come from one or another of these ancient traditions or a blend of all of them.

NOVEMBER

NOVEMBER 1 | The Land of Fire

On All Saints Day, November 1, 1520, Portuguese explorer Ferdinand Magellan, sailing under the flag of Spain, entered a strait at the southern tip of South America. He called it Estrecho de Todos los Santos (Strait of All Saints), but today it's called the Strait of Magellan. On shore he saw smoke curling up from native fires, so he called the area Tierra del Fuego, the Land of Fire. It's an archipelago, composed of one large island and hundreds of smaller ones. The indigenous people, primarily the Yaghans, arrived as early as 8000 BCE, likely crossing an ice bridge from Patagonia. After Magellan, Europeans didn't return in numbers until the nineteenth century, bringing sheep farming and then gold mining to the islands. The native population did not survive the contact. Having been an isolated community, they were susceptible to diseases introduced by the colonizers, and those who didn't die were easily dispersed. Charles Darwin, on the second voyage of the HMS *Beagle* in 1834, became familiar with the native people but could not overcome his cultural arrogance: "These poor wretches were stunted in their growth, their hideous faces bedaubed with white paint, their skins filthy and greasy, their hair entangled, their voices discordant, their gestures violent. Viewing such men, one can hardly make oneself believe they are fellow-creatures, and inhabitants of the same world." Today Tierra del Fuego is divided between Chile and Argentina, with petroleum production and tourism the main industries.

NOVEMBER 2 | Twin Sisters

The Dakota Territory was created in 1861, from land that had been the northernmost section of the Louisiana Purchase. At first, the new territory included the area from the Minnesota border west to what later became parts of Montana, Wyoming, and Idaho; after a few years, its size was reduced. Congress voted to admit North and South Dakota to the Union in February 1889 (there had been some who supported the idea of East and West Dakota, divided by the Missouri River). President Benjamin Harrison signed the statehood proclamations on November 2, 1889. He was reluctant to choose which Dakota would become a state first, so a plan was devised whereby "no one knew which of the new States was born first, that all hands at the birth of the twins were by legerdemain kept from knowing which Territory first answered the functions of Statehood. The proclamations were mixed up, then signed with the headings covered, and then mixed up again so the President himself could not tell which proclamation he first signed." Because North Dakota is first alphabetically, it became the thirty-ninth state, and South Dakota is the fortieth.

NOVEMBER 3 | An Emblem of Extinction

Dead as a dodo; that's pretty dead. The dodo (*Raphus cucullatus*, part of the pigeon family) was a large, clumsy, ugly, flightless bird first seen by Europeans around 1600 when Dutch sailors visited the island of Mauritius in the Indian Ocean. Barely eighty years later, the bird was gone, probably the first species in recorded history to be brought to

A dodo

extinction by human action. It wasn't because the explorers ate them all, though they certainly did try cooking a few (but dodos were not particularly palatable). But they did introduce cats, rats, pigs, and other animals to Mauritius that ravaged the dodos' nests and habitat. Because the birds couldn't fly and their size and stubby legs meant they couldn't even waddle very fast, they were easy prey. It was the dodos' isolation on an island without predators that had allowed them to thrive as long as they had.

NOVEMBER 4 | Mission to Mars

A seventeen-month mission to Mars ended successfully on November 4, 2011. Actually, it was fake, a simulation: six astronauts (three Russian, two European, one Chinese) spent 520 days in a chamber in Moscow so that scientists could observe and analyze the effects of isolation, boredom, crowding, and overfamiliarity. "We need to understand that in a manned flight, the people are the most vulnerable thing," said Victor Baranov of the Russian Institute of Biomedical Problems, who sponsored the *Mars 500* project, along with the European Space Agency. A similar 420-day experiment had ended badly in 2000 when two astronauts got in a fistfight, and another made an unwelcome advance on a female crew member. The 2011 experiment included only men and managed to avoid the problems of the earlier trial. The cramped quarters included computers used for both scientific experiments and for entertainment. To simulate actual conditions in space, a twenty-minute time lag was built into communications with the outside world. There was no shower; instead, the crew members would heat themselves in a saunalike chamber and then scrape off the dirt. An actual flight to Mars is still many years away, but important groundwork has been laid. One crew member proudly pointed out, "On this mission we've achieved the longest isolation ever so that humankind can go to a distant but reachable planet."

NOVEMBER 5 | The Finest Highway Ever Built

In the late 1940s, the governor of New Jersey decided that the state needed a high-speed, modern toll road, and planning began for the New Jersey Turnpike. The *Saturday Evening Post* called it "the finest highway every built" and described the route: "Arching over miles of trackless marshes, knifing through industrial areas and several cities, striding over sixty-seven creeks and rivers, vaulting 196 intersecting highways and railroad crossings, and cleaving through the heart of some of the state's richest farmlands." Constructed at lightning speed in about two years and with no public funds, the original turnpike was 118 miles long, from the Delaware Memorial Bridge to the George Washington Bridge (the original passenger car toll for the whole stretch: $1.75). The first section (about fifty miles) opened on November 5, 1951, and about 790,000 vehicles drove the pike in its first two months. The highway's first fatal accident happened about six weeks after the opening. Five U.S. Marines, traveling home from Camp Lejeune, North Carolina, for the Christmas holidays, were killed when their car hit a truck. In 2010, 235 million cars traveled a total of 5.9 billion turnpike miles with about 7,200 accidents, including 13 fatalities.

NOVEMBER 6 | Mr. First

The first person to drive on the brand-new original section of the New Jersey Turnpike in 1951 was Omero Catan—known as Mr. First. He claimed at that time to have made "more than 400 firsts of civic and historic importance," including bridge, tunnel, and subway openings, starting with the George Washington Bridge in 1931 (by 1995, his achievements numbered 573). He was also the first person to put a coin in a New York City parking meter and the first to skate on the ice rink at Rockefeller Center. In 1945, Catan was in an army hospital in England when the north tube of the Lincoln Tunnel opened, so his brother paid the toll and made the drive in his place. Catan's reaction to the new turnpike: "It's a dream. Out of this world. It feels great. It's a great thrill to go over this thing." Mr. First also collected four-leaf clovers and was a member of the Shuffleboard Hall of Fame. He died in 1996.

NOVEMBER 7 | Unique Yew Nork

Alliterative or rhymed phrases spoken rapidly can be difficult to enunciate and can tie your tongue into knots. "She sells seashells by the seashore" is perhaps the most famous English language tongue twister. The most difficult one may be, "The sixth sick sheik's sixth sheep's sick." They can be fun, but there's also a serious side to tongue twisters. For centuries, elocutionists (a profession that doesn't really exist anymore) used tongue twisters to improve their students' public speaking ability. In addition, as anyone who saw the 2010 Oscar-winning film *The King's Speech* knows, tongue twisters can be used in speech therapy as a way to help control stuttering. Lionel Logue, the Australian elocutionist who helped King George VI overcome his stammer, used several tongue twisters with his patient, including "She sifted seven thick-stalked thistles through a strong thick sieve."

NOVEMBER 8 | Hoax or History?

To say that the Kensington Runestone is a controversial artifact is putting it mildly. Since its discovery in 1898 by a Swedish-American farmer near the town of Kensington in Douglas County, Minnesota, there's been a lively debate, with both sides claiming irrefutable proof. Is it history, proving that people from Scandinavia visited America long before Columbus? Or is it a hoax? The stone is a two-hundred-pound slab of gray sandstone inscribed with runes, an ancient alphabet used in northern Europe. The text claims that thirty men on a journey from Vinland camped there in 1362, and that ten of them had been found massacred. Skeptics say the rune-forms and the vocabulary are not medieval, and there is no other archaeological evidence of Norsemen traveling that far west at that time. Proponents interpret the facts differently and contend that the linguistics and the geology prove it is authentic. The Smithsonian Institution has changed its opinion over the years—the Runestone was exhibited there from 1948 to 1953 as a significant historical object, but after criticism from scholars, the

ᚠᛜᛋ᛬ᚹ᛬ᚤᚷᛌᚼ᛬ᚹᛎ᛬ᛈᚤᚹᛎᛏ᛬ᛉᛏ᛬ᚼᛎ᛬
(We) have   10   men   by   the sea   to   look

ᚭᛒᛏᛁᛧ᛬ᚤᛎᛧᛎ᛬ᚼᛎᛁᛒᛌᚠᛮᛈᚤᚤᛎ᛬ᛧᛁᚼᛎ᛬
after   our   ships   14   days'   travel

ᚤᛧᚤᚤ᛬ᛈᚼᚤᚤᛮᚭᛎ᛬ᚤᛎᛧ᛬ᛌᚠᚠᚠᛮ
from   this   island. (In the) year   1362.

Part of the Kensington Runestone inscription

museum revised its description to say that experts consider the inscription spurious. Alexandria, Minnesota, the home of the Runestone Museum, calls itself the "Birthplace of America."

NOVEMBER 9 | The Milk Man Succeeded

Gail Borden Jr. (1801–1874) had no formal education, but that didn't stop him from trying his hand at a number of professions. He was a surveyor, a newspaperman, a customs collector, and an inventor. It was the last occupation that made him famous, but not without a number of failures. He developed a process to dehydrate meat and mix it with flour, and called it "meat biscuits." The product won a number of awards, but it didn't sell, and he soon lost his entire investment. Borden then turned his attention to another food idea, condensed milk, for which he received a patent in 1856. After two failed attempts to open a factory, he tried a third time with backing from a New York financier, and this time he was successful. The ability to store milk for longer than a day or two without refrigeration was just what the army needed once the Civil War began, and the government bought massive amounts of it. Borden marketed his canned milk under the name "Eagle Brand," and it is still being produced today. He died in 1874, and his grave marker bears the epitaph, "I tried and failed. I tried again and again and succeeded."

NOVEMBER 10 | Number, Please?

In 1951, the North American Numbering Plan (NANP) took effect for long distance calling, and you had to dial (not touch or press, but turn an actual rotary dial) a three-digit code to make a call outside your local area. Before that, you called the operator, who said, "Number, please?" and looked up the code and put the call through for you. Until the 1920s the operator had to find a pathway and route the call through a number of switchboards, and it might require several minutes to place a cross-country call (you would hang up and wait for her to call back when the connection was completed). Before that, even local calls went through an operator. Before that, in 1876 to make a telephone call you had to be Alexander Graham Bell with Thomas Watson down the hall. (Okay, this is a bit simplified, but you get the idea.) The first direct-dialed long distance call with an area code in the United States was made on November 10, 1951, when the mayor of Englewood, New Jersey (area code 201), called the mayor of Alameda, California (area code 415). The NANP administrators take their work very seriously; they track the phone number supply and demand and identify locations where numbers are in jeopardy of being exhausted. Then emergency procedures are implemented to monitor new numbers, and eventually an area code split may take place.

NOVEMBER 11 | Unknown Heroes

After World War I, a number of countries decided to honor the soldiers who had died in that conflict but whose remains were unidentified. Britain and France each buried one unknown soldier, in Westminster Abbey and beneath the Arc de Triomphe, respectively. Four bodies of unidentified American soldiers from four cemeteries in France were transported to the Hotel de Ville in Chalons. Sergeant Edward Younger, a highly decorated American soldier on duty in Germany, was selected to make the final choice. On October 24, 1921, Sergeant Younger entered the room, circled the caskets three times, and placed a spray of white roses on one of them. A French military band played Chopin's "Funeral March." The soldier's remains were brought to the United States, where on Armistice Day, November 11, 1921, he was laid to rest at Arlington National Cemetery in the Tomb of the Unknown Soldier. An inscription on the monument reads, "Here rests in honored glory an American soldier known but to

God," and the Sentinels of the Tomb, an elite battalion of the U.S. Army's Old Guard regiment, has maintained a twenty-four-hour watch since 1937.

NOVEMBER 12 | An Unknown Identified

In addition to the soldier from World War I, unidentified soldiers from World War II, Korea, and Vietnam were selected for burial in the Tomb of the Unknowns in Arlington Cemetery. In 1984, an unidentified soldier from the Vietnam War was placed there, with appropriate pomp and ceremony. Yet finding an unidentifiable soldier from that conflict had not been an easy task, as forensic technology had improved substantially by that time. Nonetheless, a soldier identified only as X-26 was selected and interred, on Memorial Day 1984. A decade later, however, a Vietnam vet and POW/MIA activist named Ted Sampley, the publisher of *U.S. Veteran Dispatch*, wrote an article arguing that the soldier buried at Arlington was not unknown, but most likely was Air Force 1st Lieutenant Michael Joseph Blassie. Sampley's extensive research inspired CBS News to investigate the case, and the producers also concluded that the unknown Vietnam soldier was Blassie. On May 14, 1998, the remains were exhumed, and a DNA test was done. It was indeed Blassie; his body was returned to his family in St. Louis, where he was reburied with full military honors. The crypt for the Vietnam unknown at Arlington remains vacant, and the marker was changed to read, "Honoring and Keeping Faith with America's Missing Servicemen."

NOVEMBER 13 | Renaissance Chat Room

The Pasquino was the first of Rome's famed "talking statues." Not the painted mimes who pose for tourist photos, these statues have provided an anonymous outlet for social criticism since the sixteenth century. Pasquino is an eroded and mutilated fragment of an ancient sculpture group that probably represents Menelaus, the husband of Helen of Troy; it sits in its own little square near the southern end of

Pasquino

the Piazza Navona. "During the Renaissance witty and sometimes libellous puns and comments would be found attached to this statue," explained travel writer H. V. Morton. "Some popes resented these pasquinades—so called from a tailor named Pasquino who was believed to be the originator." Among the more well-known of the *pasquinata* was this clever denunciation of Pope Urban VIII (1568–1644), a member of the powerful Barberini family, who repurposed ancient Roman artifacts for his family's palaces: "What the barbarians did not do, the Barberini did." Today's postings on the statue are more likely to lampoon government leaders—local and international, including American presidents—than the Vatican.

NOVEMBER 14 | A Bad Rap for Luddites

In today's digital world, calling people *Luddites* usually means they are opposed to modern technology and would be happier living in a pre-computer era. The original Luddites are remembered for their attacks against the textile industry, smashing machines in England, beginning in 1811. They were not actually antitechnology—some of them were quite adept with contemporary machinery—but they were worried about preserving their jobs in an economically depressed period. Historian Kevin Binfield explained, "They just wanted machines that made high-quality goods, and they wanted these machines to be run by workers who had gone through an apprenticeship and got paid decent wages. Those were their only concerns." The British government reacted, passing laws against destroying machinery, and bore down hard on the protests, which had spread across a wide swath of the country. The authorities also searched for the supposed ringleader of the movement, a man named Ned Ludd. But Ned Ludd didn't exist; he was a creation of some of the protesters, who likened him to Robin Hood and gave him a puckish persona with a penchant for mischief. His reputation spread quickly and both inspired the dissidents and frightened the government. The protests were deadly serious, however, and many Luddites were executed or exiled to Australia before the unrest died out after a few years.

NOVEMBER 15 | An Island of Kelp

The Sargasso Sea is almost as notorious as the Bermuda Triangle, but the legends of ships becoming tangled and trapped in the choking seaweed (*sargassum*) for which it is named are just that—unsubstantiated stories. The sea encompasses a large area in the Atlantic Ocean around Bermuda, and many boats were becalmed there in past centuries, not due to seaweed, but because of the lack of winds and currents. The area sits at about 30 degrees North latitude, a band called the "horse latitudes." (There are different theories for how that name came to be, the most logical being that when ships were becalmed, the horses onboard would get sick and die from lack of water and were then thrown overboard. There is also a similar band at 30 degrees South latitude.) The sea is circled by currents (including the Gulf Stream), so it appears rather like a large, slow-moving whirlpool. The Sargasso—the only sea without coastlines—has a high salt content and temperature and a deep blue color.

NOVEMBER 16 | Pizzly Grolars

Have you ever heard of pizzly bears? Perhaps by their other name, grolar bears? Pizzlies or grolars are hybrids of polar bears and grizzlies. The two species can interbreed and produce fertile offspring (unlike the offspring of horses and donkeys, which are sterile), something that is unusual in the animal world, because they shared a common ancestor as recently as twenty thousand years ago. DNA studies have shown that polar bears interbred with brown bears during the last Ice Age, but then they went their separate ways when the ice receded. In fact, a 2011 study showed that all polar bears are actually descended from brown bears that once lived in Ireland. Normally, modern polar bears and grizzlies in the wild don't mingle much during mating season, but climatic events are changing that, and many scientists believe that the diminishing natural habitat as polar ice melts will cause more hybridization of arctic animals.

NOVEMBER 17 | Getting a Rise Out of Bread

What's the difference between matzo and brioche; why is one flat and the other tall and fluffy? To put it simply, it's yeast, which is a living thing, a member of the fungus family. When added to a bread recipe, yeast produces carbon dioxide and alcohol as it consumes the sugars present in the dough and makes them ferment. This creates small bubbles of gas, and the dough rises, causing the gluten in the flour to stretch and contain the CO_2. The alcohol is dissipated during cooking and the bubbles break, leaving the bread with a light, airy texture. Matzo and some other flatbreads are made without yeast or another leavening agent. Yeast exists naturally in soil and air, so its effect was probably first discovered when it floated acci-

A loaf of bread

dentally into someone's resting flatbread dough. Other consumables are made with various types of yeast—beer and wine, in particular. It has nonfood uses as well: in ethanol production and to generate carbon dioxide in aquariums, for example.

NOVEMBER 18 | Tilt!

Before the advent of video games, pinball was the amusement of choice for millions of Americans. The predecessor of pinball was an eighteenth-century tabletop game called *bagatelle*, sort of a cross between bowling and billiards. Players set up pins at one end of a board and shot a ball at them with a small cue stick. In the next development, the pins were attached to the table and target holes were added, and the object became to ricochet the ball off the pins and into a hole. The spring-loaded plunger replaced the cue in 1870, and by the late 1920s, coin-operated mechanisms were added, which changed pinball from a parlor game to a gambling device in saloons. The first profitable coin-operated pinball machine was invented by David Gottlieb in 1931 and was called *Baffle Ball*; he sold fifty thousand units the first year. People were looking for cheap amusements during the Great Depression, and pinball filled the bill. A game craze spread across the country, and suddenly, machines could be found almost anywhere people congregated. The games were electrified in the early 1930s, bringing all of the accoutrements that came to be associated with pinball: flippers, bumpers, automatic scoring systems, bells, and flashing lights. With the advent of software and microchips in the late twentieth century, pinball tried to keep up with video games, but it seems to be a losing battle.

NOVEMBER 19 | From a Log Cabin to the White House

James Abram Garfield (1831–1881) was the last American president born in a log cabin and our first left-handed president. Trained in classical languages, he could simultaneously write in Latin with one hand and Greek with the other. He was an abolitionist, a general during the Civil War, and a supporter of African American education and suffrage. In his 1881 inaugural address, Garfield stated,

> The will of the nation, speaking with the voice of battle and through the amended Constitution, has fulfilled the great promise of 1776 by proclaiming "liberty throughout the land to all the inhabitants thereof." The elevation of the Negro race from slavery to the full rights of citizenship is the most important political change we have known since the adoption of the Constitution of 1787. No thoughtful man can fail to appreciate its beneficent effect upon our institutions and people. . . . It has liberated the master as well as the slave from a relation which wronged and enfeebled both. It has surrendered to their own guardianship the manhood of more than 5,000,000 people, and

James Garfield

has opened to each one of them a career of freedom and usefulness.

On July 2, fewer than four months into his term, President Garfield was shot in the back by Charles Giteau (usually described as a "disappointed office-seeker"). Garfield died from internal bleeding and infection on September 19, 1881.

NOVEMBER 20 | "Profoundly and Widely Distrusted"

Chester A. Arthur (1830–1886) was considered just another slick, machine politician when he obtained a patronage appointment as collector of the Port of New York from Roscoe Conkling, the boss of the Stalwart Republican faction. In 1880, the Stalwarts were at odds with the GOP's Reformer wing at their national convention. James Garfield, a Reformer, was nominated, and Arthur was selected for vice president as a sop to the Stalwarts. The ticket was elected, but Garfield was assassinated four months later by a "disappointed office seeker," who wanted Arthur to be president. To everyone's surprise, Arthur acted presidential, eschewing machine politics and even supporting the Pendleton Act, which reformed the patronage system by mandating competitive exams for public office, banning kickbacks, establishing a merit system, and creating the Civil Service Commission. That action lost him the support of the Stalwarts, without gaining the backing of the Reformers, and he was not renominated in 1884. Journalist Alexander K. McClure said of Arthur, "No man ever entered the Presidency so profoundly and widely distrusted, and no one ever retired . . . more generally respected."

NOVEMBER 21 | The Scold's Bridle

In the war between the sexes, an especially nasty chapter occurred in England and Scotland during the sixteenth to nineteenth centuries, when a device known as the brank or "scold's bridle" was used to punish a woman who was considered quarrelsome or a gossip or who was charged with "telling her mind to some petty tyrant in office, or speaking plainly to a wrong-doer, or for taking to task a lazy, and perhaps a drunken husband." The brank was an iron mask or cage that fit over the head, with a metal plate, sometimes with spikes, that pressed on the victim's tongue, making it impossible to talk without pain and injury. The primary intent was to humiliate the woman, and she was usually led through the streets and taunted by the townspeople; some branks had bells on them to call attention to the offender. Use of the brank spread to other areas, including Germany and the American colonies, and it was occasionally a method of punishment for men accused of offensive speech.

NOVEMBER 22 | The Czech Locomotive

Whenever he ran, he looked as if he was in great pain, grimacing and grunting as his body rocked from side to side, but Emil Zátopek (1922–2000) always managed to win. The great Czech runner had already set national records in the 2,000- 3,000- and 5,000-meter races when he entered the 1948 Olympics in London. He won the 10,000 meters and earned the silver medal in the 5,000. But it was in the 1952 Helsinki Olympics that Zátopek truly shone. He won the gold in the 5,000- and 10,000-meter races, setting Olympic records in both events, and then at the last minute announced that he would compete in a race he had never run before—the marathon. Not knowing anything about race strategy, he decided to shadow the favorite, Jim Peters of Britain. Peters set a blistering pace, but Zátopek kept up, even asking Peters at one point, "Is the pace too fast?" Peters, perhaps joking, said, "No." So Zátopek ran faster. Peters couldn't stay with him; he developed leg cramps and dropped out. Zátopek kept chugging along, winning the race by about half a mile and setting his third Olympic record of the games. No one before or since has matched his feat. In 1998, Emil Zátopek was awarded the Order of the White Lion by Czech president Vaclav Havel.

NOVEMBER 23 | *Dit Spruitjes*

Like many people, I didn't enjoy brussels sprouts as a child, but the vegetable seems less awful now, in adulthood. Botanically, they are cultivars of the species *Brassica oleracea*, the same group that includes cabbage, kale, kohlrabi, cauliflower, and broccoli. Although these vegetables appear very dissimilar, they're actually just different varieties of the same plant. *B. oleracea* evolved in the Mediterranean region and originally wasn't like the present-day cabbage with a firm, rounded head; it was a loose cluster of large leaves. The varieties developed over the centuries, not by scientific breeding, but through selective propagation by individuals, which encouraged particular desired traits. The brussels sprout plant has a straggly top that is not eaten, but along the stem are numerous miniature cabbage buds, which are the edible part. Most food historians place their development in northern Europe in the seventeenth or eighteenth century, although there are

unverified earlier claims. Some contend that they were cultivated around Brussels in the thirteenth century, thus giving them their present name (*choux de Bruxelles*, in the French-speaking parts of Belgium; in the Flemish areas, they're simply called *dit spruitjes*). Brussels sprouts have a long list of health benefits, most particularly their ability to reduce cholesterol and as a cancer preventative.

Brussels sprouts

NOVEMBER 24 | The President Flew in a Sacred Cow

It's become a potent symbol of the American presidency, but *Air Force One* isn't actually a particular airplane. Technically, it's the radio call sign assigned to any air force plane that is carrying the president. Franklin Delano Roosevelt was the first chief executive to fly while in office. The idea of a specially designated airplane was suggested in 1943, when a C-87A Liberator named *Guess Where II* was proposed as the president's personal transport. The Secret Service didn't like the Liberator's safety record, though, and it was rejected (but it was good enough for Eleanor Roosevelt to use on her South America trip). Instead, the first official presidential plane was the Douglas C-54 Skymaster, nicknamed *Sacred Cow*. Roosevelt flew in it only once, however, to the Yalta conference at the end of World War II. The designation *Air Force One* didn't come into use until 1953, after a commercial flight, Eastern 8610, entered the same airspace as President Dwight D. Eisenhower's plane, which was using the call sign Air Force 8610. President John F. Kennedy's Boeing 707 was the first to be popularly known as *Air Force One*. Today, two Boeing 747–200B planes (tail codes 28000 and 29000; Air Force designation VC-25A) are in use. The president's plane is obviously one of the most secure airplanes in the world; its four thousand square feet of space contain hardened electronics, secure communications technology, a medical office, and an extensive presidential suite.

NOVEMBER 25 | The Unforgiven

Captain Henry Wirz, the Confederate commander of the Andersonville prisoner-of-war camp in Georgia, was one of only two men executed for war crimes after the Civil War. (The other man put to death was Samuel "Champ" Ferguson, who had led a Southern guerrilla band.) In the period from early 1864 to Lee's surrender in April 1865, almost thirteen thousand Union soldiers died in Andersonville from malnutrition, disease, and exposure. Wirz was arrested and held in the Old Capitol Prison in Washington, D.C. (now the site of the Supreme Court) and hanged there, with soldiers gathered around the gallows chanting, "Wirz, remember Andersonville." He had been tried in a military tribunal—one of the country's first—in what is generally considered a kangaroo court. The trial was overseen by Major General Lew Wallace, who had also participated in the court that tried the Lincoln assassination conspirators (he is the author of *Ben-Hur*, one of the most popular books of the era). Neither the court nor the general populace in the North were in a forgiving mood. Anger over Lincoln's assassination was still very strong; photographs of the emaciated prisoners had been circulated, to great shock; and even poet Walt Whitman commented about Andersonville: "There are deeds, crimes that may be forgiven but this is not among them."

NOVEMBER 26 | A Woman of Valor

In all of American history, only one woman has been awarded the Medal of Honor. Her name was Mary Edwards Walker (1832–1919), and she was a medical doctor at a time when female physicians were rare. She graduated from the Syracuse Medical College in 1855 and, at the outbreak of the Civil War, traveled to Washington with the intention of joining the army as a medical officer. She was rejected, so she volunteered as an assistant surgeon and served in that capacity for various units through the war years, continually agitating for a commission. In April 1864, she was captured by the Confederates and held for a few months at Castle Thunder prison near Richmond. Finally, that October, she was given a commission as acting assistant surgeon, the first female physician in the U.S. Army. In 1865, President Andrew Johnson signed a bill awarding Mary Walker the Medal of Honor, because she "has devoted herself with much patriotic zeal to the sick and wounded soldiers, both in the field and hospitals, to the detriment of her own health, and has also endured hardships as a prisoner of war." She continued to practice medicine after the war and took up the cause

Mary Edwards Walker

of women's rights with great zeal. She had long preferred to wear men's clothing and was even arrested several times for "masquerading" as a man. In 1917, Congress changed the criteria for awarding a Medal of Honor, restricting it to those who had engaged in actual combat with an enemy. Hundreds of medals, including Mary Walker's, were rescinded. She refused to return hers, however, and wore it proudly until her death. In 1977, President Jimmy Carter reinstated Mary Walker's Medal of Honor, recognizing her "distinguished gallantry, self-sacrifice, patriotism, dedication and unflinching loyalty to her country, despite the apparent discrimination because of her sex."

NOVEMBER 27 | A Parade Like No Other

R.H. Macy's, the famed New York department store, decided to sponsor a Christmas parade in 1924. Clowns, acrobats, Macy's employees, and animals from the Central Park Zoo marched from Harlem to the flagship store at 34th Street and Herald Square. It was a huge success and started an annual tradition, renamed the Macy's Thanksgiving Day Parade. In 1927, large balloons joined the parade for the first time. Filled with helium, they were let go during the finale of the parade but unexpectedly burst as they rose. The next year, with redesigned valves, the balloons were again released, this time with an offer from Macy's of $100 for the return of any balloon. For decades afterward, the helium was simply discharged into the atmosphere at the parade's end. In 1958, helium supplies were low, and the balloons were filled with air and placed on trucks. Due to a combination of environmental concerns and the high cost of helium, a recovery-and-recycling program for the helium was begun by Linde North America in 2008. Millions of people line the parade route every year, and tens of millions watch on television.

NOVEMBER 28 | Easy as Cake

When a person is learning a foreign language, one of the most important and difficult aspects to master is the grasping of idioms. Idioms can reveal a great deal not only about the language, but also about the local culture and the way people think. Here are some interesting examples of idioms, with their English equivalents, drawn from Simon Ager's website Omniglot.com, the online encyclopedia of writing systems and languages:

Cheyenne: *Étaomêhótsenôhtóvenestse napâhpóneehéhame*; my tapeworm can almost talk by itself = my stomach is growling.

Mandarin/Cantonese: 杯弓蛇影 (*bēi gōng shé yǐng / būi gōng sèh yíng*); seeing the reflection of a bow in a cup and thinking it's a snake = worrying about things that aren't there.

Italian: *avere gli occhi foderati di prosciutto*; to have one's eyes lined with ham = can't see the wood for the trees.

Serbian: *Nosom para oblake*; he's ripping clouds with his nose = he's conceited, puffed up.

Russian: Вешать лапшу на уши (*Vešat' lapšu na ušy*); to hang noodles on one's ears = to tell lies, talk nonsense.

Japanese: 猿も木から落ちる (*Saru mo ki kara ochiru*); even monkeys fall from trees = even experts get it wrong.

French: *pédaler dans la choucroute*; to pedal in the sauerkraut = to spin your wheels, to go nowhere.

Dutch: *Ijsberen*; to polar bear = to pace up and down.

Hindi: अंगारे उगलना (*angare ubalna*); to excrete embers = to get very angry.

And this one, which is my editor's favorite:

French: *faire du lèche-vitrine*; to lick the windows = to go window shopping.

NOVEMBER 29 | A Very Big Hit

Thirty-five million years ago, a bolide (a large extraterrestrial object, such as an asteroid or a comet) struck the Earth at the site of Chesapeake Bay. It was huge, spraying water as high as thirty miles and spewing millions of tons of rock and sediment into the air. Gigantic tsunamis followed, and aquatic life was destroyed for hundreds of miles around. According to one scientist, the strike "fractured the crystalline bedrock below to at least a depth of 7 miles (11 kilometers) and a width of 85 miles (137 kilometers). This was a big hit." Yet this cataclysm remained unknown until 1983, when scientists drilling deep sea core samples off the Atlantic coast noticed the signatures of a meteor strike. The center of the impact seems to have been on the southern tip of the Delmarva peninsula, near the town of Cape Charles in Virginia. Did the collision actually create Chesapeake Bay? It certainly had something to do with the bay's eventual formation, because it depressed the sea bed and altered the course of rivers flowing into it. More than 150 impact craters have been identified around the globe, from various time periods. At about the same time as the Chesapeake Bay impact, a larger bolide hit Siberia; the strike in the Yucatan region of Mexico that is considered the likely cause of the extinction of the dinosaurs occurred much earlier, about sixty-five million years ago.

NOVEMBER 30 | "Untrammeled Womanhood"

The bicycle was a truly remarkable invention. Evolving from the simple mechanical hobby horse of Baron von Drais in 1817 through the high-wheeled models and tricycles to the modern pneumatic-tired safety bikes, bicycles provided ordinary people with access to horseless personal transportation. But they also offered women a freedom they had never before enjoyed, with a new emphasis on exercise and health, and they instituted a profound change in fashions. Corsets and petticoats began to be replaced by tailored blouses and split skirts. All of this came with substantial amounts of criticism, of course. Many men didn't like the idea of "mannish women" who would lose their feminine charm. In an interview in 1896, Susan B. Anthony said, "Let me tell you what I think of bicy-cling. I think it has done more to emanci-pate women than anything else in the world. It gives women a feeling of freedom and self-reliance. I stand and rejoice every time I see a woman ride by on a wheel . . . the picture of free, untrammeled womanhood."

A ladies' safety bicycle

DECEMBER

DECEMBER 1 | Cavernous Music

The Great Stalacpipe Organ is said to be the largest musical instrument in the world, covering about three and a half acres. In 1954, Leland Sprinkle was visiting the Luray Caverns in Virginia with his young son. Their tour guide tapped one of the stalactites hanging from the cave ceiling, and it produced a beautiful sound. Sprinkle had an idea. He tested thousands of the stalactites for tone, then attached rubber-tipped plungers activated by solenoids to some three dozen of them. He wired the solenoids to an organ keyboard, and the Great Stalacipe Organ was born. It took Sprinkle three years to complete it, then there were decades of tweaking to get it just right. The stalactites are tuned by sanding them until they strike a pitch-perfect note. It is not an easy instrument to play; the sound is gentle and ethereal and doesn't reach the player until a full second after the note is struck. The solenoids require constant maintenance because of the high humidity in the cave. Although the organ can be played manually, the songs are usually produced by an automated system, much like a gigantic player piano.

DECEMBER 2 | Freedom Triumphant

It can be difficult to discern from the ground whether the statue atop the U.S. Capitol depicts a Native American woman (Pocahontas?), a figure from ancient Rome (Minerva?), or something else entirely. The original wood-and-copper dome of the Capitol had been completed in 1824, but within thirty years it was seen as too small (and a fire hazard), so Congress authorized a plan to replace it. Sculptor Thomas Crawford was commissioned in 1855 to design an allegorical figure to crown the building, which he originally called *Freedom Triumphant in War and Peace*. After several mishaps, including the death of the artist, the plaster model for the statue was cast in bronze, with much of the work done by an enslaved Maryland foundry worker named Philip Reid. The sections were hoisted into place and assembled, and the project was completed in 1863. Here's the description of the Statue of Freedom, from the Architect of the Capitol website:

> [A] classical female figure of Freedom wearing flowing draperies. Her right hand rests upon the hilt of a sheathed sword; her left holds a laurel wreath of victory and the shield of the United States with thirteen stripes. Her helmet is encircled by stars and features a crest composed of an eagle's head, feathers, and talons, a reference to the costume of Native Americans. A brooch inscribed *U.S.* secures her fringed robes. She stands on a cast-iron globe encircled with the words *E Pluribus Unum*.

In 1993, the Statue of Freedom was removed for repairs and restoration and was returned to its pedestal five months later, this time by helicopter.

DECEMBER 3 | Talking Strings

The Empire of the Incas (or Inkas) in South America (1400–1535 CE) has long puzzled scholars, because it appeared that the people had no writing system to administer their territory, which stretched through the Andes from Ecuador to Chile. They did have a method for recording numbers for census, commerce, taxation, and other purposes. They used bundles of knotted strings, called khipu (or *quipu*, which means "knot" in the Quechua language), made of cotton or llama or alpaca hair. The type of knots, their location and orientation on the strings, and their color signified different numerical values, and they could be quite elaborate and complex. You can think of a khipu as an abacus made of textiles, which isn't surprising, because the Inca used fibers the way other civilizations used clay, metal, or stone. Some scholars believe that khipu also expressed nonnumerical content—narrative or verbal data presented in a sort of binary code. Unfortunately, many khipu were destroyed by Spanish conquistadores and missionaries, but researchers continue to work on about seven hundred specimens that remain, hoping one day to find a "Rosetta khipu" that will allow them to decipher their true meaning and function.

DECEMBER 4 | A Muscular Primer

What a piece of work is man—and woman, for that matter. Consider the human muscle system (from the Latin *musculus*, "little mouse"). Each of us has more than 630 muscles—accounting for at least 40 percent of our body weight—that contract and relax, allowing us to walk, breathe, and digest. Among the skeletal or voluntary muscles, the smallest is the stapedius in the ear; it's connected to the smallest bones in the body, the ossicles of the middle ear. The largest muscle is the gluteus maximus in the buttocks. The tongue (actually, a group of muscles) is the only one that's not attached at both ends, and it's one of the strongest. The jaw also has a very strong muscle, the masseter, which enables the jawbone to produce about two hundred pounds of force on the molars. Eyelid-blinking muscles are the fastest; we are able to blink up to five times a second (but most of us don't). The other muscles that control eye movement are also pretty busy,

Part of the chest and arm muscle system

moving about a hundred thousand times a day. There are two other types of muscles: smooth and cardiac. Smooth muscles, such as those in the stomach and the blood vessels, are associated with involuntary motion. Cardiac muscles are found in only one place, the heart.

DECEMBER 5 | It's All Thumbs

The African thumb piano has many different local names: *kalimba, mbira, sansa, ikembe.* The instruments vary in size and sound but are all essentially the same thing: a plucked idiophone. An idiophone ("self-sounder") is "a class of musical instruments in which a resonant solid material—such as wood, metal, or stone—vibrates to produce the initial sound." A thumb piano is a wooden box with thin metal or wooden strips mounted on the top, clamped to the box at one end, and elevated by a metal bar that serves as a bridge. The box is held with the fingers while the thumbs pluck the strips. The strips (or tongues) are of different lengths, sounding different notes. It's an ancient instrument, so old that one African myth says that metal was first given to humans by the creator when the world was young, so that they could make kalimbas. Archaeologists have uncovered a bamboo thumb piano from 1000 BCE. There are several different traditional African tunings in use, but the diatonic scale has become the most popular in the West. The kalimba can be used as a solo instrument, to accompany singers or dancers or to call on ancestral spirits.

A kalimba

DECEMBER 6 | "Running Scared"

Roy Orbison was not your typical rock star. Where most male rockers had swagger, Orbison wore thick glasses and projected a shy persona. Where most rock songs were written in a conventional format (verse-chorus-verse-chorus-bridge-verse-chorus), Orbison explored a variety of structures. Most rockers gyrate and dance to the beat as they perform, but Orbison stood nearly motionless. His voice was pure and clear, with incredible range. Nowhere are those qualities more evident than on his hit "Running Scared," recorded in 1961. He used a bolero-type repetitive rhythm, perhaps the first time it had been used in rock. There was no chorus, the song built continually until the climax—a triumphant high note (G above high C) that he intended to sing in falsetto. His producer, Fred Foster, suggested he try singing it without the falsetto so that it would cut through the full orchestra and the backup singers. Foster describes what happened: "Then we came to the end, and Roy hit that note full voice. I'm surprised the musicians didn't just lay down their instruments. Harold Bradley's eyes widened and he stood up, still playing his guitar, but with his mouth wide open. . . . I knew I had a star who could combine opera, blues, country and soul." Roy Orbison was enjoying a resurgence of his career and had a song on the charts when he died suddenly of a heart attack on December 6, 1988.

DECEMBER 7 | A Day of Infamies

Pearl Harbor, Hawaii, wasn't the only target of Japanese attacks on December 7, 1941. As part of their overall strategy to control oil and other raw materials in southeast Asia, the Japanese wanted to destroy America's military capabilities in the Pacific. Pearl Harbor was the primary target, but well-coordinated, surprise attacks were also launched on Guam, Wake Island, the Philippines, Malaya, Thailand, China, and Midway Island, in preparation for a full-scale invasion and occupation. Guam was hit by dive bombers at 8:27 a.m., and the marines' barracks, a radio station, a hotel, and several warships were struck. Japanese planes assaulted British Malaya and Thailand, landing troops in both locations with the aim of uniting them and heading south to Singapore. Artillery batteries, airfields, and a power plant were hit on Midway Island. The foreign quarter of Shanghai was occupied, and Hong Kong was bombed. The Philippine airfields were attacked and most of America's fighters and bombers were destroyed. The war in the Pacific, a struggle to control one-third of the Earth's surface that would continue for almost four years, had begun.

DECEMBER 8 | Revolutionary Artists

She is an icon of modern feminist art and Mexican identity; he is an icon of public art and political engagement. Frida Kahlo (1907–1954) and Diego Rivera (1886–1957) were destined to be one of the more interesting artist couples of the twentieth century. Born in Coyoacán, Kahlo had a difficult childhood. She suffered with polio and then the effects of a serious bus accident that caused deep pain for the rest of her life. While convalescing, she took up painting and showed great talent. Introduced to the world of art and leftist politics, she became close to Diego Rivera, already an established muralist. Rivera had been born in Guanajuato; his father was a liberal politician who supported Diego's artistic ambitions and arranged for him to study in Europe. Frida and Diego married in 1929, then divorced and remarried; their life was tempestuous. But it was their art that made them the center of Mexico's cultural and political life. Kahlo produced numerous portraits of herself garbed in traditional Tehuana dress, reflecting pride in her Mexican and her feminist individuality. Rivera's giant wall paintings were revolutionary in their political approach, particularly in his devotion to Mexican peasants and workers; one biographer called him "an evangelist-in-paint for social reform." Together, they represented a vision of the country's glorious past and contemporary culture that continues to influence the world's perception of Mexico.

DECEMBER 9 | The Man Who Never Was

The quest for the "missing link" in human evolution—the transitional stage between apes and humans—had been raging ever since Charles Darwin published *The Descent of Man* in 1871. In 1912, it appeared that the answer had been found near the town of Piltdown in southern England. Amateur archaeologist Charles Dawson brought some fossils to Sir Arthur Smith Woodward, the keeper of geology at the Natural History Museum in London. Among those fossils were a humanlike cranium fragment and an apelike jaw, so if it turned out that they came from the same individual, it would be that missing

The Piltdown skull

link. Woodward concluded that the fragments did belong to one skull. Other scientists disagreed, but they were soon overshadowed by those who hailed the new discovery, especially the press. About forty years later, scientists were finally able to prove that it was actually a modern human cranium and the jaw of an orangutan. Piltdown Man was a forgery, albeit a very clever one, and the paleontological community was greatly embarrassed. The identity of the hoaxer has remained a mystery, though there was no lack of suspects: Dawson and Woodward, of course, but also Sir Arthur Conan Doyle, who lived nearby, and Jesuit paleontologist and philosopher Pierre Teilhard de Chardin.

DECEMBER 10 | The Great Wall of Hollywood

Reusing old movie sets for new films is nothing unusual in Hollywood; sets can be expensive, and if money could be saved by recycling, the studios didn't hesitate. One set in particular has an intriguing history. For the Cecil B. DeMille 1927 silent epic *King of Kings*, a towering set was built on the Culver City back lot known as "40 Acres" to represent the Temple of Jerusalem. Five years later, when shooting began for the Merian Cooper classic *King Kong*, the temple was redressed to look like a gigantic wall, with huge wooden doors and a gong on top to summon the giant ape. The wall next appeared in the Marlene Dietrich vehicle *Garden of Allah* in 1935 and then met its final, glorious demise in David O. Selznick's classic *Gone with the Wind*. On December 10, 1938, the scenes of the burning of Atlanta were filmed, and the great wall went up in flames so high that nervous nearby residents called the Fire Department.

DECEMBER 11 | Leonardo's Copter

The first certified human-powered helicopter was developed by students at California Polytechnic State University. In December 1989, after several failed attempts, the *Da Vinci III* flew for 7.1 seconds and reached eight inches of altitude. The experiment was conducted in the university gym, because the copter was so lightweight (it was made mostly of balsa wood and plastic) that any outdoor breeze would likely have overturned the craft. The pilot reclined in a cage suspended from two rotors and pedaled a bicycle mechanism, driving the propellers on the ends of the rotors and providing the lift. The machine was named in honor of Leonardo da Vinci, who sketched an aerial screw in his notebook that's considered the first helicopter design; he never built one but made this observation, "If this instrument made with a screw be well made—that is to say, made of linen of which the pores are stopped up with starch and be turned swiftly, the said screw will make its spiral in the air and it will rise high."

DECEMBER 12 | *Die Älteste Funnie*

The longest-running comic strip of all time is *The Katzenjammer Kids*, which was first published 115 years ago. Inspired by the German children's story *Max und Moritz*, German American illustrator Rudolph Dirks created *The Katzenjammer Kids*, and it premiered in the Sunday supplement of William Randolph Hearst's *New York Journal* on December 12, 1897. It starred Hans and Fritz, two incorrigible boys who were constantly aggravating Mama; the characters spoke in an Anglicized German dialect. Dirks took time off in 1898 to fight in the Spanish-American War, and when he returned, he added new characters, including Der Captain and the Inspector, a truant officer. In 1912, Dirks wanted to travel for a year, and Hearst gave the strip to another cartoonist, Harold H. Knerr. When Dirks returned, he took Hearst to court to regain control of the strip. In the settlement, Hearst and Knerr retained *The Katzenjammer Kids*, but Dirks was allowed to use the characters under another name, so he created *The Captain and the Kids* for a rival newspaper; it ran for more than fifty years. *The Katzenjammer Kids*—during World War I, the name was changed to *The Shenanigan Kids*—is still being drawn today, now by Hy Eisman, and is syndicated by King Features.

DECEMBER 13 | Sacred Beetles

Wander through any museum with Egyptian artifacts on exhibit and you will surely notice all of the insects—amulets, jewelry, and seals crafted to look like the dung beetle or scarab (*Scarabeus sacer*). Scarabs were sacred to Egyptians from all walks of life, similar to the way that the cross is significant to Christians. The beetles lay their eggs in dung, then roll the little ball in front of them as the larvae grow. This activity reminded Egyptians of the god Khepri ("He who is Coming into Being"), who pushes the ball of the sun through the sky. Scarabs thus came to symbolize rebirth and were thought to contain magical powers and provide protection from evil. The flat bottom of the scarab was used for all sorts of inscriptions—names, wishes, mottos, prayers, or images of gods or other sacred symbols. Heart scarabs, those

included in burials, were thought to prevent the hearts from testifying against their owners when they were judged before Osiris. Part of an inscription on one reads: "Do not create opposition against me among the assessors! Do not tip the scales against me in the presence of the Keeper of the Balance! . . . When you go forth to the Hereafter, my name shall not stink to the courtiers who create people on his behalf. Do not tell lies about me in the presence of the Great God!"

Scarabs

DECEMBER 14 | Moving through Snow on Boards

Skiing—today an extremely popular recreational and competitive sport—began as a mode of transportation that predates the wheel. During the last Ice Age, about twenty thousand years ago, people in northern Europe and Asia probably began to attach long, narrow pieces of wood to their boots as a means of moving easily through snow. There's an ancient Siberian myth that explains the Milky Way as the ski tracks of a great hunter who pursued Xeglun, the elk of the heavens. Remnants of wooden skis dating back eight thousand years have been uncovered in Russia, and archaeologists have identified

Neolithic rock carvings and drawings that depict people on skis. Roland Huntford, the author of *Two Planks and a Passion, the Dramatic History of Skiing*, explains that "together with the hammer, the knife and the axe, the ski is one of the few Stone Age implements handed down to us in their original form. . . . The origins of skiing are bound up with the emergence of modern man." He also points out that Roald Amundsen and his team won the race to the South Pole in 1911 in part because they were better skiers than their English rivals.

DECEMBER 15 | One Tongue, One People

On December 15, 1859, Ludovic Lazarus Zamenhof was born in Bialystok, Poland—then part of the Russian Empire. Many different tongues were spoken in Bialystok, and the young Zamenhof displayed a facility for languages. He became fluent in Russian, Yiddish, Polish, and German and later learned French, Latin, Greek, Hebrew, and English. While in secondary school, he began working on a new international language, one that he hoped would serve as a way to bring people of different nations and cultures together in peace. Based on Romance languages, it used twenty-two letters of the Latin alphabet plus six new letters, each representing a single sound. Zamenhof attended medical school and became an ophthalmologist but continued to tinker with his creation. Finally, in 1887, he published *Lingvo Internacia* under the pen name Doktoro Esperanto ("Doctor Hopeful"). The name Esperanto stuck. In an address at the First World Congress of Esperanto in 1905, Zamenhof proclaimed,

> for the first time in human history, we, citizens of the most diverse nations, stand side by side, not as strangers, not as competitors, but as *brothers*, who, understanding each other without forcing our own languages on each other, do not regard each other with suspicion because ignorance divides us, but love each other and shake hands, not in the insincere manner of one foreigner to another, but sincerely, as human to human.

The language did not catch on as quickly as Zamenhof hoped, but it did spread slowly and steadily. Today the number of Esperanto speakers is estimated at anywhere from a hundred thousand to a few million. It may not have established world peace, but it is the most successful invented language ever created.

DECEMBER 16 | Wham-O

It's rare in the world of fad amusements to hit on one successful idea, but Richard Knerr and Arthur "Spud" Melin managed to find two in two years. Their attempt to popularize falconry had failed, but the slingshots they used to train the birds sold well. Knerr and Melin named their company Wham-O, after the sound made by the sling-shots. Then they bought the rights for a plastic flying disc called the Pluto Platter from its designer Fred Morrison. It was released in 1957 and caught on immediately. The next year they produced a new toy based on a bamboo ring that Australian children were playing with. The Hula Hoop became a true national fad, selling twenty-five mil-lion units in just four months. The hoop was nothing new; children in ancient Egypt had played with hoops of dried grapevines, and Greeks used them for exercise around 500 BCE. The Wham-O flying disc wasn't a new idea either. Kids on the East Coast had been fling-ing around pie plates from the Frisbie Pie Company for a while before Wham-O released the Pluto Platter. The new plastic discs were widely referred to as Frisbies, and Wham-O wisely chose to change the name of its product to match (with a slightly different spelling). Wham-O still produces both Hula Hoops and Frisbees.

DECEMBER 17 | The Pope's Cocaine

In the 1860s, a young Corsican chemist named Angelo Mariani was developing a variety of medicinal wine. These tonics were very popular at the time, but Mariani's was unusual—he infused his Bordeaux with coca leaves. The stimulating concoction was an immediate hit, and within two decades Mariani had become the largest importer of coca leaves in Europe. The wine wasn't successful only because of the kick it provided; Mariani also proved a master at marketing and promotion, garnering endorsements from all sorts of celebrities, including Queen Victoria, Thomas Edison, aviator Alberto Santos-Dumont, and writers Jules Verne and Emile Zola. Pope Leo XIII, who was said to carry a hip flask filled with Vin Mariani, awarded a gold medal to Mariani as a benefactor of humanity. The cocaine content was not actually very high, because the more coca leaves that were added, the worse it tasted. Many American wine companies developed their own versions of coca wine, and some started adding refined cocaine, getting a higher content without the disagreeable flavor. Mariani died in 1914, a wealthy man.

DECEMBER 18 | Delicious, Refreshing, Exhilarating

The therapeutic properties of coca were all the rage in the 1880s. Cocaine was marketed as a stimulant, a digestif, an aphrodisiac, an anesthetic, and a cure for morphine addiction, which was a growing problem in the United States. It was that last benefit that caught the eye of an Atlanta druggist named John Stith Pemberton, who was himself struggling with morphine dependence. Noting the success of Angelo Mariani's coca wine, in 1885 he developed his own imitation— Pemberton's French Wine Coca. In addition to cocaine, it also contained caffeine from kola nuts, another highly touted stimulant. The wine sold well until Atlanta and surrounding Fulton County instituted a prohibition against alcohol in 1886. Pemberton took out the wine and began to experiment with different flavorings for what he called a "temperance drink." The result was a new beverage that would eventually become a global symbol of the United States, Coca-Cola.

DECEMBER 19 | The Tree of Life

There's an African legend about the origin of the baobab tree (*Adansonia digitata*). One day it noticed how beautiful the other trees were and complained to the creator about its own odd

A baobab tree

appearance: a fat, stubby trunk; pale flowers; tiny leaves; and wrinkled bark like elephant skin. The creator, insulted and angry, lifted the tree out of the ground, turned it over, and planted it upside down to silence its whining. To make amends, the tree has given much sustenance to humans ever since. Its fruit, leaves, bark, and even its size have all proved extremely useful. The fruit (called monkey bread) is tasty and highly nutritious, the leaves are edible and also have medicinal value, the bark is used for cloth and rope, and the trunks are so big they can serve as human shelters. The baobab, the world's largest succulent plant, stores water in its trunk for use in the dry season, and that water can also be tapped by people. The trees can live up to several thousand years and provide homes for many species of birds, lizards, frogs, squirrels, monkeys, insects, and so on. No wonder it is known as the Tree of Life. Indigenous to Africa, Australia, and Madagascar, the baobab is now cultivated in many tropical areas around the globe.

DECEMBER 20 | Thanks to Haiti

At the beginning of the nineteenth century, as the enslaved people of Haiti were successfully fighting the troops of Napoleon Bonaparte, American president Thomas Jefferson was worried about French control of the Mississippi and their possible expansion into the West. He began negotiating with France to purchase the city of New Orleans for $2 million. With his plans for a renewed sugar empire disintegrating, Napoleon exclaimed, "damn sugar, damn coffee, damn colonies," and that—along with other factors—caused the emperor to rethink his western colonization strategy and decide to cut his losses. At the suggestion of his finance minister, Napoleon sold not only New Orleans, but the entirety of France's North American holdings—about 820,000 square miles—to the United States. After obtaining approval from Congress, Jefferson concluded the Louisiana Purchase for the price of $15 million, roughly three cents per acre, and doubled the size of the country. The transfer took place on this day in 1803.

DECEMBER 21 | The Lightest Substance Ever Made

In November 2011, scientists announced that they had invented the lightest solid material on Earth. A team from the University of California at Irvine, HRL Laboratories, and Caltech developed an "ultralight metallic microlattice" that is one hundred times lighter than Styrofoam but also has strength, resiliency, and the ability to absorb energy. "Ultralight" here means less than ten milligrams per cubic centimeter. "The trick is to fabricate a lattice of interconnected hollow tubes with a wall thickness 1,000 times thinner than a human hair," said Tobias Shaedler of HRL. The material is 99.9 percent air and is so light you can put a piece of it on a dandelion fluff without crushing it. The scientists don't have any practical applications for it yet, but it could be used for insulation, shock absorption, and even battery electrodes. Although the scientists used nickel for the prototype, the lattice can be made from a variety of materials. When asked what would happen if you tossed it into the air, Bill Carter of HRL explained, "It's sort of like a feather—it floats down. . . . It takes more than 10 seconds . . . to fall if you drop it from shoulder height."

DECEMBER 22 | Wales Aligned

Corduroy may sound like a French word (cord or rope of kings), but it was the British who coined it, possibly in order to imply that the cloth was from France. The French actually call it *velours côtelé*. The *Oxford English Dictionary* defines corduroy as "A kind of coarse, thick-ribbed cotton stuff, worn chiefly by labourers or persons engaged in rough work." It is a member of the textile group called fustians (such as velveteen and moleskin), with tufted cords or wales that form ridges. Fans of the fabric started the Corduroy Appreciation Club (CAC), which strives to celebrate the importance of corduroy; "All Wales Welcome" is their slogan. They had a grand celebration on November 11, 2011, because the numerical notation of that date—11/11/11— looks like corduroy; "the wales have aligned," said one CAC member. The word *corduroy* also describes a type of road made with logs or tree trunks that resembles the wales of the cloth.

DECEMBER 23 | Lost Language Revealed

Hieroglyphics was the formal pictorial writing system of ancient Egypt, the symbols we see on monuments and inside tombs. For everyday use, a simpler version had been developed, called demotic script. By the fifth century CE, both were dying out, and eventually the ability to decipher hieroglyphics disappeared. In 1799, Napoleon's soldiers stationed in the Egyptian town of Rosetta (Rashid) discovered a large basalt slab on which a text was inscribed in three scripts—hieroglyphics, demotic, and ancient Greek. A British scientist made some headway with a translation, but it was Frenchman Jean-François Champollion who achieved the breakthrough. Champollion had a wonderful facility for languages, and in comparing the two untranslatable scripts with the known Greek text, he sensed that hieroglyphics were not only pictograms but represented phonetic sounds as well. The first word he translated was the name of the pharaoh Rameses. He ran to his brother at the Institut de France and shouted, "I've found it!" and immediately fainted. The text was a decree concerning King Ptolemy V, written in 196 BCE; the first line reads, "In the reign of the young one who has succeeded his father in the kingship, lord of diadems, most glorious, who has established Egypt and is pious towards the gods, triumphant over his enemies, who has restored the civilised life of men." Because Champollion's translation reopened an ancient culture to modern eyes, the Rosetta stone remains one of the most important archaeological finds of all time.

DECEMBER 24 | Fire Plants

Dinoflagellates are a group of one-celled microorganisms, most of which are sea plankton. As such, they are a vital first link in the marine food chain, photosynthesizing light energy into consumable chemical energy. Some species are called *Pyrrhophyta*, fire plants, because they are bioluminescent. They glow, and when agitated, they glow very brightly. Bioluminescence can appear anywhere at sea, but there are only a few places where dinoflagellates congregate in large numbers with some regularity. One of those sites is Mosquito Bay in Puerto Rico's Vieques Island. It's also called Bioluminescent Bay, and regular tours are conducted where visitors can canoe and swim in the waters at night with the glowing microorganisms, which one tourist described as "neon blue champagne bubbles." Yet dinoflagellates are not completely benign. Sometimes an excess of nutrients from the ocean floor can rise to the surface, feeding the plankton and causing a population explosion or "bloom" that may turn golden or red in color and is then called a "red tide." This condition can be harmful to marine and human life, due to the toxins produced by some species of dinoflagellates.

DECEMBER 25 | "The Scintillating Evergreen"

An associate of Thomas Edison, Edward Hibberd Johnson, is said to have been the first person to put electric lights on a Christmas tree, in 1882. A reporter for the *Detroit Post and Tribune* visited the Johnsons' home and saw "a large Christmas tree presenting a most picturesque and uncanny aspect. It was brilliantly lighted with many colored globes about as large as an English walnut and was turning some six times a minute. . . . The scintillating evergreen was a pretty sight." A couple of decades later, strings of lights became commercially available

President Calvin Coolidge lighting the tree

but were very expensive. The first U.S. president to push a button and illuminate the National Christmas Tree was Calvin Coolidge, in 1923; by 2009, the National Tree was using LED (light-emitting diode) technology exclusively. Because of the energy crisis in 1973, Richard Nixon didn't light the tree; floodlights illuminated it from the base, but there were no lights on the tree itself. Jimmy Carter left the tree dark in 1979 and '80, to honor the Americans who were being held hostage in Iran. In the United States, we use about thirty billion lightbulbs in holiday decorating each year.

DECEMBER 26 | "I Have Not Killed"

Thirty-eight Native American men were hanged in a prison camp in Mankato, Minnesota, on December 26, 1862—the largest mass execution in American history. They had been taken prisoner during the U.S.-Dakota War, a six-week fight between Sioux tribes and white settlers, following years of treaty violations and attacks on settlements. Hdainyanka (Rattling Runner), one of the condemned men, wrote in a letter just before his death, "I have not killed, wounded or injured a white man, or any white persons. I have not participated in the plunder of their property. . . . When my children are grown up, let them know that their father died because he followed the advice of his chief, and without having the blood of a white man to answer for to the Great Spirit." Astoundingly, 303 men had been condemned to death, but President Abraham Lincoln commuted most of the sentences. The Sioux Wars continued in the region until 1890 and ended with the Battle of Wounded Knee in South Dakota. In 1997, the city of Mankato dedicated Reconciliation Park and a statue of a white buffalo to honor the executed warriors.

DECEMBER 27 | Child Hatcheries

Babies born prematurely have always had difficulty thriving, and for most of human history their survival rate was poor. In 1878, E. D.

Tarnier, a French obstetrician, saw a warming chamber that was used for poultry and thought it might be helpful for human preemies, so he soon introduced an enclosed incubator at a Paris hospital, where it was used successfully. Two decades later, a physician named Martin Couney set up an exhibit of incubators at the World Exposition in Berlin, with premature infants from a local charity hospital. He called the display *Kinderbrutanstalt*—child hatchery. It was a huge success and helped spread the word about incubators but also unfortunately connected them with fairs and cheap amusements. More European demonstrations followed, and in 1901, Couney arranged a display at the Pan-American Exposition in Buffalo. Others noticed the commercial potential of the baby shows, and they began to proliferate. Couney settled in Coney Island in 1903, where for the next forty years he exhibited his incubator babies every summer. He didn't charge the mothers for the infants' care but did charge admission to view them. These preemie sideshows were an odd combination of science and hucksterism, but they did help inform both medical professionals and the public at large about neonatal incubators.

DECEMBER 28 | Insects Float

Fire ants (*Solenopsis invicta*) have evolved some amazing skills in order to keep their colonies intact and safe. They can collect themselves together to function as tools—constructing temporary walls, ladders, or bridges. Perhaps the most incredible example of their cooperative behavior is their ability to float. An individual ant will founder in water, but a group can actually turn itself into a raft. By locking together their jaws and legs, they create a tight mat of ants, "a self-assembled hydrophobic surface." Each ant's body is slightly water-repellent and has a thin layer of air clinging to it, so when massed in a group, they become buoyant and waterproof and can float for days or longer, enabling them to survive floods and migrate to form new colonies.

A fire ant

DECEMBER 29 | Liquid Fire

In the nineteenth century, scientists began to experiment with passing an electric current through a gas in a glass vacuum tube, causing it to glow. This led to the development of electric discharge lamps, which used carbon dioxide, mercury vapor, or other gases to produce light. Then French inventor Georges Claude designed a lamp that used the recently discovered gas called *neon*, which he successfully demonstrated in 1910—two thirty-nine-foot-long tubes that glowed bright red. The commercial possibilities of luminous advertising were immediately apparent, and the neon sign was born. (Although they're all referred to as "neon tubes," other gases are actually used to produce other colors.) The first sign was made for a small barber shop in Paris in 1912, and the next year a larger one for Cinzano vermouth appeared on the Champs-Elysees. Ten years later, Claude sold his first neon signs in the United States, to a Packard automobile dealer in Los Angeles. The American landscape has not been the same since.

DECEMBER 30 | Bridging East and West

Isamu Noguchi (1904–1988) was a sculptor, an architect, and a man of two worlds. Born in Los Angeles to an American mother and a Japanese father, he lived in Japan when he was a child but returned to the United States and attended medical school for a short time before he realized sculpture was his true calling. He studied in Paris with Constantin Brancusi and then worked in both abstract and portrait sculpture; the portraits gained him recognition, especially a stunning bust of George Gershwin. Noguchi next traveled to Mexico to work on a mural with painter Diego Rivera and developed an affinity for large-scale pieces. In the 1930s, he began to work on public sculptures, including a stainless steel bas-relief on the Associated Press building in New York. In Japan, Noguchi created gardens and fountains that combined his interest in sculpture and architecture. In the United States, he designed sets for choreographers Martha Graham, Merce Cunningham, and George Balanchine. He never belonged to a particular school but knew and developed bonds with many artists from different disciplines. Beyond his public art, he is remembered for his domestic designs, including a free-form coffee table and Akari lamps that remain popular. The museum he founded provides this description of Noguchi's work: "Through a lifetime of artistic experimentation, he created sculptures, gardens, furniture and lighting designs, ceramics, architecture, and set designs. His work, at once subtle and bold, traditional and modern, set a new standard for the reintegration of the arts."

DECEMBER 31 | The Little Ice Age

During the years 1550 to 1850, the Earth experienced a period of cooler temperatures that is called the Little Ice Age (LIA). Although it was not a true ice age, this moderate cooling still had some obvious and some subtle effects, particularly in Europe. Many rivers and lakes—and even the Baltic Sea—froze over; encroaching glaciers caused the abandonment of some villages in Switzerland; and a shorter growing season led to famine in many areas. A study of European paintings revealed an increase in the depiction of winter scenes during the Little Ice Age: "Paintings of snow-covered landscapes are almost absent before 1565 . . . before Bruegel, winter was never painted as cold and snowy, and our traditional 'White Christmas' scene was totally absent." As for what caused the LIA, scientists are still split. Most believe cooler periods correlate with decreased solar activity (what's called a Grand Minimum), but others point to volcanic activity or changes in ocean currents. If the LIA was caused by lessened solar activity, then we need to be prepared for another cold period, because many scientists are predicting a new Grand Minimum in just a few years. Yet they also say that human-produced global warming could offset any cooling that might occur.

Acknowledgments

No author is an island. Even if you want to be, even if you sequester yourself in a dark little room and try to eliminate all outside contact as you write, it's never possible to produce a book alone. Many people advise, consult, critique, or assist the process in ways that improve the work or at least help you avoid future humiliation.

My dear husband, Robert Malesky, continues to be the best supporter any writer could have. On this project, he was my full-time researcher, and he saved me many hours of drudgery by helping me find appropriate, reputable, reliable sources among the gigantic amount of dreck that passes for information these days. I absolutely could not have produced this book without him.

Colleagues and friends provided suggestions and feedback that were enormously useful to me, especially Scott Simon, Walter Ray Watson and Carline Watson, Jim Anderson, Ken Rudin, Neal Conan, Gemma Watters, Andy Trudeau, Smokey Baer, Rick Lewis, and Jim Oliver. My editor at Wiley, Stephen S. Power, provided me with excellent notes, side notes, notes about notes, and many wonderful ideas; I'm also grateful to our production editor, Lisa Burstiner, for her thorough work, gently done.

Again with this project, as with my previous volume of facts, the NPR librarians were supportive, even though my absence sometimes meant that their days were more difficult. I want to thank our enthusiastic supervisor, Laura Soto-Barra, and my reference desk colleagues, Katie Daugert, Mary Glendinning, Jo Ella Straley, and Barbara van

Woerkom; our archivists and taxonomers, Elizabeth Allin, Denise Chen, Maureen Clements, Beth Howard, Janel Kinlaw, Lauren Sin, and Hannah Sommers; our music librarians, Robert Goldstein and Jennifer Bromley; and our transcript coordinators, Dorothy Hickson and Laura Jeffrey.

As any good librarian knows, it makes sense to turn to experts—people who know and love the facts you're researching—whenever possible. In this volume, I had help from Rachel Laribee from her story about Tibetan sky burial; Simon Ager of Omniglot.com; Aaron Bobrow-Strain at Whitman College; Mike Woodcock from the St. Andrews Links Trust; Elaine Fantham, University of Toronto; Alan Boese, Museum of Hoaxes; Larrie Ferreiro and Reverend Michael G. Witczak of the Catholic University of America; Shahriar Shahriari for his literal translation of the *Rubaiyat*; the Zion Reformed Church of Allentown, Pennsylvania; Joan Stahl, the head librarian at the Mount Vernon Estate and Gardens; Patricio D. Navia of New York University; and Liza Gross at the International Women's Media Foundation.

My language advisers include Caroline Simon, Matina Kourkoutas, Sylvia Poggioli, Nishant Dahiya, Davar Ardalan, Ned Wharton, and Katie Papadopoulos of the Belgium Tourist Office.

For permission to reproduce illustrations, I appreciate the generosity of Annette Buckley of the Student Association of the School of Information at the University of Texas at Austin, and cartoonist Ben Sargent (the reading armadillo); J. M. Ertzman and B. Wallace, courtesy of Carnegie Museum of Natural History (the Kensington Runestone); Friends of Gillette Castle State Park, secretary John Stratton, and artist Judy White (Gillette castle); Tim Brookes of the Endangered Alphabets Project (Balinese alphabet); Mike Millner from "Documenting the American South," University of North Carolina at Chapel Hill Libraries (Henry Brown's box); the Kansas State Historical Society, www.kansasmemory.org (photo of Elizabeth Jennings); S. D. Sampson of the Utah Museum of Natural History (*Kosmoceratops*); and www.antweb.org photographer April Nobile (fire ant). Botanical illustrations are from the U.S. Department of Agriculture Plants Database, from N. L. Britton and A. Brown, *An Illustrated Flora of the Northern United States, Canada, and the British Possessions* (New York: Charles Scribner's Sons, 1913).

Notes

I consulted several sources for every fact in this volume, in the hope of finding all of the good details for each story from trustworthy publications and websites. Because so many of those sources and further readings are online (and to save space and paper), we are making the complete list available on my site, www.keemalesky.com, where you can more easily access the Internet material. Links will be checked regularly and repaired, replaced, or updated as needed. Sources that are not available free online may be accessible through your local public library.

Here you will find the citations for any material that I quoted in the text, because it would be morally and ethically wrong to separate the credit from the quote.

Introduction

1 *"Young cat, if you"* Dr. Seuss, *I Can Read with My Eyes Shut* (New York: Random House, 1978), 19.

2 *"to attain the ideals"* Jacques Delors, *Learning: the Treasure Within: Report to UNESCO of the International Commission on Education for the Twenty-first Century* (Paris: UNESCO Publishing, 1996), 13–35, http://www.unesco.org/education/pdf/15_62.pdf.

January

January 4

7 *"There's a formal"* "Should It Be Burma or Myanmar?" *BBC News Magazine*, September 26, 2007, http://news.bbc.co.uk/2/hi/7013943.stm.

January 6

8 *"a plain, unadorned"* Joseph Nathan Kane, Steven Anzovin, and Janet Podell, *Famous First Facts* (New York: H. W. Wilson, 2006), 6.

January 7

9 *"Hello, London"* "Science: Eerie Voice," *Time*, January 17, 1927, http://www.time.com/time/magazine/article/0,9171,729856,00.html.

January 8

9 *"the #1 thinking sport"* World Chess Boxing Organisation, http://wcbo.org/content/e470/index_en.html.

9. *"Fighting is done"* Ibid.

January 11

11 *"cigarette smoking is"* *Smoking and Health: Report of the Advisory Committee to the Surgeon General of the Public Health Service*, U.S. Department of Health, Education, and Welfare, January 11, 1964, 33, http://profiles.nlm.nih.gov/ps/access/NNBBMQ.pdf.

11 *"I can stop"* "Smoker in Street Largely Defiant," *New York Times*, January 12, 1964.

11 *"I love these"* Ibid.

January 12

12 *"most customers will"* "Cinema: Nose Opera," *Time*, February 29, 1960, http://www.time.com/time/magazine/article/0,9171,873276,00.html.

January 14

13 *"There is a river"* Matthew Fontaine Maury, *The Physical Geography of the Sea and Its Meteorology* (New York: Harper & Brothers, 1855), 25, http://books.google.com/books?id=FpwqAAAA YAAJ&printsec=frontcover&dq=maury+% 22physical+geography+of+the+sea%22&hl =en&ei=g9jcTqKqPIyWtwfdgrDtAQ&sa =X&oi=book_result&ct=result&resnum=1 &ved=0CDkQ6AEwAA#v=onepage&q&f=false.

January 15

13 *"I heard something"* Scott Simon, "Molasses Tragedy of Boston 1919," *Weekend Edition Saturday*, NPR, January 15, 1994.

January 16

14 *"Imagine a ball"* Museum of Polo and Hall of Fame, http://polomuseum.com/welcome.htm.

14 *"In the cosmic game"* Shahriar Shahriari, trans., *Rubaiyat of Omar Khayyam*, http://www.okonlife.com/poems/page5.htm.

January 17

15 *"Of all my inventions"* "Franklin's Glass Armonica," Franklin Institute, http://www.fi.edu/learn/sci-tech/armonica/armonica.php?cts=benfranklin-recreation.

January 18

15 *"A stage or platform"* *Oxford English Dictionary*, 3rd ed., March 2005.

16 *"a high scafolde"* A. M. Nagler, *A Source Book in Theatrical History* (Mineola, NY: Dover Publications, 1959), 49.

January 19

16 *"an unparalleled wildlife"* "Pantanal," Waterland Research Institute, http://www.pantanal.org/pantanal.htm.

January 20

16 *"It was at the dawn"* Steve Inskeep, "Robert Morris: America's Founding Capitalist," *Morningx Edition*, NPR, December 20, 2010, http://www.npr.org/2010/12/20/132051519/-robert-morris-america-s-founding-capitalist.

January 25

20 *"The tree of liberty"* Thomas Jefferson to William Stephens Smith, November 13, 1787, in Bernard Bailyn, ed., *The Debate on the Constitution: Federalists and Antifederalist Speeches during the Struggle over Ratification* (New York: Library of America, 1993), 310.

January 28

22 *"At first glance"* "Happy Anniversary, Crawlers," Space Shuttle, NASA, January 13, 2006, http://www.nasa.gov/mission_pages/shuttle/behindscenes/crawlers.html.

January 29

22 *"Col. Kearny was . . . authorized"* James Knox Polk, *The Diary of James K. Polk during His Presidency, 1845 to 1849* (Chicago: A. C. McClurg, 1910), 444, http://books.google.com/books?id=wxMOAAAAIAAJ &pg=PA500&dq=polk+diary&hl=en&ei=d PbwTbSPN4fAgQe0iLHKBA&sa=X&oi= book_result&ct=result&resnum=2&sqi=2& ved=0CC4Q6AEwAQ#v=onepage&q&f=f alse.

January 30

23 *"It doesn't seem"* Sara Israelsen-Hartley, "2010 Was Banner Year for Dinosaur Discoveries," *Deseret Morning News*, January 1, 2011, http://www.deseretnews.com/article/700096887/2010-was-banner-year-for-dinosaur-discoveries.html.

February

February 1

25 *"Each person's microbial"* Rob Dunn, "Belly Button Diversity," Your Wild Life, http://www.wildlifeofyourbody.org/.

25 *"Having an appreciation"* Eleanor Spicer Rice, "What's Living in Your Bellybutton?" *Raleigh News and Observer*, May 9, 2011, http://www.newsobserver.com/2011/05/09/1184876/whats-living-in-your-bellybutton.html#storylink=misearch.

February 2

26 *"stories of gods and spirits"* "Shakespeare in China," Internet Shakespeare Editions, University of Victoria, http://internetshakespeare.uvic.ca/Library/Criticism/shakespearein/china2.html.

26 *"I do my best"* Murray Levith, *Shakespeare in China* (New York: Continuum

Books, 2004), 11–12, http://books.google
.com/books?id=v1NF9Nq0OZ4C&printsec
=frontcover&source=gbs_ge_summary_r&c
ad=0#v=onepage&q&f=false.

February 4
27 *"The smell of sizzling"* Alastair
Jamieson, "Chemical Reaction That Explains
the Appeal of the Bacon Sandwich," *Telegraph*,
April 6, 2009, http://www.telegraph.co.uk/
foodanddrink/foodanddrinknews/5111754/
Chemical-reaction-that-explains-the-
appeal-of-the-bacon-sandwich.html.

February 7
29 *"He knew, by the streamers"* Walter
Scott, *The Lay of the Last Minstrel, a Poem*
(London: Longman, Hurst, Ree, and Orme,
1805), 40–41.

February 9
30 *"their songs consist"* "Singers: The
New Madness," *Time*, November 15, 1963,
http://www.time.com/time/magazine/
article/0,9171,873176,00.html.
30 *"Yeah, yeah, yeah"* Tatiana Morales,
"The Beatles Are Coming!" *The Early Show*,
CBS News, December 5, 2007, http://www
.cbsnews.com/stories/2004/02/04/earlyshow/
leisure/books/main597992.shtml.

February 11
32 *"powerful and everlasting"* "Did You
Know? Three Stars on Noodles," Samsung
Village, Samsung Corporation, http://www
.samsungvillage.com/blog/2011/03/did-you-
know-three-stars-on-noodles.html.

February 12
32 *"There are, in our"* Lowell Dingus
and Mark A. Norell, "The Bone Collector,"
Discover, March 2007, http://discovermagazine
.com/2007/mar/the-bone-collector/.

February 13
33 *"You might just"* Allan W. Howey,
"Weaponry: The Rifle-Musket and the
Minié Ball," *Civil War Times*, October 1999,
http://www.historynet.com/weaponry-the-
rifle-musket-and-the-mini-ball.htm/1.

February 14
34 *"in principle"* Than Ker, "What
Created Earth's Oceans? Comet Offers
New Clue," National Geographic Daily
News, October 5, 2011, http://news
.nationalgeographic.com/news/2011/
10/111005-comets-earth-water-oceans-
kuiper-belt-nature-science/.

February 17
36 *"consist of a jumble"* Bolton Brown,
"Letter to the Editor: 'Art' in the Armory,"
New York Times, March 1, 1913.

February 18
36 *"The demonstration was undertaken"* "Milk Drops from Skies as Cow
Takes Air Ride," Associated Press, February
18, 1930.

February 20
37 *"a President has to"* "The Presidency:
Fanatics' Errand," *Time*, November 13, 1950,
http://www.time.com/time/magazine/
article/0,9171,821335–1,00.html.

February 26
40 *"that the genetic diversity"* "Svalbard
Global Seed Vault," Ministry of Agriculture
and Food, Government of Norway, http://
www.regjeringen.no/en/dep/lmd/campain/
svalbard-global-seed-vault.html?id=462220.
41 *"the wealth that is being"* "UN
Lauds 'Innovative' Norwegian Arctic
Vault Safeguarding World's Crop Seeds,"
UN News Centre, February 26, 2008,
http://www.un.org/apps/news/story
.asp?NewsID=25754&Cr=food&Cr1.

February 27
41 *"I never wanted"* Janet Smith,
"Interview with Elfego Baca," pt. 2, American
Life Histories, American Memory, Library
of Congress, http://lcweb2.loc.gov/ammem/
wpa/20040209.html.
41 *"Baca's bravery instilled"* Bill
Richardson, "Tribute to Elfego Baca," May
10, 1995, http://tinyurl.com/dxp3zah.

March

March 1
44 *"My eyes, what a wig!"* Linda
Greenhouse, "Ideas & Trends: The Chief
Justice Has New Clothes," *New York Times*,
January 22, 1995, http://www.nytimes
.com/1995/01/22/weekinreview/ideas-
trends-the-chief-justice-has-new-clothes.
html.
44 *"If we must"* L. B. Proctor, "First
Federal Chief Justice," *American Lawyer*,
April 1896, 152, http://books.google.com/
books?id=sOYKAQAAMAAJ&pg=PA152
&lpg=PA152&dq=scotus+wigs&source=bl
&ots=OSsxhwEx1g&sig=l4Kh1_zMVLe_
Y7ZB7rZb6kGemmI&hl=en&ei=PG_CTo

T3HtKWtwfxtYC6DQ&sa=X&oi=book_
result&ct=result&resnum=8&ved=0CEcQ6
AEwBw#v=onepage&q=wig&f=false.

March 2
45 "Kind of Blue *lives and prospers*" Ashley Kahn, *"Kind of Blue": The Making of the Miles Davis Masterpiece* (New York: Da Capo Press, 2000), 17.

March 3
46 "*All human beings*" "The Universal Declaration of Human Rights," United Nations, http://www.un.org/en/documents/udhr/.

March 5
47 "*This is a golden*" "Relationship with the West," Kurdistan, the Other Iraq, http://www.theotheriraq.com/relationship.html.

March 7
48 "*[M]y mind takes flight*" Jean-Dominique Bauby, *The Diving Bell and the Butterfly* (New York: Alfred A. Knopf, 1997), 5.

March 8
49 "*Having seen that*" "Alexander Thomas Augusta," in *Notable Black American Scientists* (Detroit: Gale, 1998).

March 10
50 "*eerie buzzing harmonics*" Andrew Gilbert, "Tuvan Rockers Go Easy on Ears with Throat Singing," *Boston Globe*, September 23, 2006.

March 11
51 "*If you put*" Phuong Le, "Flotsam from Japan's Tsunami to Hit U.S. West Coast," Associated Press, April 1, 2011, http://abcnews.go.com/US/wireStory?id=13272083.

March 12
52 "*acoustically perfect tabernacle*" "Welcome to the Integratron: The Fusion of Art, Science and Magic," Integratron, http://www.integratron.com/.

March 15
53 "*boldly cast himself*" "Andrew Jackson (1767–1845)," American President: An Online Reference Resource, Miller Center of Public Affairs, University of Virginia, http://millercenter.org/president/jackson.

March 16
54 "*the greatest ecological disaster*" Susan Freinkel, "Chestnutty: Wielding

Cutting-Edge Science and Lots of Patience, James Hill Craddock Hopes to Restore the Ravaged American Chestnut Tree to Its Former Glory," *Smithsonian*, September 2004, http://www.smithsonianmag.com/science-nature/Chestnutty.html.

March 18
55 "*Then the wind struck*" Peter S. Felknor, *The Tri-State Tornado: The Story of America's Greatest Tornado Disaster* (Lincoln, NE: iUniverse, Inc., 2004), 7.
55 "*It was almost*" Ibid., 9.

March 19
55 "*at the threshold*" Orrin C. Shane III, and Mine Küçuk, "The World's First City," *Archaeology*, 1998, https://www2.bc.edu/~mcdonadh/course/huyuk.html.
56 "*In terms of population*" Graham Lawton, "Urban Legends: Long Thought to Be the World's First City Dwellers, the Citizens of Uruk Now Face Competition from Some Out-of-Towners," *New Scientist*, September 18, 2004.

March 23
59 "*I was again placed*" Henry Box Brown, *Narrative of the Life of Henry Box Brown, Written by Himself* (Manchester, 1851), 54, http://docsouth.unc.edu/neh/brownbox/brownbox.html.

March 24
59 "*would not be practical*" "Views on Trained Cats, March, 1967," Science, Technology and the CIA, National Security Archive, http://www.gwu.edu/~nsarchiv/NSAEBB/NSAEBB54/st27.pdf.

March 28
61 "*When depicting the human body*" "The Art of Ancient Egypt," Metropolitan Museum of Art, http://www.metmuseum.org/learn/for-educators/publications-for-educators/~/media/Files/Learn/For%20Educators/Publications%20for%20Educators/The%20Art%20of%20Ancient%20Egypt.ashx.

March 30
63 "*This was a heart*" Bill Christine, "Big Red Machine: Secretariat Had the Heart of a Champion, and the Popularity of a Movie Star," *Los Angeles Times*, June 4, 1998.

March 31
63 "*No picture shall be produced*" Leonard J. Jeff, and Jerold Simmons, eds.,

The Dame in the Kimono: Hollywood, Censorship, and the Production Code from the 1920s to the 1960s, 2nd ed. (Louisville: Univ. Press of Kentucky, 2001), 286.

April

April 2
65 *"Mindful of the fact"* "Norden Bombsight," U.S. Centennial of Flight Commission, http://www.centennialofflight .gov/essay/Dictionary/NORDEN_ BOMBSIGHT/DI145.htm.

April 3
66 *"loose-fitting breeches" Oxford English Dictionary* (Oxford, UK: Oxford Univ. Press, 1989).

April 6
68 *"a monstrous system"* Roy Moxham, *The Great Hedge of India* (New York: Carrol & Graf, 2001), 3, http://books.google.com/ books?id=3BCymeSXDhoC&printsec=fron tcover&source=gbs_ge_summary_r&cad=0# v=onepage&q&f=false.

April 8
69 *"All players on a team"* Official Baseball Rules 2011, Major League Baseball, 7, http://mlb.mlb.com/mlb/downloads/ y2011/Official_Baseball_Rules.pdf.

April 9
70 *"The* moai *are not"* Paul Trachtman, "The Secrets of Easter Island," *Smithsonian*, March 2002, http://www.smithsonian-mag.com/arts-culture/Mysterious-Island .html?c=y&story=fullstory.

April 10
70 *"cars were designed to inspire"* Jane and Michael Stern, *Encyclopedia of Pop Culture* (New York: HarperPerennial, 1992), 169.

April 11
71 *"making an opening"* International Trepanation Advocacy Group, http://www .trepan.com/.

April 12
72 *"[H]e was the first"* Marie G. Young, "Lest We Forget," *National Magazine* 37, no. 1 (October 1912): 109, http://books .google.com/books?id=VnBYAAAAMAAJ& pg=PA109&dq=%22he+was+the+first+of+th e+Titanic's+martyrs%22&hl=en&ei=xdlcTr_ OLMSRgQfEvqSMAg&sa=X&oi=book_res

ult&ct=result&resnum=1&ved=0CCoQ6 AEwAA#v=onepage&q=lest%20we%20 forget&f=false.

April 15
73 *"spread out the peak"* Jessica Sung, "Why Is Tax Day April 15?" *Fortune*, April 15, 2002, 64, http://money .cnn.com/magazines/fortune/fortune_ archive/2002/04/15/321414/index.htm.
73 *"The hardest thing"* Garson O'Toole, "The Hardest Thing in the World to Understand Is Income Taxes," Quote Investigator, March 7, 2011, http:// quoteinvestigator.com/2011/03/07/ einstein-income-taxes/.

April 16
74 *"wonderful things"* Nicholas Reeves and John H. Taylor, *Howard Carter before Tutankhamun* (London: British Museum, 1992), 141.
74 *"And so, after a silence"* T. G. H. James, "The Trumpets of Tutankhamun," Museum Tours video, http://www.youtube .com/watch?v=zr_olu7chEY.

April 19
76 *"A well-tied tie"* Oscar Wilde, *A Woman of No Importance*, act 3, scene 1, http://www.gutenberg.org/cache/epub/854/ pg854.html.

April 20
76 *"areas of geologically"* Joshua Calder, "Continent or Island?" World Island Info, http://www.worldislandinfo.com/ CONTISLAND.html.

April 21
77 *"The master of the monstrous"* Wendy Beckett, *The Story of Painting* (New York: Dorling Kindersley, 2000), 123.

April 23
78 *"What's the probability"* Rebecca Hersher, "Nabokov's Blues," *Harvard Gazette*, February 17, 2011, http://news.harvard.edu/ gazette/story/2011/02/nabokov's-blues/.

April 24
79 *"After completing all"* "Soyuz-1 Conquers the Cosmos: Official Tass Communiques, April 24, 1967," Goddard Space Flight Center, National Aeronautics and Space Administration, http://ntrs .nasa.gov/archive/nasa/casi.ntrs.nasa .gov/19670017082_1967017082.pdf.

79 *"this devil ship"* Robert Krulwich, "A Cosmonaut's Fiery Death Retold" *Krulwich Wonders*, NPR, May 3, 2011, http://www.npr.org/blogs/krulwich/2011/05/03/135919389/a-cosmonauts-fiery-death-retold?sc=fb&cc=fp

April 26

80 *"My painting* Guernica*"* George Sewell, "The Glove That Changed *Guernica*," *London Evening Standard*, May 8, 2009, http://www.thisislondon.co.uk/arts/review-23687477-the-glove-that-changed-guernica.do.

April 27

81 *"a tomb before which"* Arthur Judson Brown, *Rising Churches in Non-Christian Lands* (New York: The Presbyterian Department of Missionary Education, 1915), 9, http://books.google.com/books?id=c7gPAAAAIAAJ&printsec=frontcover&source=gbs_ge_summary_r&cad=0#v=onepage&q&f=false.

April 28

81 *"Any such exercise"* Carl Haub, "How Many People Have Lived on Earth?" Population Reference Bureau, October 2011, http://www.prb.org/Articles/2002/HowManyPeopleHaveEverLivedonEarth.aspx.

April 29

82 *"[A]pparently there is"* "Industrial Art in America," *Chicago Daily Tribune*, June 8, 1925.

April 30

83 *"Since both Asia"* Toby Lester, "The Waldseemüller Map: Charting the New World," *Smithsonian*, December 2009, http://www.smithsonianmag.com/history-archaeology/The-Waldseemuller-Map-Charting-the-New-World.html?c=y&story=fullstory.

May

May 5

87 *"the image of a rabbit"* Patricia Rieff Anawalt, "Flopsy, Mopsy, and Tipsy," *Natural History* (April 1997).

May 11

90 *"had contributed little"* Erik Larson, *The Devil in the White City* (New York: Crown Publishers, 2003), 156.

90 *"out-Eiffel Eiffel"* Ibid.

May 12

91 *"industrial lubricant"* "Marmite: Ten Things You'll Love/Hate to Know," BBC News, May 25, 2011, http://www.bbc.co.uk/news/uk-13541148.

May 14

92 *"There were female"* Steven Murray, "Female Gladiators of the Ancient Roman World," *Journal of Combative Sport*, July 2003, http://ejmas.com/jcs/jcsart_murray_0703.htm.

92 *"gladiatorial shows by torchlight"* Suetonius, *The Twelve Caesars*, trans. Robert Graves (London: Penguin, 1957; revised 1979), 305.

92 *"to be burnt"* Michael Grant, *Gladiators* (London: Weidenfeld & Nicolson, 1967), 31.

May 17

94 *"was one of the most notable"* "Colonel Clark Kills Himself," *New York Tribune*, April 23, 1899.

May 19

95 *"I just like"* Matt Schudel, "Betty Skelton, 'Fastest Woman on Earth,' Dies at 85," *Washington Post*, September 3, 2011, http://www.washingtonpost.com/local/obituaries/betty-skelton-fastest-woman-on-earth-dies-at-85/2011/09/03/gIQAyv83zJ_story.html.

May 21

96 *"one of the leading"* "Lindenthal Dies: Bridge Designer," *New York Times*, August 1, 1935.

May 22

97 *"An atlatl is essentially"* "What Is the Atlatl?" World Atlatl Association, http://www.worldatlatl.org/WhatisAtlatl.html.

May 23

97 *"patients gathered"* M. Best, D. Neuhauser, and L. Slavin, "Evaluating Mesmerism, Paris, 1784; The Controversy Over the Blinded Placebo Controlled Trials Has Not Stopped," *Quality and Safety in Health Care*, June 2003, http://www.ncbi.nlm.nih.gov/pmc/articles/PMC1743715/pdf/v012p00232.pdf.

May 24

98 *"There are no obvious"* Jerome Sueur, David Mackie, and James F. C. Windmill, "So Small, So Loud: Extremely

High Sound Pressure Level from a Pygmy Aquatic Insect (*Corixidae, Micronectinae*)," PLoS [Public Library of Science] ONE, June 15, 2011, http://www.plosone.org/article/info%3Adoi%2F10.1371%2Fjournal.pone.0021089.

98 *"Remarkably, even though"* "World's Loudest Animal Is Recorded for the First Time," University of Strathclyde, June 30, 2011, http://www.strath.ac.uk/press/newsreleases/headline_455782_en.html.

May 26

99 *"We are born"* "George Mortimer Pullman," Pullman State Historic Site, http://www.pullman-museum.org/theMan/.

100 *"[T]he idea of Pullman"* Richard T. Ely, "Pullman: A Social Study," *Harper's*, February 1885, http://www.library.cornell.edu/Reps/DOCS/pullman.htm.

May 27

100 *"Its unprecedented size"* Morrow and Morrow, Architects, *The Golden Gate Brige; Report on Color and Lighting*, April 6, 1935, http://www.goldengatebridge.org/research/documents/ReportColorLighting.pdf.

May 28

101 *"The administration is trying"* James McGrath Morris, "A Tribute to the 'First Lady of the Black Press,'" *Washington Post*, August 14, 2011.

101 *"You are either"* Donald A. Ritchie, "Ethel L. Payne," in *American Journalists: Getting the Story* (Oxford: Oxford Univ. Press, 1997), 266, http://books.google.com/books?id=E3IM-YLtyFAC&printsec=frontcover&source=gbs_ge_summary_r&cad=0#v=onepage&q&f=false.

May 30

102 *"[I]nduced by bodily necessity"* Robert Wirth, ed., "Primary Sources and Context Concerning Joan of Arc's Male Clothing," *Joan of Arc*, Primary Sources Series, Historical Academy (Association) for Joan of Arc Studies, 2006, 10, http://primary-sources-series.joan-of-arc-studies.org/PSS021806.pdf.

June

June 1

104 *"We've got feathers"* "Dinosaur Feather Evolution Trapped in Canadian Amber," BBC News, September 15, 2011, http://www.bbc.co.uk/news/science-environment-14933298.

105 *"We're getting more"* Ibid.

June 3

105 *"a violently rotating"* Roger Edwards, "The Online Tornado FAQ," Storm Prediction Center, National Oceanic and Atmospheric Administration, http://www.spc.noaa.gov/faq/tornado/.

June 7

108 *"national peacockery"* Giles Tremlett, *Catharine of Aragon: The Spanish Queen of Henry VIII* (New York: Walker and Company, 2010), 198.

June 9

110 *"I am only"* William McBrien, *Cole Porter: A Biography* (New York: Alfred A. Knopf, 1998), 381.

June 10

110 *"It's us against"* Guy Raz, "Miami Invaded by Giant, House-Eating Snails," *All Things Considered*, NPR, September 17, 2011, http://www.npr.org/2011/09/17/140540662/miami-invaded-by-giant-house-eating-snails.

June 11

111 *"Improving the urban"* Yarn Bombing, http://yarnbombing.com/.

June 13

112 *"The sandy spot"* Alexandra Topping, "Turtle Chaos; Terrapins Delay Flights at JFK," *Guardian*, June 30, 2011, http://www.guardian.co.uk/world/2011/jun/30/turtle-chaos-delays-flights-jfk.

112 *"We got a couple turtles"* Bill Sanderson and Jeremy Olshan, "Yo, Get the 'Shell' Out of the Way! Turtle Invasion Brings JFK Jets to a Crawl," *New York Post*, June 30, 2011, http://www.nypost.com/p/news/local/yo_get_the_shell_out_of_the_way_yPGvyUwynrokkx05V3LH2I.

June 14

112 *"This is full-body"* Melissa Block, "Preserving the Sacred Harp Singing Tradition," *All Things Considered*, NPR, December 5, 2003, http://www.npr.org/templates/story/story.php?storyId=1534280.

June 15

113 *"of the dead rising"* John William Polidori, *The Vampyre: A Tale* (London:

Sherwood, Neely, and Jones, 1819), http://www.gutenberg.org/files/6087/6087-h/6087-h.htm.

June 17

114 *"We've got to wake up"* Cameron McWhirter, "America Forgot James Weldon Johnson," The Root, July 22, 2011, http://www.theroot.com/views/america-forgot-james-weldon-johnson?page=0,0.

June 18

115 *"Tibetans believe that"* Rachel Laribee, "Tibetan Sky Burial, Student Witnesses Reincarnation," *River Gazette*, St. Mary's College of Maryland, April–May 2005, 9, http://www.smcm.edu/rivergazette/_assets/PDF/may05/tibetanskyburial.pdf.

June 19

115 *"the first theater"* E. W. Lightner, "Pittsburg Gave Birth to the Movie Theater Idea," *Dispatch*, November 16, 1919, Carnegie Library of Pittsburgh, http://www.clpgh.org/exhibit/neighborhoods/downtown/down_n71.html.

June 20

116 *"No one who has"* Frederick Law Olmsted, "Public Parks and the Enlargement of Towns," a paper read before the American Social Science Association, Boston, February 25, 1870, Franklin & Marshall College, http://www.fandm.edu/dschuyle/electronic-course-materials/ams-env-280-american-landscape/public-parks-and-the-enlargement-of-towns.

June 21

117 *"[I]nstead of stressing"* Robert Malesky, *Island of Dreams; A Coney Island Perspective*, NPR, September 1979.

June 22

118 *"Camel-breeding nomads"* Richard W. Bulliet, *The Camel and the Wheel* (New York: Columbia Univ. Press, 1990), 90–91.

June 23

119 *"To hear the Didjeridu"* Joe Cheal, *The Didjeridu, a Guide*, The G-Wiz Learning Partnership, 2009, 1, http://www.gwiztraining.com/Didj%20Book.pdf.

June 29

122 *"Hollywood was given"* Historical Marker Placed by the Broadway-Hollywood Department Store and the Board of Supervisors of the County of Los Angeles, November 1955, http://www.earthsignals.com/Collins/0015/0010_1.jpg.

July

July 2

125 *"They're slow dreamers"* "Sunfish Sighted Far from Home Seas," UPI, December 7, 2009, http://www.upi.com/Science_News/2009/12/07/Sunfish-sighted-far-from-home-seas/UPI-49321260229525/.

July 3

126 *"It's a bad looking"* Steve Inskeep, "A Yacht, a Mustache: How a President Hid His Tumor," *Morning Edition*, NPR, July 6, 2011, http://www.npr.org/2011/07/06/137621988/a-yacht-a-mustache-how-a-president-hid-his-tumor.

July 4

126 *"Connecticut was . . . the victim"* Helen M. Carpenter, "The Origin and Location of the Firelands of the Western Reserve," *Ohio Archaeological and Historical Quarterly*, no. 2 (April 1935: 165), http://publications.ohiohistory.org/ohstemplate.cfm?action=detail&Page=0044163.html&StartPage=163&EndPage=203&volume=44&notes=&newtitle=Volume%2044%20Page%20163.

July 6

128 *"was a bridge"* Gil Griffin, "Godfather of African Soul on U.S. Safari," *Los Angeles Times*, August 24, 1994.

128 *"in recognition of"* "Manu Dibango," Artists for Peace, UNESCO, http://portal.unesco.org/en/ev.php-URL_ID=20677&URL_DO=DO_TOPIC&URL_SECTION=201.html.

July 7

128 *"the greatest forward step"* Catherine Stortz Ripley, "Happy Birthday, Sliced Bread!" *Chillicothe News*, July 8, 2009, http://www.chillicothenews.com/news/x135743963/HAPPY-BIRTHDAY-SLICED-BREAD.

128 *"So neat and precise"* Chillicothe *Constitution Tribune*, July 6, 1928.

July 8

129 *"We're moving into"* "NASA's Hubble Finds Most Distant Galaxy

Candidate Ever Seen in Universe," Hubble Site, Space Telescope Science Institute, http://hubblesite.org/newscenter/archive/releases/2011/05/full/.

July 9

129 *"the Recreation & delight"* "Bowling Green," New York City Department of Parks and Recreation, http://www.nycgovparks.org/parks/bowlinggreen/highlights/6421.

July 10

130 *"forced to write"* Aphra Behn, "To the Reader," *Sir Patient Fancy*, in *The Works of Aphra Behn*, vol. 4, Montague Summers, ed. (London: William Heinemann, 1915), 7.

130 *"All women together"* Virginia Woolf, *A Room of One's Own*, annotated by Susan Gubar (New York: Harcourt, 2005), 65.

July 11

130 *"Cooking increased the value"* Richard Wrangham, *Catching Fire: How Cooking Made Us Human* (New York: Basic Books, 2009), 2, http://www.scribd.com/doc/50009885/Catching-Fire-How-Cooking-Made-Us-Human-Richard-Wrangham.

July 12

131 *"a Resort, where the infirm"* American *Apollo* (Boston), July 12, 1793, http://upload.wikimedia.org/wikipedia/commons/d/d0/1793_JuliensRestorator_Boston_AmericanApollo_July19.png.

July 14

132 *"Born in a slave state"* "Frederick Douglass Describes the Life of a Negro Tailor, 1859," Hofstra University, http://people.hofstra.edu/alan_j_singer/Gateway%20Slavery%20Guide%20PDF%20Files/5.%20Abolition_Complicity%201827–65/5.%20Documents%201827–1865/1859a.%20(A)%20Jennings%20Obit.pdf.

July 15

133 *"sore and stiff"* "Outrage upon Colored Persons," *New York Tribune*, July 19, 1854.

133 *"Colored persons if sober"* "City Items: A Wholesome Verdict," *New York Tribune*, February 23, 1855.

July 18

135 *"That's my story"* David H. Onkst, "Douglas 'Wrong Way' Corrigan,"

U.S. Centennial of Flight Commission, http://www.centennialofflight.gov/essay/Explorers_Record_Setters_and_Daredevils/corrigan/EX16.htm.

July 19

135 *"archetypal violators of"* Simon Price and Emily Kearns, eds., "Tantalus," in *The Oxford Dictionary of Classical Myth and Religion* (Oxford: Oxford Univ. Press, 2003), 532.

July 20

136 *"You got a bunch"* "The First Lunar Landing," *Apollo 11 Lunar Surface Journal*, NASA, http://www.hq.nasa.gov/alsj/a11/a11.landing.html.

July 21

137 *"Day had just dawned"* Ammianus Marcellinus, *The Later Roman Empire (A.D. 354–378)*, trans. Walter Hamilton (London: Penguin Books, 1986), 333.

July 22

137 *"When the train"* "The Insect Plague: Ravages of Insects in the West," *New York Times*, August 3, 1874, http://query.nytimes.com/mem/archive-free/pdf?res=F00812FE3B541A7493C1A91783D85F408784F9.

July 25

139 *"The clicking of the two"* "Contest for a Prize of $500—the Remington Operator Wins the Battle," *Cincinnati Commercial Gazette*, July 26, 1888.

July 27

140 *"devoted to the interests"* Ken Schlager, "Billboard: Always No. 1," Billboard History, http://web.archive.org/web/20051213024449/http://www.billboard.com/bbcom/about_us/bbhistory.jsp, 1.

July 29

141 *"It's kind of a strategy"* Annie Feidt, "The Kittiwake: Winging It, Survival-Wise." *Weekend Edition Saturday*, NPR, July 23, 2011, http://www.npr.org/2011/07/23/138574244/the-kittiwake-winging-it-survival-wise.

July 31

143 *"It has been the prayer"* Winfield Scott, "General Orders, No. 13," *The War of the Rebellion: A Compilation of the Official Records of the Union and Confederate Armies* (Gettysburg, PA: National Historical Society, 1972), 430.

August

August 1

144 *"From certain cloistered"* Herman Melville, *Moby Dick; or, the White Whale* (Boston: St. Botolph Society, 1892), 135–136, http://tinyurl.com/45drseh.

August 2

145 *"Since there is no"* "The Geographical Center of the Lower 48 United States, at Lebanon, Kansas," *The Lay of the Land,* Spring 1999, Center for Land Use Interpretation, http://www.clui.org/sites/default/files/16_spring1999.pdf.

August 3

146 *"[t]hey shall find"* John Fedele, "The Cathedral of Learning: A History," *Pitt Chronicle,* March 12, 2007, http://www.chronicle.pitt.edu/?p=65.

August 5

147 *"the Tycoon is grieved"* John Hay, *Lincoln and the Civil War in the Diaries and Letters of John Hay* (New York: DaCapo Press, 1988), 67.

August 7

148 *"family that dominated"* Donald C. Johanson, "Anthropologists: The Leakey Family," *Time,* March 29, 1999, http://www.time.com/time/magazine/article/0,9171,990619,00.html#ixzz1TJh6WjpK.

148 *"It is only"* L. S. B. Leakey, *Adam's Ancestors* (London: Methuen, 1953), 218.

August 8

149 *"The Overture will be"* Kseniia Iur'evna Davydova, Vladimir Vasil'evich Protopopov, and Nadezhda Vasil'evna Tumanina, *Muzykal'noe nasledie Chaikovskogo. Iz istorii ego proizvedeniĭ,* trans. Brett Langston (Moscow: Akademiĭ Nauk SSSR, 1958), 295, http://www.tchaikovsky-research.net/en/Works/Orchestral/TH049/index.html.

149 *"I'm undecided as to"* Ibid.

August 9

149 *"Solicited and obtained"* "Articles of Impeachment against Richard M. Nixon," http://classes.lls.edu/archive/manheimk/371d1/nixonarticles.html.

August 10

150 *"The maze of lines"* Anthony F. Aveni, "Solving the Mystery of the Nasca Lines," *Archaeology* (May/June 2000), http://www.archaeology.org/0005/abstracts/nasca.html.

August 11

151 *"In an online poll"* Adam Barrows, "Time Wars: How a Huge New Clock in Mecca Is Reviving a Century-Old Clash over What Time It Is," *Boston Globe,* June 19, 2011, http://www.boston.com/bostonglobe/ideas/articles/2011/06/19/time_wars/?page=full.

August 12

151 *"the Dorchestrians gave up"* Louis C. Elson, "Early Musical Organizations," in *The History of American Music* (New York: Macmillan Company, 1904), 28, http://books.google.com/books?id=YXouAAAAMAAJ&printsec=frontcover&source=gbs_ge_summary_r&cad=0#v=onepage&q=%22early%20musical%20organizations%22&f=false.

August 13

152 *"The North West Passage"* "Arctic Passage," *Nova,* PBS, February 28, 2006, http://www.pbs.org/wgbh/nova/arctic/.

August 15

153 *"most fearless animal in the world"* Colleen and Keith Begg, "The Honey Badger: Conserving 'the Most Fearless Animal in the World,'" *Science in Africa,* March 2003, http://www.scienceinafrica.co.za/2003/march/badger.htm.

August 16

154 *"[S]he was truly"* Walter Terry, "Princess Firebird," *Los Angeles Times,* February 4, 1951.

August 17

154 *"Look to Africa"* Jérémie Koubo Dagnini, "Rastafari: Alternative Religion and Resistance Against 'White' Christianity," *Études caribéennes,* April 2009, http://etudescaribeennes.revues.org/3665.

August 19

156 *"indispensable that the Government"* Alexander Tabarrok, ed., *Entrepreneurial Economics: Bright Ideas from the Dismal Science* (New York: Oxford Univ. Press, 2002), 250.

August 20

157 *"And I do further proclaim"* Frederick E. Hosen, "A Proclamation by the President of the United States of America, No 4

August 20, 1866," in *Federal Laws of the Reconstruction: Principal Congressional Acts and Resolutions, Presidential Proclamations, Speeches and Orders, and Other Legislative and Military Documents, 1862–1875* (Jefferson, NC: McFarland and Company, 2010), 49.

August 23
159 *"The screams of the affrighted"* Lorenzo Dow, *History of Cosmopolite; or, the Four Volumes of Lorenzo Dow's Journal* (Wheeling: Joshua Martin, 1848), 344, http://books.google.com/books?id=SYNllIx56rUC&printsec=frontcover&dq=%22Lorenzo+Dow's+Journal%22&hl=en&ei=3stcTuWwKIjq0gHr-IiYAw&sa=X&oi=book_result&ct=result&resnum=1&ved=0CC0Q6AEwAA#v=onepage&q&f=false.

August 24
159. *"Seeing one explode"* Linda Vu, "Berkeley Scientists Discover an 'Instant Cosmic Classic,'" News Center, Lawrence Berkeley National Laboratory, August 25, 2011, http://newscenter.lbl.gov/feature-stories/2011/08/25/supernova/.
159 *"an instant cosmic classic"* Ibid.

August 26
160 *"a vibrant, if niche"* Georgiana Cohen, "What Is Filk? The Answer, My Friend, Is Blowin' in the Diurnal Atmospheric Disequilibrium," *Boston Phoenix*, March 20, 2008, http://thephoenix.com//Boston/Life/58308-What-is-Filk/.

August 27
161 *"Suddenly, it became"* Alwyn Scarth, *Vulcan's Fury: Man against the Volcano* (New Haven: Yale Univ. Press, 1999), 143, http://books.google.com/books?id=oRgF3SQI8DoC&printsec=frontcover&source=gbs_ge_summary_r&cad=0#v=onepage&q&f=false.

August 29
162 *"Kinkering Congs"* "Who Was Dr. Spooner of 'Spoonerism' Fame?" Science Advisory Board, Straight Dope, June 11, 2002, http://www.straightdope.com/columns/read/2010/who-was-dr-spooner-of-spoonerism-fame.

August 30
163 *"the most feminine"* Adam Bernstein, "Nancy Wake, 'White Mouse' of World War II, Dies at 98," *Washington Post*, August 9, 2011, http://www.washingtonpost.com/local/obituaries/nancy-wake-white-mouse-of-world-war-ii-dies-at-98/2011/08/08/gIQABvPT5I_story.html.

August 31
164 *"[B]efore night, I who"* Olaudah Equiano, *The Interesting Narrative of the Life of Olaudah Equiano, or Gustavus Vassa, the African, Written by Himself*, vol. 2 (London: 1789), 16–17, http://docsouth.unc.edu/neh/equiano2/equiano2.html.

September

September 1
166 *"would dash his head"* Suetonius, *Suetonius*, trans. J. C. Rolfe (London: William Heinemann, 1914), 155, http://books.google.com/books?id=NJv_zeFbFi4C&pg=PA154&dq=%22Quintili+Vare,+legiones.

September 2
166 *"A cold, uncaring"* Roger Dobson, "Thinking Yourself Sick," *Times* (London), August 25, 2007, http://www.timesonline.co.uk/tol/life_and_style/health/article2321071.ece.

September 5
168 *"who from rude nature"* "The History of Labor Day," U.S. Department of Labor, http://www.dol.gov/opa/aboutdol/laborday.htm.

September 7
169 *"Are the yachts"* Alfred F. Loomis, "Ah, Your Majesty, There Is No Second," *American Heritage*, August 1958, http://www.americanheritage.com/content/"ah-your-majesty-there-no-second".

September 8
170 *"I get frustrated"* Nicholas D. Kristof, "His Libraries, 12,000 So Far, Change Lives," *New York Times*, November 5, 2011, http://www.nytimes.com/2011/11/06/opinion/sunday/kristof-his-libraries-12000-so-far-change-lives.html?_r=1&ref=nicholasdkristof.

September 10
171 *"Naturism is a way"* "Your Gateway to Naturism," International Naturist Federation, http://www.inf-fni.org/.

September 11
171 *"I have faith"* "Salvador Allende: Last Speech to the Nation," Marxists

Internet Archive, http://www.marxists.org/archive/allende/1973/september/11.htm.

September 12

172 *"characterized by artificiality"* "Mannerism," *Encyclopædia Britannica*, vol. 7 (Chicago: Encyclopædia Britannica, 2003), 784.

September 13

173 *"Then commenced the battle"* Rear-Admiral Charles Holmes, "Letter from the Plains of Abraham, September 18, 1759," University of Waterloo, http://www.lib.uwaterloo.ca/discipline/SpecColl/archives/holmes/holmes.html.

September 15

175 *"I guess the train"* Steve Harvey, "It Was a Train Wreck of an Event," *Los Angeles Times*, May 29, 2011, http://articles.latimes.com/2011/may/29/local/la-me-0529-then-20110529.

September 16

175 *"It is a story"* Griel Marcus, "Sly Stone: The Myth of Staggerlee," in *Mystery Train* (New York: Dutton, 1975), 76.

September 17

176 *"Mr. Brady has done"* "Brady's Photographs," *New York Times*, October 20, 1862.

September 18

177 *"[T]his is not my fight"* Leon Claire Metz, *Dallas Stoudenmire: El Paso Marshal* (Austin: Pemberton Press, 1969), 42.

177 *"a most quarrelsome"* "Telegrams to the *Times*: An El Paso Feud," *Los Angeles Times*, September 20, 1882.

September 19

178 *"They wanted a better"* Mark Roth, "Real Pirates Bore Little Resemblance to the Legends, Pitt Scholar Says," *Pittsburgh Post-Gazette*, July 23, 2006, http://www.post-gazette.com/pg/06204/707401–51.stm.

September 20

178 *"such knowledge is important"* Robert M. May, "Why Worry about How Many Species and Their Loss?" PLoS Biology, August 23, 2011, http://www.plosbiology.org/article/info%3Adoi%2F10.1371%2Fjournal.pbio.1001130.

September 21

178 *"She sits on the bed"* Mo Costandi, "Alois Alzheimer's First Case,"

Neurophilosophy, *Science Blogs*, November 2, 2007, http://scienceblogs.com/neurophilosophy/2007/11/alois_alzheimers_first_case.php.

September 23

180 *"The object of the game"* Elizabeth Magie Phillips, "Game Board," patented September 23, 1924, United States Patent Office, 1,509,312, http://www.google.com/patents?id=lD1cAAAAEBAJ&printsec=abstract&zoom=4&source=gbs_overview_r&cad=0#v=onepage&q&f=false.

September 25

181 *"patients with FAS"* Diane Garst and William Katz, "Foreign Accent Syndrome," *ASHA Leader*, American Speech-Language-Hearing Association, August 15, 2006, http://www.asha.org/Publications/leader/2006/060815/f060815c/.

September 27

183 *"Then you finally"* Larry Schwartz, "Didrikson Was a Woman Ahead of Her Time," Top North American Athletes of the Century, ESPN, http://espn.go.com/sportscentury/features/00014147.html.

September 28

183 *"Let us . . . stand"* Frances Willard, "Address before the Second Biennial Convention of the World's Woman's Christian Temperance Union," October 1893, Gifts of Speech, Women's Speeches from around the World, Sweet Briar College, http://gos.sbc.edu/w/willard.html.

September 29

184 *"unquestionably one of"* Brendan Gill, "A Fast Full Life," *New Yorker*, February 9, 1998.

September 30

185 *"are due to the ignorance"* Jerome to Lucinius, Letter LXXI, in *The Principal Works of St. Jerome*, Christian Classics Ethereal Library, http://www.ccel.org/ccel/schaff/npnf206.v.LXXI.html.

October

October 1

186 *"Of all precious"* John Bostock and H. T. Riley, trans. *The Natural History of Pliny*, vol. 6 (London: Henry G. Bohn, 1857), 416–417.

October 4

188 *"resembleth the noise"* C. Plinius Secundus, *The Historie of the World*, Book VIII, Philemon Holland, trans. (London: Adam Islip, 1601), http://penelope.uchicago.edu/holland/pliny8.html.

188 *"It is so strong"* T. H. White, *The Book of Beasts: Being a Translation from a Latin Bestiary of the Twelfth Century* (Madison, WI: Parallel Press, 2002), 51–52, http://books.google.com/books?id=7egVUaj2oyUC&printsec=frontcover&source=gbs_ge_summary_r&cad=0#v=onepage&q&f=false.

October 6

189 *"No. 1 source of germs"* Denise Mann, "Germs in the Kitchen," WebMD, October 18, 2007, http://www.webmd.com/food-recipes/features/germs-in-kitchen.

October 7

190 *"The greatest of these"* Ernest Vincent Wright, *Gadsby: A Story of Over 50,000 Words without Using the Letter "E"* (Los Angeles: Wetzel Publishing, 1939), http://www.holybooks.com/wp-content/uploads/Gadsby-by-Ernest-Vincent-Wright.pdf.

October 9

191 *"looks like the sea"* Wayne Curtis, "The Old Man and the Daiquiri," *Atlantic*, October 2005, http://www.the-atlantic.com/magazine/archive/2005/10/the-old-man-and-the-daiquiri/4257/.

October 10

192 *"the product has"* Jonathan Miner and Adam Hoffhines, "The Discovery of Aspirin's Antithrombotic Effects," *Texas Heart Institute Journal* (2007), http://www.ncbi.nlm.nih.gov/pmc/articles/PMC1894700/?tool=pubmed.

October 11

192 *"The recovery of these"* Rossella Lorenzi, "An Ancient Art Studio Found in Cave in Africa," Discovery News, October 13, 2011, http://news.discovery.com/history/art-studio-111013.html.

October 13

194 *"The Republic endures"* "The Court Building," Supreme Court of the United States, http://www.supremecourt.gov/about/courtbuilding.aspx.

October 14

194 *"Since they must rely"* Orlando O. Espin and James B. Nickoloff, *An Introductory Dictionary of Theology and Religious Studies* (Collegeville, MN: Liturgical Press, 2007), 619.

October 16

196 *"discovery that the inhaling"* "Ether Monument," Roadside America, http://www.roadsideamerica.com/story/15438.

October 17

196 *"It has been observed"* Noah Webster, "An Essay on the Necessity, Advantages, and Practicality of Reforming the Mode of Spelling and of Rendering the Orthography of Words Correspondent to Pronunciation," in *Dissertations on the English Language: With Notes, Historical and Critical, to Which is Added, by Way of Appendix, an Essay on a Reformed Mode of Spelling, with Dr. Franklin's Arguments on That Subject* (Boston: Isaiah Thomas & Company, 1789), 391, 393–394, http://www.archive.org/stream/dissertationsone00websrich#page/n3/mode/2up.

October 18

197 *"Fire is the rapid"* Cecil Adams, "What Exactly Is Fire?" Straight Dope, November 22, 2002, http://www.straightdope.com/columns/read/2425/what-exactly-is-fire.

October 20

198 *"a magical or scientific"* "Voynich Manuscript," Beinecke Rare Book and Manuscript Library, Yale University, http://beinecke.library.yale.edu/digitallibrary/voynich.html.

198 *"No one has worked"* John Whitfield, "World's Most Mysterious Book May Be a Hoax," *Nature*, December 17, 2003, http://www.nature.com/news/1998/031215/full/news031215-5.html.

October 21

198 *"the toughest biological"* "Top Ten New Species—2011," International Institute for Species Exploration, Arizona State University, http://species.asu.edu/Top10.

October 22

199 *"hard, durable, and bright"* Marie Louise Handley, "Luca di Simone Robbia," in *The Catholic Encyclopedia*, vol. 13 (New York:

Robert Appleton & Company, 1912), http://www.newadvent.org/cathen/13095b.htm.

199 *"seeing that the profit"* Giorgio Vasari, "Luca della Robbia," in *Stories of the Italian Artists from Vasari*, trans. E. L. Seeley (London: Chatto & Windus, 1908), 46.

October 23
200 *"blithering saphead"* "Gillette Will Requests His Home Not Be Sold to 'Blithering Saphead,'" *Hartford Courant*, May 4, 1937.

October 27
202 *"The razor-edged teeth"* Theodore Roosevelt, *Through the Brazilian Wilderness* (New York: Charles Scribner's Sons, 1914), 42, http://books.google.com/books?id=lWwCAAAAYAAJ&printsec=frontcover#v=onepage&q=piranha&f=false.

October 28
203 *"began to unreel"* "The Sights and Sightseers," *New York Times*, October 29, 1886, http://query.nytimes.com/gst/abstract.html?res=F60A11F7355410738DDDA00A94D8415B8684F0D3&scp=1&sq=%22curling%20streamers%22&st=cse.

October 30
204 *"The meter was now"* "Weights and Measures," Virtual Museum, National Institute of Standards and Technology, http://museum.nist.gov/exhibits/ex1/index.html.
204 *"the International Meter"* Ibid.

November

November 1
206 *"These poor wretches"* Charles Darwin, "Tierra del Fuego," in *A Naturalist's Voyage Round the World* (London: John Murray, 1913), 224, http://www.gutenberg.org/files/3704/3704-h/chx.html.

November 2
207 *"no one knew"* "They Are Twin Sisters: Nobody Knows Which of the Dakotas First Became a State," *Chicago Daily Tribune*, November 5, 1889.

November 4
208 *"We need to understand"* Richard Hollingham, "Inside the *Mars-500* 'Spaceship,'" BBC News, March 3, 2008, http://news.bbc.co.uk/2/hi/science/nature/7267689.stm.

208 *"On this mission"* Alissa de Carbonnel, "Pale-Faced Mars Crew 'Lands' after 520 Days in Isolation," Reuters, November 4, 2011, http://www.reuters.com/article/2011/11/04/uk-russia-mars-isolation-idUSLNE7A303V20111104.

November 5
209 *"the finest highway ever built"* Richard Thruelsen, "How New Jersey Built Its Dream Road," *Saturday Evening Post*, December 8, 1951.

November 6
209 *"more than 400"* Russell W. Baker, "Veteran 'Mr. First,' on Hand Again, Finds New Jersey Turnpike 'Thrill,'" *Baltimore Sun*, November 6, 1951.
209 *"It's a dream"* Ibid.

November 9
211 *"I tried and failed"* Sue Shephard, *Pickled, Potted, and Canned: How the Art and Science of Food Preserving Changed the World* (New York: Simon and Schuster, 2000), 152.

November 13
214 *"During the Renaissance"* H. V. Morton, *A Traveller in Rome* (London: Methuen, 1957), 290.
214 *"What the barbarians did"* Verity Platt, "Shattered Visages; Speaking Statues from the Ancient World," *Apollo*, July 1, 2003.

November 14
214 *"They just wanted"* Richard Conniff, "What the Luddites Really Fought Against," *Smithsonian*, March 2011, http://www.smithsonianmag.com/history-archaeology/What-the-Luddites-Really-Fought-Against.html?c=y&story=fullstory.

November 19
217 *"The will of the nation"* James A. Garfield, "Inaugural Address," March 4, 1881, http://www.presidency.ucsb.edu/ws/index.php?pid=25823#axzz1LPOiE1ED.
218 *"disappointed office-seeker"* James P. Pfiffner, *The Modern Presidency*, 6th ed. (Boston: Wadsworth, Cengage Learning, 2011), 122.

November 20
218 *"No man ever entered"* "Chester A. Arthur 1881–1885," Presidents: The White House, http://www.whitehouse.gov/about/presidents/chesterarthur.

November 21
219 *"telling her mind"* William Andrews, *Old-Time Punishments* (Hull, UK: William Andrews & Company, 1890), 39, http://www.archive.org/stream/oldtimepu nishmen00andruoft#page/38/mode/2up/ search/branks.

November 25
222 *"There are deeds"* Walt Whitman, *The Complete Writings* (New York: G. P. Putnam's Sons, 1902), 121.

November 26
222 *"has devoted herself"* "Mary Edwards Walker," Hall of Valor, *Military Times*, http://www.militarytimes.com/ citations-medals-awards/recipient .php?recipientid=2319.
223 *"distinguished gallantry, self-sacri-fice"* "Mary Edwards Walker," Women in History, Lakewood Public Library, http:// www.lkwdpl.org/wihohio/walk-mar.htm.

November 28
224 *"Cheyenne*: Étaomêhótsenôhtóven-estse" Simon Ager, "Idioms and Sayings in Various Languages," Omniglot, http:// omniglot.com/language/idioms/index.php.

November 29
224 *"fractured the crystalline bed-rock"* Hillary Mayell, "Chesapeake Bay Crater Offers Clues to Ancient Cataclysm," *National Geographic News*, November 13, 2001, http://news.nationalgeographic.com/ news/2001/11/1113_chesapeakcrater.html.

November 30
225 *"Let me tell you"* Susan B. Anthony interview, *New York World*, February 2, 1896.

December

December 2
227 *"[A] classical female figure"* "Statue of Freedom," Architect of the Capitol, http:// www.aoc.gov/cc/art/Statue-of-Freedom-Page-Set.cfm.

December 5
229 *"a class of musical"* "Idiophone," *Encyclopædia Britannica Online*, Encyclopædia Britannica Inc., 2011, http://www.britannica .com/EBchecked/topic/281985/idiophone.

December 6
230 *"Then we came"* Ralph Emery, *The View from Nashville* (New York: William

Morrow, 1998), 234, http://books.google .com/books?id=0UIJLX2dL9kC&printsec=f rontcover&source=gbs_ge_summary_r&cad =0#v=onepage&q&f=false.

December 8
231 *"an evangelist-in-paint"* Anne E. Neimark, *Diego Rivera: Artist of the People* (New York: HarperCollins, 1992), 106.

December 11
233 *"If this instrument"* Edward MacCurdy, ed., *The Notebooks of Leonardo da Vinci*, vol. 1 (New York: Reynal and Hitchcock, 1938), 500.

December 13
234 *"Do not create"* Elaine A. Evans, "The Sacred Scarab," Frank H. McClung Museum, University of Tennessee, http:// mcclungmuseum.utk.edu/research/reoccpap/ scarab.htm.

December 14
235 *"together with the hammer"* Roland Huntford, *Two Planks and a Passion: The Dramatic History of Skiing from Paleolithic Times Until Today* (London: Continuum, 2008), 2.

December 15
235 *"for the first time"* Aleksandr Korzhenkov, *Zamenhof: The Life, Works, and Ideas of the Author of Esperanto*, trans. Ian M. Richmond (Esperantic Studies Foundation, 2009), 24, http://www.esperantic.org/ dosieroj/file/LLZ-Bio-En(1).pdf.

December 20
238 *"damn sugar, damn coffee"* Jon Kukla, *A Wilderness So Immense: The Louisiana Purchase and the Destiny of America* (New York: Alfred A. Knopf, 2003), 249, http://books.google.com/books?id=BWaB HTLTdmgC&pg=PT342&dq=%22Dam n+sugar,+damn+coffee,+damn+colonies% 22&hl=en#v=onepage&q=%22Damn%20 sugar%2C%20damn%20coffee%2C%20 damn%20colonies%22&f=false.

December 21
239 *"The trick is"* Deborah Netburn, "Scientists Invent Lightest Material on Earth. What Now?" *Los Angeles Times*, November 17, 2011, http://latimesblogs .latimes.com/technology/2011/11/lightest-material-on-earth.html?track=lat-pick.
239 *"It's sort of like"* Ibid.

December 22

239 *"A kind of coarse"* "corduroy," *Oxford English Dictionary* (Oxford: Oxford Univ. Press, 1989).

240 *"The wales have aligned"* Liz Robbins, "Corduroy Fans Prepare for the Fabric's Day of All Days," *New York Times*, November 10, 2011, http://cityroom .blogs.nytimes.com/2011/11/10/corduroy-fans-prepare-for-the-fabrics-day-of-all-days/.

December 23

240 *"I've found it"* Giles Milton, "Solving the Great Puzzle of Our Time," *Daily Mail*, September 1, 2000.

240 *"In the reign"* "The Rosetta Stone: Translation of the Greek Section," Ancient History Sourcebook, Fordham University, http://www.fordham.edu/halsall/ancient/rosetta-stone-translation.asp.

December 24

241 *"neon blue champagne bubbles"* Leigh Ann Henion, "Puerto Rico Holds One of the Planet's Last Bright Spots," *Washington Post*, September 17, 2011, http://www.washingtonpost.com/lifestyle/magazine/2011/08/25/gIQALpVxUK_story.html.

December 25

241 *"a large Christmas tree"* Ace Collins, *Stories behind the Great Traditions of Christmas* (Grand Rapids, MI: Zondervan, 2003), 120.

December 26

242 *"I have not killed"* Douglas Linder, "The Dakota Conflict Trials," Famous American Trials, University of Missouri-Kansas City School of Law, http://law2.umkc.edu/faculty/projects/ftrials/dakota/dakota.html.

December 28

243 *"a self-assembled hydrophobic"* Nathan J. Mlot, Craig A. Tovey, and David L. Hu, "Fire Ants Self-Assemble into Waterproof Rafts to Survive Floods," *Proceedings of the National Academy of Sciences* 108, no. 19 (May 10, 2011): 7669, http://www.me.gatech.edu/hu/Publications/Hu11TM.pdf.

December 30

245 *"Through a lifetime"* "Biography," Noguchi Museum, http://www.noguchi.org/noguchi/biography.

December 31

245 *"Paintings of snow"* John E. Thornes, *John Constable's Skies: A Fusion of Art and Science* (Birmingham, UK: Univ. of Birmingham, 1999), 160, http://books.google.com/books?id=gbElMVjhzQC&pg=PA31&dq=art+weather+climate+Neuberger&cd=2&hl=en#v=onepage&q=art%20weather%20climate%20Neuberger&f=false.

Illustration Credits

Page 8, E. Duperrex; pp. 11, 28, 33, 40, 66, 70, 76, 93, 105, 121, 125, 138, 145, 169, 188, 190, 202, 216, 225, 229, Dover; pp. 13, 17, 26, 52, 56, 114, 143, 218, 241, Library of Congress; pp. 15, 136, 156, 161, 177, Wikimedia Commons; p. 19, Jacopo Amigoni; p. 23, Public Library of Science; p. 37, Student Association of the School of Information at the University of Texas-Austin, and cartoonist Ben Sargent; p. 46, Tim Brookes of the Endangered Alphabets Project; p. 49, http://www.blackpast.org/?q=aah/augusta-alexander-t-1825–1890; p. 50, Friedrich Eduard Bilz, *Das neue Naturheilverfahren* (Dresden: Verlag, 1894); pp. 54, 86, 140, 158, U.S. Department of Agriculture Plants Database, from N.L. Britton and A. Brown, *An Illustrated Flora of the Northern United States, Canada, and the British Possessions* (New York: Charles Scribner's Sons, 1913); p. 56, G. Sundback, Patent #1,219,881; p. 59, University of North Carolina at Chapel Hill Libraries; p. 61, Travelers in the Middle East Archive (TIMEA); p. 74, J. P. Adolf Erman, *Life in Ancient Egypt* (New York: Macmillan and Co., 1894); p. 81, Felice A. Beato; p. 83, André Thévat; p. 90, C. E. Waterman; p. 97, H. G. Wells, *The Outline of History* (New York: P. F. Collier & Son, 1922); p. 100, http://www.picturehistory.com/product/id/4829; p. 103, Régine Pernoud, *Joan of Arc, by Herself and Her Witnesses* (New York: Stein & Day, 1966); p. 108, Theodor de Bry; pp. 110, 208, 220, 234, Pearson Scott Foresman, donated to the Wikimedia Foundation; p. 118, Friedrich Ratzel, *The History of Mankind* (New York: Macmillan and Co., 1898); p. 130, Charles Gildon, *All the Histories and Novels Written by the Late Ingenious Mrs. Behn, Entire in One Volume* (London: R. Wellington, 1705); p. 133, *American Woman's Journal,* July 1895; p. 149, Edwin Evans, *Tchaikovsky* (London: J.M. Dent & Co. and New York: E.P. Dutton & Co., 1906); p. 153, R. Lydekker, *A Geographical History of Mammals* (Cambridge: Cambridge Univ. Press, 1896); p. 164, Project Gutenberg eText 15399; p. 165, Guillaume Rouillé, *Promptuarii Iconum Insigniorum* (Lyon, 1578); p. 175, http://www.free-scores.com/partitions_telecharger.php?partition=16964; p. 181, James D. McCabe, *The Pictorial History of the United States* (Philadelphia: National Publishing Co., 1877); p. 182, *A History of the Pioneer and Modern Times of Ashland County* (Philadelphia: J. B. Lippincott & Co., 1862); p. 185, William Blades, *Pentateuch of Printing with a Chapter on Judges* (London: E. Stock, 1891); p. 195, WPClipart, http://www.wpclipart.com/plants/mushroom/mushrooms_2/mushrooms.png.html; p. 197, Project Gutenberg eText 16667; p. 200, Friends of Gillette Castle State Park, artist Judy White; p. 211, J. M. Ertzman and B.Wallace, courtesy Carnegie Museum of Natural History; p. 214, Antonio Lafreri, *Speculum Romanae Magnificentiae* (Rome, 1560); p. 222, National Library of Medicine, http://www.nlm.nih.gov/changingthefaceofmedicine/physicians/biography_325.html; p. 228, Mikael Häggström; p. 232, the Gutenberg Project eText 20417; p. 238, *Popular Science Monthly,* July 1873; p. 243, April Nobile, http://www.antweb.org/bigPicture.do?name=casent0005804&shot=p&number=1

Index